ETHNOS AND SOCIETY

ALEXANDER DUGIN

ETHNOS
AND
SOCIETY

ARKTOS
LONDON 2018

Printed in the United Kingdom.

ISBN	978-1-912079-21-6 (Softcover)
	978-1-912079-06-3 (Hardback)
	978-1-912079-20-9 (Ebook)
TRANSLATION	Michael Millerman
EDITING	Sam Richardson
	Martin Locker
COVER AND LAYOUT	Tor Westman

www.arktos.com

TABLE OF CONTENTS

1 THE *ETHNOS* AND ITS STRUCTURES

2 THE *ETHNOS* IN COMPLEX SOCIETIES: DERIVATIVES OF THE *ETHNOS*

1

The *Ethnos* and Its Structures

CHAPTER ONE

Ethnostatics: The Ethnic Structure

SECTION ONE

Phenomenology of the *Ethnos*

General Sociology as a Subdivision of Ethnosociology

In this section we will study the *ethnos*[1] as the simplest form of society, the *koineme*. The *ethnos* is the original form of society as such, so its structures can serve as "the measure of things" for the analysis of more complex social forms. If we correctly describe and interpret the basic structure of the *ethnos*, we will produce a conceptual matrix by means of which we can study the constant (i.e. properly ethnic) elements of any society as well as the forms that result when these elements are deviated from or built on. The *ethnos* understood as *koineme* is the invariable structure of more complex and changing societies (like the atom in substances). If we successfully describe the *ethnos* in its fundamental aspects, we will acquire a reliable methodological instrument of analysis for all actual or possible sociological models.

---

1   In *The Fourth Political Theory*, Dugin defines the *ethnos* as "a community of language, religious belief, daily life and the sharing of resources and goals." The term most specifically describes archaic cultures.

The ethnos is the structure of society. As a structure, it is invariable, constant and "eternal." And even when this structure becomes more complex, transforms and is overcome, it remains the initial algorithm, influencing (as the starting conditions) all phases of the unfolding process of changes. This is obvious: to speak of changes, there must be a subject of changes, i.e. knowledge of the initial structure that is subject to changes. Only in this case can we say that something changes (we have a point of comparison), while something else remains unchanging.

This logic leads to the following interesting conclusion or, rather, hypothesis: isn't sociology as a whole only one variant of ethnosociology and not vice versa, as is customarily thought? If the *ethnos* is the *koineme*, sociology deals only with its derivatives. Lévi-Strauss had something similar in mind when he said that the real sociologist must necessarily be an anthropologist, i.e. he must study the cultures of archaic, preliterate peoples (as Durkheim, Mauss, Hubert, Levy-Bruhl and others did) in order to then make judgements about more complex societies on the basis of ethnographic knowledge.

Even if we do not take such an extreme position, the significance of the *ethnos* and the study of its structures are a crucial component of sociological knowledge.

Forms of Study of the *Ethnos* as *Koineme*

The *ethnos* as *koineme* can be considered from various perspectives. They can be reduced to three main approaches: ethnostatics, ethnodynamics and ethnokinetics.

Ethnostatics studies the *ethnos* in its invariable foundation, as an "ideal type" (Weber) or "normal type" (Sombart). Ethnostatics considers the *ethnos* as a sociological paradigm, constant and invariable in its principal parameters. In reality, there is no strictly static *ethnos*. This is an abstract concept but it helps fashion an effective model, by means of which real *ethnoses* can be studied.

Ethnostatics relies on the comparative method of the study of archaic societies and by detecting common features, qualities, markers and characteristics it constructs an ideal object: the *ethnos* as such. Such a path led Shirokogorov[2] to make "*ethnos*" a fundamental anthropological category, on which ethnology and later ethnosociology were developed. Ethnosociology is important for describing the constant and invariable part of the *koineme*, the variations of which historical sociology deals with when it considers diverse types of complex societies.

Ethnodynamics introduces into the study of the *ethnos* the factor of changes but these changes are thought of as fluctuations or oscillations of ethnic processes, not changing the basic structure of society. Ethnodynamics are the vibrating force processes occurring inside the *ethnos* but remaining within the limits of its stable and invariable structural constancy. Ethnodynamics unfolds only within the limits of ethnostatics, i.e. the *ethnos* as an "ideal" type. It does not lead to its qualitative change.

Ethnokinetics is a specific domain of ethnic processes, which in contrast to ethnostatics *change* the normative structure of the *ethnos*, force the *ethnos* to change *irreversibly* and qualitatively. It describes the transition phase from the *ethnos* into its derivatives (most often into the *narod*[3]).

Ethnostatics considers the *ethnos* as a fixed structure; ethnodynamics, as a structure that vibrates, fluctuates and oscillates around a fixed axis; ethnokinetics, as a structure that changes its fundamental proportions, as a structure in motion, in change, in transformations.

All three approaches — ethnostatics, ethnodynamics, and ethnokinetics — are equally necessary for the full-fledged analysis of the *ethnos* and the processes occurring in it and they should be applied simultaneously for accurate scientific knowledge of the *ethnos* as a multi-dimensional and living, existential and historical phenomenon.

---

2   Sergei Mikhailovich Shirokogorov was a Russian anthropologist noted for his work on the Tungusic peoples. He was a White émigré who lived in China from 1922 until his death in 1939.

3   Dugin discusses the concept of the *narod* in his book *Ethnosociology*. The term means people, in the sense of peoplehood ("the Russian people"), not an aggregate of individuals ("many people think"). It is therefore akin to the German term "Volk." The Russian has been transliterated to avoid the ambiguity of the English word "people."

The Ethnostructure and the Problem of Ethnocomparison

Ethnostatics describes the *ethnos* in its invariable synchronic form. Its object is the basic, unchanging structure of the *ethnos* or the ethnostructure taken generally. An ethnostructure is the totality of the main characteristics of the *ethnos* as *koineme*. We can divide it into the following layers:

- Ethnic *thought* (consciousness) and ethnic phenomenology;

- The ethnic *"life world"*;

- The ethnic *narrative* (language and myth as a synthesis of the ethnic worldview);

- Ethnic *space* (ethnospatiality);

- Ethnic *time* (ethnotemporality);

- Ethnic *sacrality* (ethnonuminism);

- Ethnic *anthropology* (ethnoanthropology);

- The ethnic system of dividing gender roles (ethnogender);

- The ethnic model of economic activity (ethnoeconomics and, included in it, ethnotechnics).

An ethnostructure is formed of these basic elements. We can easily detect them all among every *ethnos* but their form, type, content, meaning, proportions and interconnections can vary substantially. This allows us to compose a *structural typology of ethnoses* through the comparison of concrete ethnostructures.

At the same time, we have to hold fast to the rule of "the simplest society." Ethnostructures change qualitatively during transitions to more complex forms of society. But if we begin to compare the structures of the *ethnos* (the ethnostructure) with the structures of more complex societies (for instance, the laosstructure or structure of the *narod*), we will transgress the logic of our analysis. Of course, we can and should compare the structures of the *ethnos* and the structures of more complex societies

(earlier we called that post-ethnic analysis). But then we must limit our-
selves to those *ethnoses* that have directly and actually participated in
laogenesis. The structures of other *ethnoses*, at an insurmountable historical or geographical distance from these processes, must be considered as
local structures, relating to entirely different sociological categories.
In other words, we cannot confuse two types of analysis: "horizontal"
and "vertical." The comparative juxtaposition of *ethnoses* as *koinemes*
is a horizontal analysis. Here, analysis remains legitimate so long as we
do not go beyond the limits of the *koineme* (the zone of ethnokinetics
as a process in which the *ethnos* becomes something other than itself).
Vertical analysis compares an *ethnos* or group of *ethnoses* with the more
complex post-ethnic form that formed on their basis. This analysis is also
legitimate and useful but it can concern only a limited circle of *ethnoses*,
those that had a direct temporal (historical) and spatial (geographic) relation the emergent *narod* (later nation, civil society, etc.).

Ethnophenomenology and Ethnic Thought

Let us now consider the ethnostructure as the fundamental and general
model of the *ethnos*, comprising its essence, making it what it is. We will
begin with "ethnic thought."

To describe the special character of an *ethnos'* thinking, we should
turn to Edmund Husserl (1859–1938), an outstanding twentieth-century
philosopher and founder of the phenomenological approach in philosophy. Husserl and his method are interesting because they meticulously describe the structure of the actions of consciousness preceding all spheres
of concrete logical, rational thought, which became the norm in modern
European societies but can clearly already be distinguished in antiquity,
particularly among the Greek philosophers Plato and Aristotle. Husserl
develops the ideas of his teacher Franz Brentano (1838–1917), who introduced into contemporary philosophy (a rethought scholasticism) the
concept of *intentionality*, on which Husserl builds his phenomenology.

The term "intentionality" is formed from the Latin word "*intentio.*" Intentionality is a way of apprehending the world not as it is but as desired by the one apprehending, as he wishes it to be.

The philosophical method of phenomenology is the optimal approach for describing the structure of ethnic thought. Intentionality is a form of prelogical thought, the special character of which is that the thinker does not distinguish between the representation of an object of thought (something inside the psychic world) and the object itself (located without). Only rational, logical, reflexive thought can carry out this procedure and draw a line between the representation and the thing itself. Intentional thought cannot do this and is not inclined to do it. It operates with the representation as though it were the thing itself.

Ethnic thought is intentional. This is its main quality. The *ethnos* thinks the world in the limits of intentional structures. Georg Hegel (1770–1831) calls this "natural consciousness,"[4] which takes the *model* of the world and its things as the very world and its things.

The Reversibility of Ethnic Intentionality

There is nothing in the *ethnos* and its structure that would be able to make a judgement about the correlation between representations and the world in itself, because in the *ethnos* there is neither the world in itself nor thought in itself, i.e. there is neither object nor subject. The *ethnos* thinks of itself as a "whole" in which there is no fracture.

This ethnic thought, *the process of ethnointentionality*, has an orientation. It is directed "from" and "toward." It is a vector, not between one strictly determined thing and another but simply a vector, by itself, as the independent structure of the non-equilibrium of an intentional act. There is orientation "from" and "toward" but from *what* and toward *what* remains, in the limits of the *ethnos*, unclear, general and conditional.

Moreover, the intentional vector of ethnic consciousness is (relatively) *reversible*. It permits, though it does not require, inversion. And then

---

4   Georg Wilhelm Friedrich Hegel, Arnold V. Miller, J. N. Findlay, and Johannes Hoffmeister, *Phenomenology of Spirit* (Oxford: Clarendon Press, 1979).

the thinking instance becomes *the thought* instance, "from" and "toward" change places. The *ethnos* does not insist on the reversibility of the intentional act but it allows it. This is expressed in many rituals of initiation, when, for instance, the hunter, regularly killing forest animals for sustenance, becomes a victim of these animals in rites. The killer becomes the killed; the understanding, the understood; the thinking, the thought. Such reversibility is possible because intentionality as a phenomenon unfolds within the psyche. Man is not undone by an object but by the "content of an intentional act," i.e. an animated, active representation [or notion] rooted in man himself. In the structure of the *ethnos*, there are no distinctions among representations of things, symbolic things, the names of things and the things themselves. All of these are aspects of the intentional act.

This explains the problem of anthropologists coming to an impasse when the natives they study are unable to explain to them clearly whether they are talking about myth, the soul, representations, symbols or real objects in the environment. For people of a contemporary rational civilization, a great distance separates these things. But for ethnic thought, there is no such distance. The world of the *ethnos* and the surrounding environment are endopsychic phenomena. They are within the *ethnos*, not outside it, since the gnoseological distance required to give ontological place to this "outside" simply does not exist.

The *ethnos* does not simply believe that the symbol, the representation [idea, notion], and the model correspond to the thing they represent. It knows neither symbol, nor things, since the distinction between sign and signified belongs to entirely different structures of consciousness, which can be determined as "postethnic." The symbol, model and representation are the thing, and the thing, in turn, is a symbol, model and representation.

This reversible intentionality can be taken as the main feature of the *ethnos*. Such an assertion has tremendous philosophical significance because it shows that the intentional level of thought (even in complex societies) is *ethnic*.

Ethnos and Noesis

Husserl describes the structure of intentionality through the Greek term "nous" ("intellect") and its derivatives. Husserl defines "nous" as intentional, unreflexive thought, which does not make a judgement about the correlation between representation and object (i.e. pre-rational thought). Rational thought, characteristic of complex societies, he proposes to call "dianoia." The terms "intellect/reason" can convey the sense of the pair "nous/dianoia." Intellect is simple thought. It can be called "ethnic." Reason is complex, reflexive, lying at the basis of philosophy, theology, science, logic and, accordingly, those societies that build their structures on rationally differentiated principles.

Intentional thought is noetic thought. Husserl distinguishes two aspects in noetic thought: the active and the passive. He calls the active "noesis" and the passive "noema" (the object that in simple thought corresponds to the external object and is apprehended as such an object).

When applied to the *ethnos*, this gives us a key instrument for deciphering the functioning of its fundamental structures. The world of the *ethnos* is a noetic world; it consists of processes of ethnonoesis, which construct a system of noemata, ethnonoemata. Anthropologists and sociologists often interpret these ethnonoemata, i.e. the world as the *ethnos* apprehends it, as "symbols" or "magic objects," endowed with special power. Clifford Geetz in particular builds his theory on this basis (elaborating a "symbolic anthropology"). But this can lead us into confusion, as if the *ethnos* distinguishes between its representation (symbol) and the object of the "real world," which it is called upon to symbolize. This distinction belongs to the domain of reflexive, logical thought, reason, "dianoia," and cannot be an attribute of ethnic structures. So it would be much more precise to use the term "ethnonoemata" to signify the world that the *ethnos* experiences as the world itself.

The Operative Magic of Language and Myth

The importance of language and names in the *ethnos* follows. Language, its structures and its names do not comprise a system of signs but a structure of ethnonoemata. In naming something, the member of a simple society evokes it. He does not indicate it; he constructs it noetically. There is not simply a magical connection but a direct equivalence between the names of fish, bears, plants, and all natural phenomena and actual fish, bears, plants, and natural phenomena, since the name of an animal or thing is a noema but the animal or thing itself is also a noema. The unnamed does not exist. The named exists by the fact of naming as naming-summoning.

The central importance of myth as story and narration also follows. The *ethnos* lives by a myth, thanks to which a world, language and society are constructed. In narrating a myth (the Greek word "μῦθος," "myth," is formed from the verb "μυθέιν," to tell, to narrate), the member of a simple society unfolds a noetic structure, arraying noemata such that they fall into a paradigmatic chain, constituting a world. The persons, situations and objects mentioned in a myth are as "real" as the objects in the environment; they are also ethnonoemata. This is the source of the magic force of language, regarded as a dangerous, active, powerful force. Language is a world — not signs of the world but precisely the world itself as the totality of structured noemata.

To think — to speak — to evoke (into being) — to produce: in an ethnic society, these are the same act.

Ethnos and the Lifeworld

The "late" Husserl[5] described the structures of intentional thought taken as a whole through the concept "lifeworld." The "lifeworld" is the domain of noemata and noetic acts, not examined mentally but as though we were

---

5   Edmund Husserl, *The Crisis of European Sciences and Transcendental Phenomenology: An Introduction to Phenomenological Philosophy* (Evanston: Northwestern University Press, 1970); Edmund Husserl, "Philosophy as Rigorous Science," *New Yearbook for Phenomenology and Phenomenological Philosophy* 2 (2005): 249–295.

dealing with objective reality that is not subject to doubt. Husserl discovered the "lifeworld" and its structures in complex, particularly modern European, societies where man leaves the zone of highly differentiated scientific practices and is immersed in the element of everyday existence. In ordinary life, even a scientist is guided by the rules of the "lifeworld," while in his professional scientific activity he proceeds from rational strategies, based on dianoia.

The *ethnos* knows only one world, which we can perfectly well correlate with Husserl's "lifeworld." The ethnic world is a *lifeworld*. This world is not so much comprehended as experienced and it is constituted by this experience, in which noetic thought plays a central role.

Thus, it is incorrect to think of myth as a set of symbols and symbolic situations. Myths are noetic modes of experience. Myth is experience, the centration of vital energies in their active and saturated form. Myth doesn't indicate anything. It is not meant to be applied. Its function is a vital function. Through myth and the language in which it is set forth, ethnic society lives and experiences the world. Myth is the world as life.

Ethnos and Noesis

Constituting the world through the experience of myth, unfolding the field of noemata, the *ethnos* constitutes itself on the other pole as an active center. We can call this active side of the noetic process ethnonoesis. In studying the simplest societies, anthropology describes this dimension as "man," "culture" and "society," juxtaposed with the "milieu," "environment" and "nature," reproducing under these terms the Cartesian dualism of "subject/object," familiar to modern philosophy. But the *ethnos* does not know the operation that imparts to things or the thinker an independent, autonomous reality. Intentional thought occurs in a field without internal or external borders. It is always located *between*; not between this and thought but simply *between*.[6] And this "between" constitutes not so much

---

6　The modern French sociologist Gilbert Durand calls this the "*trajet*" [trajectory], i.e. something intermediate between the subject and object but regarded as an independent phenomenon. Durand equates the "*trajet*" to the "*imaginaire*," the main

its limits as its orientations "from" and "towards," which, as we showed, are reversible.

If the orientation of the intentional act "toward" produces a noema, and ethnonoema, then appeal to the "from," i.e. to noesis itself and to its source, hypothetically constitutes noesis in its center. This center of the noetic process is the *sacred* or *numinal* (according to Otto) and the *ethnos* in its most concentrated expression.

Ethnocentrism and Holy Space

Now we can describe more concretely the parameters of the *ethnos* through the main aspects of its structure. They are all diverse aspects of ethnic intentionality, embodied in concrete spatial, temporal, anthropological and religious notions. We can consider them as a few layers of the *ethnos*. Let us begin with space. The *ethnos'* notion of space is a synchronic expression of the structure of ethnic thought. So these notions are a synchronic map of ethnic consciousness, a range of noetic processes, imprinted simultaneously in a whole picture. This space is the space of myth, sacred space.

Wilhelm Muhlmann introduced the special term "ethnocentrum"[7] to describe this space.

The ethnocentrum is ethnic thought in its synchronic form. It dominates the entire structure of the *ethnos*. The spatial expression of ethnic thought is dominant and decisive for the structure of the *ethnos* as such. We can say with a measure of approximation that the ethnocentrum is the structure of the *ethnos* in stasis. As a result, *the correct description of the ethnos can be reduced to the description of the ethnocentrum,* i.e. its spatial notions. French sociologist and philosopher Henri Lefebvre (1901–1991)

---

anthropological creative agency. See Alexander Dugin, *Sociology of the Imagination: Introduction to Structural Sociology* (Moscow: Academic Project, 2010).

7   Wilhelm E. Mühlmann *Erfahrung und Denken in der Sicht des Kulturanthropologen*; Wilhelm E., Mühlmann Ernst Muller, *Kulturanthropologie* (Köln/Berlin: Kiepenheuer & Witsch, 1966), 157.

studied the central significance of the spatial factor for the structure of societies (with an emphasis on complex societies, it is true).[8]

The structure of the ethnocentrum can be represented as a circle (Figure 1).

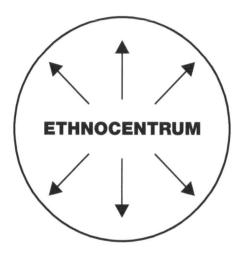

Figure 1. The Ethnocentrum.

In this circle, there is no clearly defined pole and no clearly defined periphery, although there is a bundle of vectors, indicating "from" and "towards," thanks to which the ethnocentrum acquires an orderliness and a certain symmetry. The ethnocentrum includes in its horizon everything that the member of the *ethnos* sees, the whole "surrounding world." Everything that "is" (and we know that in the *ethnos*, everything that exists is the totality of ethnonoemata) is located within the ethnocentrum. That is why it has no borders but on the other hand this endlessness takes shape in the range of visibility or surveyability of the specific landscape in which the *ethnos* lives. The ethnocentrum includes the "universal all" in the concrete limits of the clearly defined area where the life of the *ethnos* unfolds. It is an ethno-universe. Within the ethnocentrum, sun, moon, stars, wind, mountains, lakes and forests mix with souls, ancestors, progeny, etc. This

---

8   Henri Lefebve, *La production de l'espace* (Paris: Anthropos, 1974); *The Production of Space* (Cambridge: Blackwell, 1991).

is possible only if we understand that the space of the ethnocentrum is a noetic, intellectual, mythological and sacral space. The distances and connections among all things in the ethnocentrum are not determined by size or scale but by form, function and noetic characteristics. Such a space is a map of thought and language, and not an analog (even a remote one) of physical geography.

The ethnocentrum is entirely self-sufficient and stable. Within it, the static involvement of the world in the *ethnos* dominates; the world is understood as the *ethnos*, and the *ethnos* is understood as the world. In ethnostatic analysis this is a strict identity. The structure of the ethnocentrum is the structure of the world (cosmos). That means that the *ethnos* is the world and the world is the *ethnos*. It is not that the *ethnos* exists in the world or projects its notions about the world onto it; the *ethnos* and the world are inseparable and one. They are the indivisible and general process of ethnic thought, an integral "lifeworld."

People, animals, stars, weather conditions, climate, soil, technical equipment, social establishments, the dead, the unborn, mythological figures, spirits—they all have an equal ontological status, they all "are," just as they have names, myths tell of them and intentional thought is directed toward them. If rational thought judges what actually exists or does not (what only seems, is imagined or is fancied), ethnic thought neither performs nor wants to perform this operation. Thus, in studying the *ethnos* it is practically impossible to distinguish clearly what people see, feel and experience from what they believe and hope. Everything the *ethnos* believes in it sees and experiences. Everything it experiences and sees it believes in and hopes for.

That is why the ethnocentrum is not an abstraction or "symbol" but an experienced space, a "life space," a "living space," space as life.

Lefebvre, who considered mostly more complex societies, said that society at first "produces" space and then experiences it as a given[9] (and this is entirely right for complex societies). But in the case of the *ethnos*, society experiences space and *eo ipso* creates it. These are not two moments but one.

---

9   Ibid.

The Structure of the Ethnocentrum among the Evenki

We can take the Evenki[10] model of the world as a typical example of an ethnocentrum. This extremely archaic model resembles in a certain sense the general "ideal type" of the *ethnos*, which in one form or another and with many variations is met with among the majority of *ethnoses* as the deepest and most basic layer of the vision of the world.

The German ethnosociologist Adolph Friedrich (1873–1969) described this picture in his article *Das Bewusstsein eines naturvolkes von Haushalt und Ursprung des Lebens*,[11] relying on the materials of the Russian and Soviet ethnographers and ethnologists Shirokogorov, Anisimov,[12] Ksenophontov,[13] Prokofieva[14] and others.

The picture of the Evenki ethnocentrum is as follows.

At the center of the map of the world is a river. At the midway point of this river is a tribe, an *ethnos*. At this same place is territory for hunting (the Evenki belong to the most archaic mode of society, with a hunter-gatherer economy).

At the middle of the river is a camp of the living. There is a similar camp at the lower reaches of the river with the same housing, except that deceased Evenki live there. At the upper reaches of the river is another analogous camp, but the "new souls" of those Evenki still to be born live there.

---

10 A Tungusic line who are one of the indigenous peoples of northern Russia and are also found in China and Mongolia.

11 Adolph Friedrich, "Das Bewusstsein eines naturvolkes von Haushalt und Ursprung des Lebens," *Paideuma: Mitteilungen zur Kulturkunde* 6, no 2 (1955): 47–54; Mühlmann, *Kulturanthropolgie*, 186–194.

12 Arkady Anisimov, "Predstavleniia evenkov o shingenakh i problema proiskhozhdeniia pervobytnoi religii" *Sbornik Muzeia Anthropologii i Etnografii* 12 (1949): 160–194.

13 Gavriil V. Ksenofontov, *Legends and Tales about Shamans among the Yakut, Buryats, and Tungus* (Moskva: *Bezbozhnik*, 1930).

14 Ekaterina D. Prokof'eva "K voprosu o sotsial'noy organizatsii sel'kupov" *Trudy instituta etngrafii* 18 (1952): 88–107.

The three camps at three points of the river are considered the *ethnos*, i.e. the Evenki. The dead, the living and those yet to be born prove to be arrayed in a synchronic order in relation to one another. They exist. Here we see that the ethnocentrum includes in its space the worlds of the dead and the worlds of the unborn, which are parts of a single, continuous whole.

The Evenki distinguish three types of soul (or three doubles) in man: (1) the soul-shadow or soul-reflection, (2) the soul-body, and the soul-fate. These three souls correspond to three layers of society.

The soul-shadow can abandon the body, hunt and wander in the woods. This happens in sleep or in a trance. The soul-body is inseparably bound to the body and expresses itself through the body. All bodily manifestations are associated with the action of this soul. The soul-fate abides at the sources of the river in ideal conditions. Here, there is always an abundance of game and lovely weather. Man's fate depends on how this soul lives in the world of the source (which is thought of synchronically, i.e. simultaneously with the world of people). This soul is connected to man by an invisible thread.

After death, the soul-body swims along the river to the world of the dead, while the soul-shadow is sent to the upper reaches of the river, to become a new soul ("omi") there. This "omi" climbs into the body of a woman of the tribe and manifests as a baby.

In this way, a cycle is completed. The river and the stages of life are looped in a closed circle, the structure of which is the ethnocentrum.

The Evenki honor a sacred tree, called "bugady," which is also embodied in the three camps of the *ethnos*. Its roots are the camp of the dead; its trunk, the camp of the living; its branches, the camp of those to be born.

The cycle goes along the river (the horizontal projection of the ethnocentrum) and along the sacred tree (the vertical projection of the ethnocentrum). In both cases, the structure of the ethnocentrum includes visible and invisible objects: the visible river intersects the invisible river; the visible sacred tree intersects the invisible one. The visible and invisible are not in a state of opposition or hierarchical subordination: the visible and the invisible merge like two sides of the same ethnonoema.

There is reason to think that the original structures of the ethno-centrum among the most diverse *ethnoses* resemble in their general features the Evenki model of the world. The river and tree are topics that comprise the core of the mythological complex among the majority of known archaic cultures, although sometimes other figures correspond to them functionally. But the fact that the *dead/living/coming* are thought of spatially, as synchronous zones of the ethnocentrum, and precisely their totality comprises the *ethnos*, is a general property of all cultures. The *ethnos* thinks of itself spatially, as spatially multidimensional, including visible and invisible layers (intertwined with one another). In this space, ancestors and progeny exist not sequentially but simultaneously, compris-ing the total sacred core of the *ethnos*, its identity.

The Evenki describe the world tree as follows. Its roots reach into the lower world; its branches, into the upper world; its trunk is located in the middle world. The animal-mother and horned and animal souls abide there. People live on the trunk. Future people live on the branches in bird form.

The *Ethnos* and Time: Ethnotemporality

The spatiality of the *ethnos* as ethnocentrum predetermines the structure of ethnic time, ethnotemporality. Time in the *ethnos* has a secondary character, subordinated to spatial simultaneity. There are archaic *ethnoses*, in particular certain tribes of Australian aborigines, who do not know how to gauge time at all. They do not count time and although they constantly observe lunar phases, they do not have the slightest idea how many days are in a lunar month. Such an "absence of time" is characteristic of a number of hunter-gatherer *ethnoses*, which live in latitudes where changes of season do not greatly affect climatic conditions. Most often these zones are located near the equator.

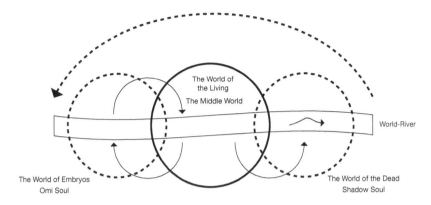

Figure 2. The World River and the Structure of the Ethnocentrum Among the Evenki. Horizontal Presentation.

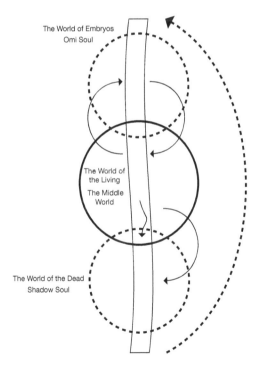

Figure 3. The World River (World Tree) and the Structure of the Ethnocentrum among the Evenki. Vertical Presentation.

In this case the *ethnos* has no notion whatsoever about time or temporality; the *ethnos* can get on quite well without time. Space answers all necessary questions. The ethnocentrum and its structure prove to be enough for the *koineme* to exist. There are no *ethnoses* without a prohibition on incest and without dances. But without time, some *ethnoses* get on rather freely.

This is an important point about the *ethnos* as such. Ethnic time can exist or not but the ethnocentrum is space that always exists and practically coincides with the noetic structure of the *ethnos*, with its thought and the experience of the apprehended world. In the *ethnos*, space is fundamental and primary, and time is derivative, instrumental and secondary.

The predominance of space over time is expressed in the fact that when the *ethnos* has a notion of time, it is cyclical, i.e. subordinate to a spatial indication. Time is closed in on itself; it rotates around its axis in a closed orbit. This circular, cyclical time is nothing other than a diachronic description of space.

Archaic calendars are an example of this. They are most often depicted as a circle or tree; i.e. in the form of the ethnocentrum.

Even when ethnotemporality is present, it is thought of analogously to space. Time is a map, each segment of which, repeating itself, acquires constancy and a spatial character. Ethnotemporality is always reversible. Everything in it is repeated as though it were immutable. Differences of detail in seasonal phenomena do not impact the general fixity of temporality.

Ethnotemporality and the Ethnocentrum in Agrarian and Hunter Societies

We already said that we can introduce into the domain of the simple society (the *ethnos*) two types of archaic culture; the hunter-gatherer and the peasant-gardener. As Thurnwald shows,[15] practically every agrarian

---

15   Richard Turnwald. *Die Menschliche Gesellschaft in ihren ethno-soziologische Grundlagen* [Human Society in its Ethnosociological Foundations, five volumes] (Berlin&Leipzig: Walter de Gruyter & Co, 1931–1935).

society has cyclical temporality, which is connected, to a certain extent, with the specific character of their fundamental economic practices. Seasonal, closed group time is a distinguishing feature of precisely such agrarian *ethnoses*. Among hunters and gatherers, in turn, cyclical temporality can be present or absent. This depends on the most various causes: the surrounding environment, the contrasts of seasons, climate, etc.

We can also observe differences in the both types of *ethnoses'* relation to the ethnocentrum. The society of hunters and gatherers relates to the surrounding world immediately, so their ethnocentrum is more connected, whole, reversible and continual. They live in the world and in thought as in a spatially expressed noesis. So their space is more living and integral.

Agrarian *ethnoses* introduce nuance into the structure of the space of the ethnocentrum by the fact that they distinguish a third, intermediary factor between society and nature: the field, garden, vegetable garden, cattleshed, which act as a special space; fruits and cereals grow there not of themselves and animals must not necessarily be tracked down and hunted but can be bred. In agrarian society, the structure of the ethnocentrum changes qualitatively: the vector of noesis, going "from" and "towards" gradually begins to move "toward" nature, away "from" society itself as "not-nature," and their meeting place becomes a special milieu where human noesis is an instrument of production, which allows them to transition from a reversible model of ethnic thought to an irreversible one.

Nomadic *Ethnoses* and the Specific Character of their Ethnocentrum

Nomadic *ethnoses* and cultures are an entirely special phenomenon. They arise from the one-sided development of numerous tendencies, each of which, in a harmonious state with other tendencies, is present in settled agrarian societies. Thurnwald shows[16] that nomadic *narods* are formed

16   Ibid.

from a core of herdsmen, who breed cattle in settled societies but gradually shift the emphasis to cattle breeding and separate from the stationary settlements in search of new pastures.

Nomads form a specific type of nomadic *ethnos*, characterized by a particular ethnocentrum and specific understanding of ethnotemporality. These *ethnoses* are mobile and constantly relocate in space (this makes them resemble hunter-gatherer societies) but they also have an intermediary layer in the structure of their ethnocentrum: the herd, which separates them from the surrounding environment (which makes them resemble settled agrarian cultures). But if the intermediate zone in the ethnocentrum of agrarian *ethnoses* is static and fixed, among nomadic *ethnoses* it is dynamic and mobile. Moving around in the surroundings of his herds, the nomad constitutes a peculiar type of ethnocentrum, where the "from" and "towards" of the ethnic process of noesis tends towards greater fixity and autonomy than in ethnic societies. The nomadic, pastoral *ethnos* has in its core a prototype of the subject and in the environment in which it moves a prototype of the "object."

The nomadic *ethnos* is the most differentiated form of ethnic structure, where reversibility is limited and the differentiation of society and the surrounding environment reaches a maximum.

Serious transformations also occur with temporality. Among nomadic *ethnoses* it is cyclical, as it is among agrarian ones. But this cyclicity tends toward being open-ended. The relocation of the nomadic *ethnos* in space does not allow one to see the coincidence of the end and the beginning of the cycle as evidently as is the case among settled cultures. Migration disturbs the obviousness of the static picture and gives rise to special phenomena that we will consider in the section on ethnokinetics.

Nomadic *ethnoses* can be thought of as the limit case of the *ethnos*; further, we transition to the first derivation from the *ethnos*, the *narod*. Precisely nomadic *ethnoses* will play a crucial role in the formation of the *narod*, as we will see, and the reasons for this lie in particular in the structure of ethnic space and ethnic time, intrinsic only to nomadic, cattle-rearing cultures.

Ethnoreligious Structures

In the simplest societies, religious structures are not separated into a special social institution or even zone and in principle coincide with the structure of the ethnocentrum. The *ethnos* and ethnocentrum themselves are sacred, sacral. The sacred is mixed with the world as the thinking experience of a multilayered integral presence and does not require any particular fixity. Only those articles, phenomena and beings that are the most concentrated expressions of the structure of the *ethnos* invest the *ethnos* as such with additional meanings and become singled-out zones. Therefore things like rivers, trees, hills (mountains, cliffs), certain animals, plants, stones and spirits (the invisible layer of the ethnocentrum) can act as models of the *ethnos* as such, expressing its entire phenomenal presence.

Thought itself is sacred and in this sense "religious" or pre-religious. Levy-Bruhl emphasizes precisely this point when he speaks of "mystical participation" as the main feature of pre-logical thought.[17] Man participates in the ethnocentrum as an integral part of the whole; each separate member of society is dissolved in the *ethnos*, becoming identical to it. This condition is the source of the religious feeling of the integration of the part in the whole, which possesses attributes of eternity, endlessness, fullness, and immutability. Lacking theology and clearly formulated religious cults, the simplest societies are through and through "religious," in the sense that their very being, including profane economic practices, are integrated into the context of a single, absolute whole. Only as societies become more complex does this diffuse religiosity become concentrated in more concrete and distinct rites, authorities, functions, etc.

Numinousity and Sacrality

To describe the structure of the *ethnos'* religiosity, we should turn to the works of the German historian of religion and Protestant theologian Rudolph Otto (1869–1937), who, following Durkheim, formulated

---

17   Lucien Lévy-Bruhl, *Primitive Mentality* (London: Allen & Unwin, 1923).

and developed the important sociological concept of "the holy" ("*das Heilige*").[18] Otto asserts that there are two aspects to religion: the rational and the irrational. The rational aspect consists of theology, the hierarchy of gods, spirits, angels, demons and other beings on which religious doctrines are based, in the teaching concerning salvation, in religious morality, in sacred history, and in the justification of certain religious institutions, customs and rites. Despite the fact that the preconditions of religion are often irrational, the body of religious ideas itself is, as a rule, a philosophically elaborated logical system.

At the same time, religion has another, irrational dimension. This is what Otto mainly studies, calling it the "holy" ("*das Heilige*").

To describe the essence of the holy, Otto introduces a number of parameters, above all the concept of "*numinousity*" from the Latin "*numen*," which in Latin means "god." But what "god"? Not "*Deus*," the god of the bright sky, the "big god" of theology, the god of the fundamental pantheon. *Numen* is, as a rule, a deity of mid-rank. However, as often happens, the term itself is open to various interpretations. A "big god," the spirit of a river or sacred grove, of rocks, lakes, hearths, strigoi — these can all be called "*numen*." As a rule, *numen* is a deity in a lowered, concrete, near-to-man sense.

From the concept "*numen*" Otto produces the concept "*numinousity*" as a quality of *numena*. Numinousity consists of the peculiar feelings, emotions, conditions and experiences, on the basis of which ancient people distinguished a holy object from a *profane* one.

Numinous experience provokes a certain gamut of very strong emotions. This is not a rational state, not an idea, but precisely a deep *feeling* touching all levels of the human psyche. Otto describes this feeling phenomenologically.

To characterize it, he draws on the Latin expression "*mysterium tremendum*." *Tremendum*, from the Latin *tremor* (literally "tremor," "trembling"), signifies "panicked horror." *Mysterium tremendum* is the feeling

---

18 Rudolph Otto, *The Idea of the Holy: An Inquiry into the non-rational factor in the idea of the divine and its relation to the rational* (London: Oxford University Press, 1958).

of panicked, causeless horror that seizes man, for instance, in darkness, in an unfamiliar, empty home or in a wild forest, and which has no visible cause. The presence of numinousity, the encounter with a "numen," makes itself known through total, senseless, primordial fear, forcing man to fall into a stupor, a tremor, a panicked fear.

We should search for the sources of more complex, developed religious institutions in numinousity as the distinct characteristic of the *ethnos* to experience a sudden, staggering, elemental psychical fear.

The historian of religion Mircea Eliade and the psychoanalyst Carl Jung borrowed from Otto the idea of numinousity as the main trait of the holy. Eliade wrote a whole series of later works on the basis of the study of numinousity among archaic *ethnoses* and cultures (African and Australian in particular).[19] Jung relied on the idea of numinousity to ground his theory of the collective unconscious, where at certain points there are areas responsible for special ecstatic states.

SECTION TWO
The Anthropology of the *Ethnos*: The Shaman, Gender, Identity

Status, Person, Mask

Now, let us consider the anthropological problem in the *ethnos*, taken as a static phenomenon.

The stance towards the individual in the *ethnos* is determined by the basic aim of minimalizing or altogether denying individual identity. This theme was studied thoroughly by anthropologists on the example of many archaic societies. Practically none of them knows the social status of the

---

19 Mircea Eliade, *Australian Religions: An Introduction* (Ithaca, New York: Cornell University Press, 1966); Mircea Eliade, *Aspects du Mythe* (Paris: Gallimard, 1963); Mircea Eliade, *Rites and Symbols of Initiation: The Mysteries of Birth and Rebirth* (New York: Harper & Row, 1975).

individual. The anthropological circle of the American anthropologists Ruth Benedict and Abram Kardiner proposed to use the special term "personality" to describe the status of the human in the simplest society. They understood "personality" as a purely social phenomenon, consisting of a set of statuses and roles (Linton), which in turn possess a collective, supra-individual nature.

Society contains the set of possible statuses. This set is apprehended so evidently and "objectively" that it serves, as a rule, as a basis for a universal taxonomy including not only society but the external world. The status-set of the *ethnos* is cosmic; i.e. it connects the structure of culture and nature as an indivisible unit. Social status is possessed not only by people but animals, plants, spirits, the souls of the dead and natural phenomena. In the same way, special traits and qualities of the non-human world are applied to humans as a kind of status. Examples of this are totemism, i.e. the acknowledgement of some animal ancestor of the tribe or genus (in the case of the totem character of the generic chain, the phratries or clans), "spirit dances" and shamanic trances and rites, in which masks symbolizing animals are used.

Masks can serve overall as the main taxon of status in the ethnos. Claude Lévi-Strauss studied this theme in detail in his work *The Way of the Masks*.[20] It is significant that the Greek word for "persona" or "person," περσονα, literally means "mask."

In the *ethnos*, everything is a mask. The structure of ethnic being is personified. Ethnic thought does not raise the question of who the mask conceals or whom the mask indicates. "Personality" is a moment of ethnic noesis and possesses qualities but not substances. Kardiner called it "basic personality," which differs from the "personality" of more complex societies in that it is considered apart from its bearer; i.e. it is not unique but typical, or "basic."

That is why in the majority of archaic languages there is not a term even closely analogous to "human" and all the more so "individual." Even

---

20 Claude Lévi-Strauss, *The Way of the Masks* (Vancouver: University of British Columbia Press, 1999).

the tribe does not have its own name and is defined as a status: totemic, economic, visual, etc.

Redfield defined "folk society" (a synonym for *ethnos*) as a community, all relations inside of which are personalized. He meant not only that all members of society know each other personally but that the relations among them, and also with the external, natural world, are built on the basis of status and statuses. Relations among people and relations between people and the surrounding environment are a carousel of masks, a single dance in which statuses and roles rhythmically come together and separate.

The principle of the personality-mask guarantees the *ethnos* constancy and invariability. There is no room in the *ethnos* for individuality, originality and singularity. If the *ethnos*, abiding in a static equilibrium (homeostasis) encounters striking individuality, it perceives this as threat and danger and classifies the phenomenon as deviance, anomaly, a challenge demanding removal and other repressive measures. Whatever transgresses the limits of the status-set, the codified structure of a concrete *ethnos*, is either ignored or repressed and crushed.

For precisely this reason the explanation of social regularities on the basis of the interrelations among separate members of society, on which many sociological theories are built (in the first place, that of the American Chicago School sociologists and the "understanding sociology" of Max Weber) is inapplicable to the study of the *ethnos*. The individual appears as a social phenomenon only in the societies derived from the *ethnos* and only in those more complex social systems does the individual begin to play some role. In ethnic society, there is neither individual nor collective (as a collection of individuals); there is not even a separate society and separate nature. There is only the world of masks, coming together and coming apart in self-sufficient semantic sequences.

People, spirits, animals, plants and stars can be related to one of two of these masks or basic personalities. Man becomes man (a personality) by wearing a mask — in some cases a ritual mask, a less noticeable one in other cases — in which he proves to be in the structure of the *ethnos*. But becoming a man, man in the *ethnos* becomes something more than man. He is connected to the general sum of cosmic knowledge contained in status; he becomes a cosmic personality. Status integrates man into social-cosmic orders and masks show visibly how this happens.

The Duality of Masks: Swaihwe, Dzonokwa

Figure 4. Swaihwe Mask.   **Figure 5.** Dzonokwa Mask.

In *The Way of the Masks*, Lévi-Strauss illustrates the dual character of the ritual masks of a few tribes of North American Indians, the Cowan, Kwak'wala and others in the Salish linguistic family. The duality of masks predetermines a certain anthropological duality of the *ethnos*. This dualism, the main concretization of the status model, is not limited to human society but extends to the entire environment, including natural phenomena and myths.

Lévi-Strauss describes two types of mask and two associated sets of myths, rites, beliefs and taboos. In the language of the Salish, the first type is called "Swaihwe" and depicts a face with bulging eyes, protruding nose, teeth that stick out and horns, and which is bordered by feathers. The second type is called "Dzonokwa." It has empty, sunken eye sockets, an open mouth and hair or feathers on top. These masks represent the two general status sets of the *ethnos*, two versions of "basic personality."

The version of the swaihwe mask is functionally, ritually and semantically connected with fullness and overflowing abundance. The dancers who wear this mask are thought to be able to provoke earthquakes, tempests and dreadful catastrophes if they are not stopped in time. This is the pole of the saturation and fullness of the world.

The dzonokwa mask, on the other hand, depicts insufficiency, damage and failures in the field of existence. It is as dangerous as the first mask, not from power but from its oppressive weakness.

The two status sets expressed in the two masks and the mythological and ritual complexes associated with them generalize the complex chains of statuses, reducing them to paradigmatic abundance and insufficiency, vital energy and dying (entropy), movement outward from within and from without inward, etc. It is a kind of basis for the grammar of society, manifest in social pairs one way or another associated with masks.

Ethnic Dichotomies

The duality of masks as a summary of the basic status sets splits up into a number of secondary internal dichotomies, through which the human (or more precisely cosmo-human) principle is realized in the *ethnos*. These secondary dichotomies all somehow relate to gender. Thus, *ethnos* and its structures are to a significant extent built around gender.

Gender dualism and the status dualism associated with it also have a cosmic dimension. Animals, stars, plants, stones, natural phenomena and also articles, rites and social institutions in the *ethnos* necessarily have a sex. This sex has a status quality and is "personal": sex as a place is reserved in a series from which the world and society are formed [пол — как место, зарезервированное в рядах, из которых складывается мир и общества]. In the *ethnos*, sex is status.

In the masks studied by Lévi-Strauss, the swaihwe is the male mask and the dzonokwa is the female. But it is important to notice that it is not accurate to say that the former "depicts a man" and the latter a "woman." The semantics of the *ethnos* first considers the general and only then the particular. The man "depicts" the swaihwe, plays its role, bears its status and the woman accomplishes the same with respect to the dzonokwa. "Personality" as a socio-cosmic phenomenon is much broader than sex in the purely human sense.

Thus, ethnic gender is a socio-cosmic taxon.

This fundamental, dual status quality manifests in the following ways:

- In the *exogamous structure of the genus*, which presumes a simple or more complex structure of characteristics;

- The resultant *zoning of the social space of the ethnos' habitation*, in which one way or another *generic* territories are distinguished (often organized dichotomously or in relation to more complex symmetries, elevated into dichotomies);

- *The functional understanding of the statuses* of men and women;

- The gendered *division of labor*;

- The gendered *organization of space*.

Homo Exogamous

The ethnic human is an exogamous human. V. V. Ivanov wrote about this colorfully in his public lecture *Dual Structures in Society*. We will adduce some excerpts from there.[21]

> With my friends and my co-author Vladimir Nikolaevich Toporov, I made an expedition in 1962 to study the Ket, a somewhat mysterious Siberian people. Today, they live on the Yenisei… We arrived in one of the little villages, to which these nomads found their way in the past… A few people came to us in the school. Among them were an old lady and a young man of about twenty, already fully Soviet. He was a member of the Komsomol and spoke Russian well. We sat together all evening and they would translate for me some phrases that I would say to them in Russian but then I grew tired of this and understood that the whole time I was telling them something of my own. And I told the young man, 'You know, it is better if you say something to me in your own language but

---

21   Vycheslav Vsevolod Ivanov, *Dual Structures in Society*, Available online at http://www. polit.ru/lectures/2005/09/06/ivanov.html [Accessed July 31, 2017].

something that in its content seems essential to you; the first thing that comes to you but something of your own.' And, having thought it over, the first thing he said to me was, 'Always take a wife from the other half of the tribe.' And this is the slogan on which is built what we call the dual organization of the society of ancient and primitive peoples.

Here, Ivanov describes the basis of ethnic anthropology, governed by the most important rule: exogamy ("always take a wife from the other half of the tribe"). "The other half of the tribe" means "the other genus," which is not one's own and which allows the marriage to be legitimate.

There are two very important points to be observed. The anatomic duality of sex — male and female — is not enough for marriage. This duality is not basic and cannot be regarded as the core of status. The core of status, in the words of the Ket, reported by Ivanov, is "the half of the tribe," which acts as "other" in relation to the first half.[22] Only a woman of "the other half of the tribe" is a *social woman* (a bride, a wife) in the *ethnos*. The woman of "this half of the tribe" is not a social woman in the full sense. She can become a social woman only in the process of being married into the other half and only for the members of the other half.

Ivanov develops this thought in the continuation of his lecture:

Society was divided into two halves. Each half knew about itself. What concerns these Ket, I can say that they also related certain animals to humans. In particular, the bear has a few souls, as people do. Hence, when a bear is killed, there is a bear festival after the hunt, during which they fortune-tell. They throw bear bones and determine in this way to which half of the tribe the bear belonged. A part of the animal world is also divided into these halves. And in general the whole world is divided in two halves. That is what we call dualistic mythology. All mythological beings and elements — sky, earth, etc. — are also divided into two groups, which correspond to the halves of the tribe.[23]

The concretization of status in the *ethnos* was therefore a necessary belonging to one of the two halves. And in certain cases precisely this

22   Aleksandr M. Zolotarev, *Rodovoy stroy i pervobytnaya mifologiya* (Moskva: Nauka, 1964).

23   Ivanov, *Dual Structures in Society.*

status was decisive. What is important is not whether one is talking about a human or a bear but whether the given "personality" belongs to one or another half of the tribe.

Homo Ludens in Ethnic Duality

The anthropological dualism of exogamous genera predetermines the dual structure of the settlement, where differences among exogamous groups are spatially emphasized. This predetermines the localization of the genus and, correspondingly, matriarchal and patriarchal structures, about which we spoke when reviewing the ideas of Lévi-Strauss.

The binary organization of social space leads to the same dualism of masks discussed above. This was often underscored by a certain hierarchization in the totem symbols of genera and in local legends and rites. An extremely important task for the *ethnos* was to draw a clear line between two status complexes, by means that included the localization of generic settlements. This physical border was supplemented by numerous methods of drawing the line on the level of inter-genus relations.

Here we must draw on the works of the Dutch cultural theorist and historian Johan Huizinga (1872–1945), who in his book *Homo Ludens*[24] studied the meaning of games for the establishment of human culture. Huizinga shows that the game lies at the foundation of many social and cultural institutions, including philosophy, music, theater, religion, etc. The basic algorithm of the game, according to Huizinga, comes down to the playing field (play space) of the two exogamous groups of the *ethnos*, which through competition, content, opposition and even rivalry and enmity organize the social field such that the unity of the *ethnos* is preserved, while a strict internal divide between the two (or more) parts is drawn. This combination of moderated opposition, which does not pass over into direct enmity and does not disturb the integral harmony of the *ethnos*, lies at the basis of culture as a phenomenon.

---

24 Johan Huizinga, *Homo Ludens: A Study of the Play Element in Culture* (London: Maurice Temple Smith Ltd., 1970).

This explains perfectly the structures of the *ethnos'* dual anthropology, embodied in the duality of the basic status sets. The group of one mask (personality) competes with the group of another mask in order to emphasize their difference within a general unity. The possibility of full-fledged exogamy is realized only thanks to this game. But the most important thing here is the *proportions* of the game, i.e. the game itself, which is called on to make the distinction but such that it does not provoke a schism and transition to direct enmity and aggression, i.e. to the cleavage of the *ethnos*. After all, the second (opposed) group/mask is an "in-law" and source of women and wives for the other group/mask. Enmity and contention between phratries are thus inseparably connected with marital symbolism.

If we use Huizinga's expression, we can say that "ethnic man is playing man," "*homo ludens*," who in the course of the game realizes all his main "personal" functions. The *ethnos* is the space of interphratrial and simultaneously marital games.

Gender and Labor

A gendered division of labor is observed in the most simple and archaic societies. Men primarily hunt and women gather. At the same time, it is thought that the most ancient forms of hunting are catching wild animals with the help of snares, traps and nets, like fishing. The bow and arrow and the spear are invented, among the most archaic societies, under the influence of external impulses.

Women in such societies gather fruit or collect edible roots (in particular, yam). Bound to their children and often pregnant, the women of archaic *ethnoses* do not wander far from their home. Men, at any rate, move further away.

Care for children and maintenance of the hearth, as well as preparing food, are considered female labor even where light sheds or natural shelters are used for housing. In archaic hamlets, the "home" is the hearth and care for it is practically always and without exception the woman's prerogative.

These gender functions are also an integral part of gender status. The figure of the "digger," "gatherer," "caretaker of the hearth," the one who "tends to the children," and "prepares food," is a female gender set. The one who "leaves far from home," "hunts for animals" and "has snares" is a male gender set.

In agrarian societies, the gender division of labor changes qualitatively. The significance and value of women grow, since agrarian *ethnoses* depend vitally on gardens and fields, with which women are predominantly occupied. They secure the stable provision of products, developing their gender labor (gathering close to home) in the direction of artificial organization around the settlement of a cultivated, worked space. In archaic societies, the working the soil by hoe is a woman's affair. The men, as a rule, engage in planting garden trees, which they place into holes dug by women.

If in agrarian societies the woman cares for the garden and field, the man breeds cattle. Overall, in agrarian societies the woman's status increases substantially, which can produce either a matriarchal or patriarchal outcome. In the first case, the status set of "women's masks" acquires an additional degree of freedom, which shows itself in particular in the heightened erotic freedom of girls before marriage and more public functions for primarily older women. In the second case, men begin to relate to woman as an "instrumental value," leading to polygamy and patriarchy.

Finally, in societies of nomad-herdsmen, the structuring of a strict and asymmetrical patriarchy occurs. Male status is placed in a clear vertical position above female status, producing the specific social quality of nomadic *ethnoses*, polygamous without exception, where women are related to as property and the first legal and economic codes take shape, firmly anchoring masculine status as the norm in the social order.

In nomadic society, the role of women first becomes entirely subordinate and unambiguously secondary, which is not the case with either hunter or agrarian *ethnoses*, where a gender balance of status is somehow preserved. Male and female masks there supplement each other. In nomadic, pastoral societies, the gender dichotomy acquires for the first time an irreversible masculine form.

The Shaman: The Main Figure of the *Ethnos*

From the perspective of the anthropology of the *ethnos*, we should distinguish that figure in whom all the major statuses are simultaneously concentrated and who can thus be considered the direct expression of "basic personality," as the predominant "person." This is the figure of the shaman.

The shaman stands at the center of the *ethnos* and is its principal "mask," "the mask of masks." The shaman is the personification and functional synthesis of the *ethnos*. He fulfills the *ethnos'* main task: he takes care to preserve the constancy of the ethnic structure. The shaman expresses *balance*, that which makes the *ethnos* an *ethnos* — invariability, continuity, the translation of the code, the transmission of knowledge (myths, rites, traditions) and the correction of the *ethnos'* social and natural faults. The shaman ensures the invariability of the stasis. He is the expression of the *ethnos* as a static phenomenon.

All private functions — healing, prophecy, rites, driving out spirits (the functions of psychopomp), trance, participation in marriage ceremonies, religious cults, magical operations, etc. — stem from the main function: the shaman must exist. His existence-presence ensures that which is the *ethnos*. An *ethnos* without a shaman is so fragile a phenomenon that it threatens to fall apart at once. In one of his works about shamanism among the Tungus, Shirokogorov writes that the Tungus fear nothing more than the period when one shaman dies and another has not yet been initiated or has yet to assume his duties.[25] This interval of "existence with a shaman" is considered a catastrophe and the most dreadful ordeal.

---

25 Sergei M. Shirokogorov, *Versuch einer Erforschung der Grundlagen des Schamanentums bei den Tungusen* (Verlag von Dietrich Reimer, 1935).

The Shaman: Leader of Souls and Protector of the Ethnocentrum

We can observe the integral significance of the shaman as the center of ethnic anthropology in the case of the Evenki. Precisely the shaman, in Evenki thinking, is in change of the most important processes in the circulation of souls through the force-lines of the ethnocentrum.

When an Evenk dies, his body is placed on a special platform in a distant place in the Taiga.[26] It is thought that the soul-body remains with him until only the skeleton is left of the corpse. In that moment, the shaman performs the "anan" ritual. He enters into a trance and leads the soul-body of the dead Evenk to the mouth of the river, to the camp of the ancestors. There, he gives it to the "ancients," after which, having returned, he carefully closes the passage with the help of spirit-helpers.

Another soul of the dead, the soul-shadow, becomes invisible and transforms into something new, an omi-soul. "Omi" means "coming to be," "origination," "embryo." The omi-soul moves to the sources of the river of the *ethnos* and settles there (in the "omiruk" world).

Then, a very important moment in the posthumous drama is played out. After some time, the chief of the settlement of ancestors, the great "mangi" (the ancestor-bear) observes that the shaman brought him not the whole person but only his shadow, the soul-body; the soul-shadow is missing. Mangi raises himself to the sources of the river, finds the missing soul and commands it to go to him. Along the way, the soul-shadow fools "mangi," transforms into a bird or animal and returns to "omiruk," to the sources of the river. From there, the omi-soul flies into the middle settlement of living Evenki, slips into the chimney of a yurt to the altar of the female spirit "togo mushun," to whom sacrifices are constantly brought, and then jumps imperceptibly into the body of the yurt's woman-proprietess.[27] As a result, she gives birth and everything is repeated anew.

---

26   Friedrich, *Das Bewusstsein eines naturvolkes von Haushalt und Ursprung des Lebens*, 188.

27   "The spirit of the tribal fire [...] is called *togo mushun*. The first word, "*togo*," literally means "fire"; the second, "*mushun*," is translated in Russian-Evenki dictionaries as

The shaman fulfils a vital function: he leads the soul-body into the dwelling-place of the ancestors at the delta of the river of the *ethnos* and "fools" mangi, so that another soul, the soul-shadow, would have enough time to transform into an omi and fly away to the sources of the river. If someone dies in the period when the tribe has no shaman, the process of the circulation of souls stops. All souls would go the world of the ancestors, and there would be no one to be born.

The shaman also ensures the protection of the ethnocentrum. He encloses the territory in which the *ethnos* lives with a certain invisible fence, which passes along the rivers, knolls, meadows and thickets. This fence is called a "marylya" and it prevents evil spirits from entering the *ethnos'* territory and upsetting its equilibrium. The shaman is helped in this by bird spirits, animal spirits, fish spirits and earth spirits. They build the fence of the ethnocentrum through all the elements, reorganizing the sacred strata of the cosmos.[28]

The Shaman and Reintegration

The rite of shamanic initiation is very meaningful from the perspective of the anthropology of the *ethnos*. When an old shaman dies, his animal double (hargi) goes to the lower reaches of the river and sends word of this event to the first-ancestor-bear (mangi). Then mangi commands one of the souls of the earlier deceased shamans to go the settlement of the living and to find there a fitting young man or woman for embodiment. Having tracked down a candidate, the spirit falls on him and invites or forces him to become a shaman. Thus begins the period of testing for

---

"a spirit, a lord of natural phenomena" (*mu mushin*: "a spirit, the lord of water," *ure mushun*: "a spirit, the lord of mountains," etc.). We cannot pass by the fact that the Evenki use the word *mushun* as an expression for the concept "spirit-lord" only for natural phenomena." Arkady Anisimov, *Religiya evenkov v istoriko-geneticheskom izuchenii i problemy proiskhozhdeniya pervobytnykh verovaniy* (Moscow-Leningrad: Academy of Sciences of the USSR 1958), 102.

28 Arkady Anisimov, "Shamanskiye dukhi po vozzreniyam evenkov i totemisticheskiye istoki shamanstva" in *Sbornik Muzeia Anthropologii i Etnografii* 13 (1951), 226.

the chosen one. This is called the "shaman disease."[29] The young man or woman stops working, runs into the forest, eats nothing and acts abnormally from the perspective of all of the tribe's usual ways. The Evenki think the soul-shadow of this person, together with the soul of the old shaman, begins its journey through the mountains of the ancestors, until both souls reach the primordial center, the first-mountain of the *ethnos*.

There, at the foot of the shaman tree, surrounded by horned animal spirits, there is the great animal-mother, most often depicted as a mother-deer. The spirit of the initiated enters the animal-mother and she begets him as a four-legged animal, fish or bird, and occasionally as a human. This depends on the totem structure of the genus to which the shaman belongs.

When the mother-deer begets a new shaman in animal form, the mountain transforms into a house, the mother-deer into an old woman and the spirits into human figures. They all dismember the future shaman, tear out his bones, temper them on the fire, forge them and gather them into a new anthropomorphic form.

Afterward, the newly assembled shaman, together with the spirit-helpers and animal-helpers received from the animal-mother, returns to his tribe and is solemnly initiated there. From that moment, he becomes the heart of the *ethnos*.

In the description of the ritual of shamanic initiation, we should note the alternation of forms: human, animal and spiritual (spirits). Many archaic *ethnoses* have a legend according to which "there was a time" when people, spirits and animals were one and the same species and could freely change form, depending on the situation. But then, as a result of some tragic event, they all lost their freedom. Whomever this event (its form and meaning are rather difficult to reconstruct correctly) caught in human form remained human; whomever in animal form, animal; whomever in spirit form, spirit.

---

29   Mircea Eliade, *Shamanism: Archaic Techniques of Ecstasy* (Princeton: Princeton University Press, 1972).

In his initiation, the shaman returns to the state when this separation had not "yet" happened. He integrates in himself all world-levels, animal, human and spiritual, re-establishing primordial nature through the rite of initiation. But now his three-fold nature is expressed through spirit-helpers and animal-helpers. Entering into a trance, the shaman becomes integrated anew and in his wanderings and battles he is transformed now into a spirit, now into an animal and then once again to human.

Here is the key to the normative anthropology of the *ethnos*. The *ethnos* is fully integral and includes both the human and the nonhuman (animal, spiritual). And in the *ethnos* only that person is of full value who is simultaneously living and dead, ancestor and offspring, human and animal. This unification of opposites is expressed in the shaman, who often wears clothes of the opposite sex and in general acts according to rules differing significantly from the rules of the rest of the members of the *ethnos*. The shaman, re-establishing himself as the primordial human, gets the ability to re-establish other members of the *ethnos* too. This is expressed in healings, in the protection of the ethnocentrum through the magic fence, in battles with evil spirits, in conducting the deceased to the foot of the great river, etc. The shaman is the concentrated figure of the ethnocentrum. He is the ethnocentrum.

Summary

The static structure of the *ethnos* is formed of a few fundamental elements:

- Ethnic intentionality, the paradigm of mythological thought;
- The ethnocentrum, a spatially synchronic model of the world, a multi-layered map;
- Ethnotemporality, the organization of ethnic time, most often in the form of cycles and the "eternal return";
- The "basic personality" of the *ethnos* as a status set, the "mask";
- The binary model of society, in the form of exogamy, the gender division of labor, etc.;

- Ethnic anthropology, expressed most clearly in the figure and function of the shaman, the normative cosmo-human.

We encounter this clear structure in its pure guise only in the simplest *ethnoses*. As a rule, the real structure is more complex and nuanced. But if we consider this structure as a kind of model, a conceptual map of ethnic analysis, then it will help us significantly in studying the infinite variety of archaic *ethnoses*, which can be classified and studied in accordance with this model. It will also help us in investigating the structure of more complex societies, derived from the *ethnos*.

This is easy to check, if we pay attention to the fact that contemporary sociology makes its analysis of complex societies on analogous principles, in which:

- Ethnic intentionality corresponds to "collective consciousness," "public opinion," or "mentality";

- The ethnocentrum is the organization of social space, for instance city or industrial architecture;

- Ethnotemporality is the sociology of time, studied, for instance, by Gurvich;

- "Basic personality" is the "sociological man" (Dahrendorf);

- The binary model is the sexual differentiation of contemporary society and the dual code in law, philosophy, technology, morals, religion, etc.;

- Ethnic anthropology is the figure of the autonomous individual, as "fantastical" in its normative features and ontological characteristics as is the figure of the shaman.

The difference is only that classical sociology begins by considering contemporary society (i.e. from sociology) and projects its norms onto archaic society (the *ethnos*), while ethnosociology proposes to reverse this procedure and consider contemporary society as a version of archaic society. These approaches do not exclude but rather supplement each other.

Thus, often in the twentieth century the thin line between sociology and anthropology (i.e. ethnosociology) was blurred and many major authors (Durkheim, Mausse, Lévi-Strauss, Malinowski, Evans-Pritchard, Marcel Granet, Ralph Linton, Abram Kardiner, Richard Thurnwald, etc.) can easily be related to one or the other scientific branches.

CHAPTER TWO

Ethnodynamics

The Meaning of Ethnodynamics in the Preservation of the Invariable Structure of the *Ethnos*

The Will to Stasis

The static picture of the *ethnos* is a normative model, a kind of ideal, toward which ethnic society strives. The *ethnos* strives to be itself, i.e. invariable and constant, a structure of perfect equilibrium. The essence of the *ethnos* consists in harmony and permanency. Thus, the static structure of the *ethnos* can be regarded as its existential goal. The purpose of the *ethnos* is to be static. At its basis lies the *will to stasis*.

The invariability of the *ethnos* and the permanence of its structures cannot be thought as a sociological fatality. The dimension of freedom is intrinsic to all human types. Man can always say "yes" or "no" to what he is, to his environment, to the social order that affects him, etc. So, we can speak precisely of the *will* to stasis as a certain value-choice and realization of human freedom. Invariability is not fate for the *ethnos* but a result of a kind of work of the spirit, asserting a certain norm and striving to embody it in reality, thereby producing that reality.

The *ethnos* produces invariability and lives it. So there is always space for choice in the *ethnos*: to say "yes" or "no" to invariability. Conservatism, the maintenance of some order of things or another, in contrast with the ordinary understanding of it, demands tremendous effort, a resolute choice imbued with constant value-quality, intensive labor, effort and social work. The *ethnos* works for the structure of the *ethnos* to be constant. This work forms a certain dimension of the *ethnos*, which can be called ethnodynamics.

The Definition of Ethnodynamics and the Concept of "Danger"

Ethnodyanmics is the sphere of processes that:

- Emerge from the *ethnos* both in its relations with its environment and within its social structure;

- Aim at to preserve the structure of the *ethnos* unchanged;

- Oppose the appearance in the *ethnos* of what can be called "the new," "the event" or "the social dimension."

Ethnodynamic processes have a reactive character (they are most often responses to challenges and not challenges themselves) and are fluctuations, i.e. oscillations around a strictly given point or axis. In the dynamics of the *ethnos*, forces participate and energy is expended. But these forces and this energy are called on to ensure the preservation of the invariable, static picture of the *ethnos*, the constancy of the structure of the ethnocentrum.

The Greek word δύναμις, from which the term "dynamics" and "ethnodynamics" are formed, means "force." The Russian word for force, "sila," stems from an Indo-European root shared by the German term "die Seele" and the English "soul." The *ethnos* thinks of the presence of force as animacy, the activity of the soul. In Greek, "soul" is "ψυχη" — "psyche," from which we get "psyche." Connecting these words with each other, we get an idea of the unified complex "soul-force" or the "psychic" dimension of the *ethnos*. The domain of ethnodynamics can be called the zone of the *intensive psychic activity of the ethnos.*

The *ethnos* as *koineme* recognizes to a certain extent that the invariability of its structure, taken as a norm and existential goal, is threatened by "danger." In stasis, this "danger" is discarded and thought of as something "overcome." That is why the ethnocentrum is a zone of safety. Everyone in the ethnocentrum is safe and the ethnocentrum, theoretically, includes everyone. But that is the norm. In reality, "danger" occasionally arises and makes itself known. Resistance to this "danger," its removal and overcoming, comprises the main meaning of ethnodynamics. The *ethnos* moves and changes to overcome the "danger" contained in movement and change. This is movement in place, which is often not that simple.

We can observe this in the circulation of souls in the ethnocentrum. The death and birth of the person are thought of as included in the general invariable structure of the cycle: new souls, old souls, and both are eternal souls. While there is the *ethnos*, there is no death and the constancy of an eternal return of souls is preserved. The eternity of souls is thought of concretely as the eternity of life and the eternity of the *ethnos*, as the eternity of the ethnocentrum. There is no danger within it: everything inside the ethnocentrum lives eternally and remains eternally itself and the same.

But in order for eternity to be ensured, serious efforts must be undertaken, directed at maintaining unchanged the general structural of the ethnocentrum. This is the domain of ethnodynamics.

The Shaman and His Ethnodynamic Functions

The shaman plays the main role in ethnodynamics.[1] Precisely he, as we already saw, ensures the closure of interethnic processes, helps guard the *ethnos* against external influences, facilitates the circulation of souls and heals sicknesses. The shaman is the basis of the *ethnos*, its existential focus point, its life axis. The shaman is responsible in the first place for making sure that no "social changes" occur in the *ethnos*, that the "new" is excluded outright. Thus, his main function consists in the realization of dynamic conservatism.

---

1   Eliade, *Shamanism*.

This is most clearly expressed in shamanic initiation.

At the start of this initiation, the shaman falls ill with the "shamanic disease," i.e. he shows signs of anomalous, deviant behavior. He takes on himself "danger," "risk." This is something "new" as unforeseen in the *ethnos*' normative structures. The shaman acts "oddly" (i.e. uncommonly, unusually) and this feature becomes a mark of his chosenness. He falls ill to recover and later to heal others.

Later in the process of initiation, the shaman overcomes the "primordial catastrophe," during which the ancient synthetic beings were divided into spirits, people, and animals. That is, the shaman copes successfully with danger and mends the general all-embracing structure of the ethnocentrum, which was threatened by "transformation." The division of the primordial beings into three types was "new," an "event," a "social change," the original catastrophe and splintering of the ethnocentrum. This was "danger" in its paradigmatic expression and any "danger" the *ethnos* encounters repeats to a certain extent this tragic algorithm of division: the separation of soul from body, loss, deprivation, the disintegration of social institutions, etc. The differentiation of the *ethnos* as an indivisible, continuous whole is thought of as "evil." "Evil" begets "danger" and the shaman removes this danger.

In the shamanic initiation, the shaman re-establishes the primordial unity of souls, people, and animals through the discovery of helpers. He undergoes reintegration, overcomes the threat and himself becomes the bearer of wholeness. This inner wholeness, won in the course of initiation, is what guarantees his ability to heal (make whole) others. The Latin saying "*medice, cura te ipsum*" ("physician, heal thyself") is fully realized in the shaman's case. His initiation is his healing, the realization of an anthropological norm, the restoration of the fullness and wholeness of the ethnocentrum. Becoming "healthy," "whole," the shaman furthers the recovery and healing of everything else.

The essence of ethnodynamics consists in this: overcoming the "new," which is thought of only and always as a "catastrophe," even if only because the "new" is different from the old and not reducible to it, and hence a differentiation, a division of a whole, indivisible unity.

SECTION TWO

Ethnosocialization

Ethnosocialization as a Process

The psychic work of the *ethnos* can be reduced to *the process of ethnosocialization*. Any institution, any rite, any human act in the *ethnos* can be regarded as a moment of ethnosocialization. In this process, there are essential, cardinal points and secondary ones. But in any case, ethnic being unfolds as a continuous and constant process of ethnosocialization.

Ethnosocialization expresses the essence of ethnodynamics. In order to be, the *ethnos* must become. Thus, the *ethnos* is constantly becoming itself, constantly striving toward its own self-identity and invariability. Ethnosocialization aims at this end. It continuously confirms the identity of the *ethnos*, its self-identity. In this process, the members of the *ethnos* say "yes" to the *ethnos* and give their assent and support to the ethnic structure as a standard, normative and "good," and hence also real. In ethnic intentional thought, the good, the normative and the "real" (actually existing) correspond.

So the process of ethnosocialization consists not simply of the constant embedding of the individual in the *ethnos* but the constant assertion, through this embedding or embeddedness, of the *ethnos*' identity itself.

The French ethnosociologist Maurice Leenhardt wrote of *Do Kamo* as a general and super-individual ethnic "subject," embracing separate sacred articles and phenomena.[2] Ethnosocialization can be regarded as the constant affirmation of the being of *Do Kamo*, its constitution through the use of the social injunctions of the *ethnos*. *Do Kamo* actually exists but at the same time it *should* exist, it is a good, a moral imperative. So, free from and incommensurably surpassing each person, *Do Kamo* depends on the

---

2   Maurice Leenhardt, *Do Kamo: Person and Myth in the Melanesian World* (Chicago: Chicago University Press, 1979). See also Alexander Dugin, *Sotsiologiya voobrazheniya. Vvedeniye v strukturnuyu sotsiologiyu* (Moskva: Akademicheskiy Proyekt, 2010), 222–224.

whole ethnic community, which it itself is. The individual is a mask, a sign but a functional sign, which, recognizing and acknowledging itself as such, secures the general order of things. The *ethnos* disappears if it refuses to say "yes" to *Do Kamo*, to honor it, to bring it sacrifices, to observe its taboos, to follow its arrangements. Thus, the whole *ethnos* depends on the ethnosocialization of each of its members separately. Living, the *ethnos* produces and upholds *Do Kamo*.

Name and Situation

A principal form of ethnosocialization is the acquisition of a "name." The possession of a "name" in the *ethnos* is the main condition of belonging to it. The name is the place of the individual in the ethnic structure. As is the name, so is the individual. The same name can be given to different individuals but their status in ethnic society in this case will be regarded as something identical. And since status in the *ethnos is* the person, these two individuals will be regarded as the same individual, with all the consequences that follow. That is why in the *ethnos* practically no one has identical names; in the opposite case, they would be the same person.

This helps us understand the difficulty connected with the idea of reincarnation of souls or people, the elements of which many anthropologists discover in diverse archaic and religious cultures (in particular, in Hinduism and Buddhism, especially Tibetan, in which the translation of the status of the Dalai Lama and other elites of the hierarchy of the Lamaists is based on reincarnation). Most archaic thought does not regard the soul or human as individual substance. The soul is a function, a mask, signifying a certain concrete element in the general structure of the ethnocentrum. Since the ethnocentrum is integral, holistic, this element can be found correlated with spatial orientations, the landscape, animals, plants, natural phenomena and also with technical instruments, spirits, or temporary, cyclical factors. The element of the ethnocentrum, defined by one or a few parameters (for instance, Black Deer, Big Crow, Flying Arrow, Fire Steel, Winter Snow, etc.), is a name. But inasmuch as the ethnocentrum is general, in naming some marker of its element the remaining markers are implied and are easily recognized in ethnic culture. That is, the name is always a metonym, explicitly naming one or a few markers of the ethnocentrum's element but implying the remaining, unnamed manifold, perfectly apparent to the members of the *ethnos*. The elements of the ethnocentrum are constant in ethnostatics but in ethnodynamics they depart and return. This can sometimes be depicted as "reincarnation" but since there is no individual substance in the *ethnos*, there is also nothing that would reincarnate. We are dealing with the theoretical constancy of functions (an ensemble of names, coinciding with language), manifested through their permanent circulation.

Accordingly, the individual in the *ethnos* has no separate being, distinct from his name (as a sign, mask, function). Man is only a function and name. Without a name, he does not exist. The *ethnos* gives a name and the name contains a meaning and function clearly indicating a place in the ethnocentrum. Only the ethnocentrum and its "places" exist. These places are names. The individual exists to the extent to which he occupies a place in the ethnocentrum.

We can draw an important conclusion from what we have said. *Man in the ethnos is thought of as situation.* The Latin word "situatio" means "arrangement," "placement." Situation in this case should be thought of in the context of the ethnocentrum as a place fixed in its general structure. Precisely a place in the ethnocentrum is the being of name. And an individual begins to participate in being by bearing a name as an ontological place.

As a result, the receipt or change of name is a crucial moment, a turning point in ethnosocialization. Acquiring a name in the *ethnos*, the individual acquires being. Losing his name, he loses everything. This is much worse than death, since physical death is regarded as a transition to a new status and new name, to the name "ancestor," "spirit." But loss of name means dissolution of the ties with the ethnocentrum and complete disappearance.

The Mirror Taboo

The understanding of man as name and the lack of being of individual substance is the essential feature of the *ethnos*. It would be inaccurate to say that the *ethnos* does "not yet" know the individual as a phenomenon. It knows it but consciously rejects it, crosses it out, destroys it as an element of the "new," which breaks up the unity and integrity of the ethnocentrum. The *ethnos* abolishes the individual as a possibility. It is arranged so that the individual cannot appear, so that the masks would not suspect that their wearers exist, that there theoretically might exist "being without a mask." If "without a mask," "without a name," then we are dealing with non-being. A sign has meaning only in the context of the ethnocentrum. In itself, outside of context, it means nothing.

Connected with these are the various taboos about the use of mirrors and the demonization of reflection.[3] Reflection was "dangerous" for two reasons: it doubled the object, splitting the mask, removing its wholeness, and at the same time it put the wearer of the mask in the foreground. Both operations undermined the notion of personality as name and situation in the ethnocentrum and, consequently, threatened the ethnocentrum. As a result, even in the Middle Ages the mirror was regarded as an instrument of witchcraft and possession of one could be equated with unlawful practices of sorcery.[4]

The reflection taboo was called on to prevent the objectification of the world, the ascription to it of self-sufficient being beyond its sign-meaning. Intentional thought did not permit self-reflection, i.e. the process of consciousness attending to consciousness itself. So the process of ethnosocialization excluded the very possibility of philosophical doubt. Affirming oneself in the *ethnos* guaranteed the reliability and certainty of endowment with being, no questions about the authenticity of which could arise even theoretically. The question of thing and image (representation) and their correspondence did not and could not arise; both were strictly identical.

---

3   Sabine Melchoir-Bonnet, *The Mirror: A History* (New York: Routledge, 2001).

4   Ibid.

Ethnosocialization and Language

Language fulfills the main function of ethnosocialization. It is a potential ordered set of names and is an equivalent of the ethnocentrum and itself an ethnocentrum (since there is no duality in intentional thought between signified and signifier). Any space — ordinary, technical or ceremonial — in the *ethnos* is a route delineation within the *ethnos*, something new, a new description of a fragment of its structure. Each utterance in the *ethnos* constitutes the *ethnos* as language and the speaker as its part and "place." The very process of speaking can be likened to the depiction on a map of ordinary objects, their correlations and the correspondences among them. Speech traces again and again the general map of language and its integral structure. Ritual and steadfast turns of speech, sacred formulas and other figures are called on to secure the basic nodes of the map of the ethnocentrum, serving as system coordinates. Their constant repetition serves precisely to secure the constancy and invariability of the static ethnic structure.

Linguistic relations in the *ethnos* are a major psychical phenomenon. In the exchange of words, names and speeches there occurs the soul's ethnic work of constantly making more precise the situationalization of name in the ethnocentrum, including those who speak, those spoken to and those spoken of. Any discussion in the *ethnos* is an arrangement of ethnonoemata (ethnic things) in their place in the ethnocentrum, a ceremonial ordering of the world. The individuality of the speaker and the practical knowledge (in the extra-linguistic sphere) of the discussion are secondary in the ethnic community and do not have much independent value. Speech is an autonomous exchange of names and their arrangement on the map of ethnic language. If this arrangement of names according to places demanded action of the participations of the discussion or influenced the practical sphere, this would happen as a self-evident consequence, already contained in intercourse. Exchanging names of things and phenomena, the members of the *ethnos* do not "signify" them but affirm their being in the fact of the utterance itself, drawing it out from the potentiality of language into the actuality of speech. But since potentiality is always broader than actuality, speeches were repeated, precisely or with variations, as acts, gestures and deeds were repeated in ethnic society. The general structure was a set of constantly told myths, which can be called "the speeches of the basic personality." One speaking a language produces the language and himself in the very process of speaking. Since the speaker himself, the narrator, is a name among names, uttering names, he accomplishes ontogenesis, i.e. he produces being. The being of the *ethnos* is constituted in the course of the process of speaking. The *ethnos* exists so long as there is speech built on the laws of language and so long as that speech is heard.

Initiation

The most important task of ethnosocialization is the inclusion of everything in the *ethnos*. Everything must receive a name and place in the *ethnos*. The *ethnos* does not permit the presence of another. Everything must be defined, named, measured, put in its place. Thus, ethnodynamics is a process of uninterrupted *inclusion*.

Initiation is a principal element of ethnosocialization. This rite exists in practically all *ethnoses*, with only very rare exceptions (it is absent from several groups of Eskimo).

Initiation is a rite undergone by youths of the tribe upon reaching puberty (sexual maturity).[5] Initiation anticipates their entry into adult life and is a necessary condition for their full social value. For the youths of almost all known *ethnoses*, initiation is the major rite of ethnosocialization.

A typical scenario of the rite of the initiation is as follows.[6] The adult members of the "male union" take the youth a certain distance away from the settlement as family members bid him farewell and bewail him, accompanying this with the same rites performed over the deceased. The entire scene of initiation symbolizes death, torment and immersion into another world. At the place of initiation, there is a special structure, usually

---

5   Mirce Eliade, *Rites and Symbols of Initiation: The Mysteries of Birth and Rebirth* (New York: Harper & Row, 1975).

6   Ibid.

in the form of a monster. Sometimes the initiated are buried, suspended from a tree, exposed to physical torments. They almost always receive physical trauma: they are cut, their teeth are knocked out, their fingers are crippled, etc. Sometimes they are beaten, choked, poisoned with smoke, inundated with water, left in the hot or cold. The purpose of this phase of initiation is the realistic experience of pain and death, in suffering and the transition to a state of helplessness, passivity, insignificance. A funeral is often imitated in this phase.

In the next phase of initiation, birth or resurrection is imitated. The youth crawls out of the tomb, emerges alive from the dummy monster, he is removed from the tree, washes from himself the funeral paint, etc. Often a grave, monster and other initiatory structures are made to sym-bolically resemble the womb. That is why initiation is consistently referred to as a "second birth."

After this "resurrection" the members of the "male union" accept the initiated into their circle. He is told the "secret" myths of the tribe, which he swears under penalty of death to conceal from outsiders. He is instructed in the rules and tricks of the trade (hunting, rearing cattle). He is given a new name as a confirmation of his status as a full-fledged adult member of society. He is instructed in the sacred dances and receives a mask. The meaning of magical ceremonies is revealed to him.

Only after initiation does the youth receive the right to marry, to participate in the tribal councils, to hunt together with adults, to share equally in the spoils, to possess property, to carry out religious ceremo-nies, to dance the male dances of hunters and warriors, to listen and to narrate to other members of the "male union" the tribal myths.

Returning to his kin, the initiated often gets a separate dwelling and is considered an "ancestor" returning from the other side. He is surrounded by taboos, especially for his kin.

In initiation, we see all the aspects of socialization, united in a gen-eral procedure.[7] Passing through initiation guarantees the youth prestige, education, economic self-sufficiency and rightful status in adult society.

---

7   Vladimir Propp, Istoricheskiye korni volshebnoy skazki (Leningrad, 1946).

The initiated is born in the most direct sense: not as an organism but as a social phenomenon, as status, as "personality," as a rightful "place" in the ethnocentrum. The *ethnos* and its structures are organized around the moment of initiation: ethnosocialization reaches its critical, culminating point therein. Before initiation, the youth is a potential member of the *ethnos*. After, he is a firm part of the ethnocentrum, its point, a name in the series of names. The model of initiation is so important, in the course of which the initiate passes through the whole process of the creation of the *ethnos* from "chaos," pain and death. Dying and resurrecting, the initiated constitutes the life of the *ethnos* as cosmos.

Initiation is the essence of ethnodynamics. In it, the initiated encounters danger, outcry, "nonbeing" as the nonbeing of the *ethnos*, and he overcomes it, thereby consolidating the *ethnos* as an invariable structure and himself in the *ethnos* as part of its invariable structure. We can call this the work of initiation, constitutive of the *ethnos* as such.

In a certain sense the initiation of each youth in the tribe repeats in an easier and reduced form the initiation of the shaman and, hence, its ethnodynamics semantics.

Female Initiations

In some *ethnoses*, male and female "secret unions" exist side by side. There are "sisterhoods," and, accordingly, female initiations. As a rule, their rituals have a softened character and the forms of symbolic death and resurrection are most often connected with rivers or other bodies of water. The Russian "cuckoo funeral" rites recall these "sisterhoods." In this ritual, girls, on the eve of the marriage of one of them, gathered in a secluded place far from the settlement and arranged rites to mourn the loss of girlhood, the culmination of which was throwing a certain doll called a "cuckoo" into a river or stream. It symbolized the girl herself, bidding farewell to her girlish life and its becoming dead to her. The contemporary "hen party" is a distant echo of female initiations in archaic societies.

However, female initiations were not performed in every *ethnos* and the ethnosocialization of women was gradual, continuous and extended over time. But, on the other hand, in almost all archaic cultures girls, upon reaching sexual maturity, were exposed to temporary isolation, during which they had to live in certain conditions, avoiding certain articles, distant from the rest of the tribe, without having any direct contact or discussions with anyone (except for certain old women selected for this purpose). This was often accompanied with dwelling in dark quarters (a basement, cellar or special hut), symbolizing a grave and the stage preceding a new birth.

Marriage

Marriage is another crucial element of ethnosocialization. Since the maintenance of the *ethnos* requires the birth of new members, or more precisely the possibility for the embodiment of "ancestors," "old-new" souls, marriage has a fundamental significance for the *ethnos*. For the *ethnos* to continue being invariable, it is necessary ever to release new members. That is why marriage and the creation of a family are regarded as the basis of ethnodynamics, as the principal form of the *ethnos'* work of consolidating its constant self-identity.

Only youths who had undergone initiation could marry, and we can consider marriage a direct consequence of initiation. In the *ethnos*, only the one who has passed through initiation is thought of as a man. Indeed, it was the rite of becoming a man. Having become a man, the tribe member realized the possibilities contained in this status.

In our presentation of Lévi-Strauss' ideas we paused over the structures of kinship in archaic ethnoses and in speaking of ethnostatics we noted the ethnic dualism of the binary model of society, in which the presence of two exogamous phratries or clans is posited, the generic and one's own. Here, we can regard marriage as the most important instrument for including kin (subethnic) groups, genera, in the *ethnos*.

Concluding a marriage between two exogamous genera, these genera establish between themselves ties of *property* ["svoistvo," from "svoi," one's own].[8] Thereby, they become *proper* to one another. *Property* presupposes

---

8   Claude Lévi-Strauss, *Les Structures élémentaires de la parenté* (Paris: PUF, 1949).

the possibility of consolidating efforts in hunting, labor, the use of certain articles and instruments of labor, participation in shared ethnic rites, dances, ceremonies, etc. Becoming *propers*, the genera constitute the *ethnos* as an endogamous unit. One could say, Huizinga sees in the games of the phratries-propers the paradigm of culture as such.[9] Thus, marriage integrates exogamous genera in a general structure, accomplishing an act of dynamic integration.

By producing descendants, the family replenishes the genus with potential bearers of names and functions, acquired after initiation and sexual maturity. Thus, marriage is an active force in the reproduction of the genus and simultaneously the reproduction of the *ethnos*. The *ethnos* regenerates through *property* and the genus [kin group] through kinship. So two fundamental lines in the dynamic of the *ethnos* lead to marriage: the constancy of the genus and the constancy of the *ethnos* as an endogamous structure.

The Socialization of the Dead

Including the dead in the *ethnos* is one of the important tasks of ethnosocialization.[10] The *ethnos* does not know death as non-life. It knows death as invariant life, i.e. as a specific form of life. The dying one is thought of as changing place and the born anew as returning to his place. Hence the idea of the circulation of souls, shadows, doubles, masks. The place from which people are born and the place to which the dead go are thought of as an enclosed domain, an enclosed cyclical trajectory. Thus, "dead" is also an ethnic status and "to be dead" in the *ethnos* is rather honorable and prestigious.

In many archaic languages, the words "dead person" or "deceased" often have the same meaning as "ancestor." In dying, a man becomes an "ancestor," he acquires the status of "ancestor." This status has a big burden, since an honorable and often central place in the ethnocentrum

9   Huizinga, *Homo Ludens.*

10 Philippe Ariès, *The Hour of Our Death* (New York: Vintage Books, 2008).

is allotted to ancestors: customs, rites, myths, legends and institutions are rooted in the world of the ancestors. This world to which the deceased go has a sacred significance and its functions constantly influence the world of the living. These worlds are intertwined. "Ancestors" participate in certain rites and rituals. Through certain procedures, they are consulted for advice or for a decision. They are brought sacrifices and are mentioned in prayers and invocations.

In some *ethnoses*, among ancient Slavs in particular, ancestors were buried under the threshold of the house or in the house itself, since they were the "force" of the genus, its "soul," called on to secure the house and its inhabitants. When the deceased were buried in some allotted place, this place, cemetery or graveyard often became a place for tribal gatherings, the center of the socium. So members of ethnic society did not fear death, especially when the deceased were guaranteed their proper status in existence beyond the grave. Much more terrible was banishment from society for some act or other forms of desocialization.

Burial rites and appeals to the deceased, to "ancestors," play a major role in the structure of the *ethnos*.

The Socialization of Nature

We saw that the ethnocentrum does not distinguish between the social (cultural) and the natural.[11] The integrity of the *ethnos* as ethnostatic consists in the absence of this distinction. On the ethnodynamic level, we can note a substantial gap, i.e. a certain suspicion of the *ethnos* that culture and nature can have different ontological statuses. This suspicion is "new" and "dangerous," since it threatens to undo the unity of the ethnocentrum. So the *ethnos* strives to actively overcome this gap. We can call this overcoming "the ethnosocialization of nature."

Nature, animals, stones, light, stars, mountains, forests, plants, rivers, etc., are integrated through myth, becoming participants of language

---

11   Émile Durkheim, *The Elementary Forms of the Religious Life, a Study in Religious Sociology* (London: G. Allen & Unwin, 1915), Aleksandr Krasnikov, *Mistika. Religiya. Nauka. Klassiki mirovogo religiovedeniya* (Moskva: Kanon+, 1998).

and narration and acquiring thereby a personified place in the general structure of names. The *ethnos* simply does not see the distinction between culture and nature, it does not want to see it; it strives to abolish the distinction. So nature becomes not only social but even more social than society. In totemism, animals are not only numbered among members of the *ethnos* but are thought of as its founders, as "ancestors" (for instance, among the Evenki Mangi, a bear or great-mother deer, is the first ancestor). Here, we can see precisely the dynamic work of the *ethnos'* socialization of nature, which is integrated into the very heart of the *ethnos* in order to be included surely in the structure of the *ethnos* and to avoid the possibility of escaping from its outer borders.

The ethnosocialization of nature is also realized through rituals, rites, dances, ceremonies, animal masks, names and nicknames referring to animals (many families, even contemporary ones, have an animal origin: Volkov, Zaitsev, Medvedev, Kuritsyn, Svin'in, Kabanov, Voronin, etc.).

In agrarian societies, the ethnosocialization of nature is established through seasonal celebrations connected with the agricultural cycle. Tillage, sowing, harvest, etc., became sociocosmic events, in which people, spirits and the forces of nature participated.

Shirokogorov describes the symbiosis between people and animals with the formula "taiga society," using the example of the tribes of northern Manchuria.

In northern Manchuria, there are two species of bear, a dark brown big bear and a small brown one. There are also tigers and people there. Depending on the time of year, animal, tiger and man change places, as they are compelled to do by the movement of game man eats. The big bear goes ahead and occupies the best places. He is followed by the tiger, who sometimes contests for his territory. The small brown bear and, finally, the Tungus-hunter settle into the worst places in relation to game but good enough in other respects. This movement from one place to another and in that same order continues daily. But sometimes there is a conflict between young individual tigers and bears for territory (each of them takes for himself a small brook). The matter is settled with a duel, as a result of which the weaker concedes the place to the stronger. These duels sometimes last for three years. What is more, for competition the bear nibbles at one tree and the tiger scratches the tree, and if it can scratch a spot higher than the bear has nibbled, either the bear leaves or the issue is settled in the same way next year. If neither backs off, a violent battle ensues. The local Tungus hunters, having well learned this order of the territorial division between young individuals, willingly participate in the fight, knowing when they occur (daily at the end of April) and where (at a tree gnawed and scratched up in the previous year). The hunter usually kills both fighters. There are well-known cases where the man has to cede his occupied place, if it is taken away from him by the tiger or bear as a result of violent and systematic attacks on his domestic animals or home. So it is entirely understandable that many Tungus consider certain rivers inaccessible to them for hunting, since they are occupied by tigers or big bears.

Thus, because the bear cannot but wander, since it is fit for precisely this kind of life, while the other kind of bear, the tiger, and the man are also all fit to wander, competition arises among them, and finally they enter into a certain relationship, become dependent on one another, and produce a peculiar organization, 'taiga society,' guided by its own norms, rites, etc. This organization allows man to live alongside bear, which does not touch man if it does not see any signs of aggression, while the latter gathers berries, and neither brings the other harm.[12]

Other Forms of Ethnosocialization

Practically all aspects of the life of the *ethnos* can be interpreted as processes of ethnosocialization. Ethnosocialization is realized through:

- Labor practices;

- Religious cults;

- Joint tribal holidays;

- Participation in military excursions;

- Medical rites, in which the entire tribe often participated;

- Tribal councils;

---

12 Sergei M. Shirokogorov, *Etnos. Issledovaniye osnovnykh printsipov izmeneniya etnicheskikh i etnograficheskikh yavleniy* (Moskva, Kafedra Sotsiologii Mezhdunarodnykh Otnosheniy Sotsiologicheskogo fakul'teta MGU, 2010), 70–71.

- Belonging to "Taiga" society;

- Collective games, competition between phratries, etc.

In all these cases, the issue is the constant fortification of ethnic identity.

In addition, for individuals outside the *ethnos*, there were special forms of inclusion, which we mentioned earlier: adoption, "blood brotherhood," according refuge in the tribe ("asylum"), etc.

Banishing "the New"

The most terrible punishment in the *ethnos* was renunciation of ethno-socialization, its reverse process. The case of exclusion from the *ethnos* or deprivation of ethnic status is a rather rare and extraordinary occurrence. The procedure of depriving status (as a name) was envisaged as punishment for the most serious infractions, something used in the most extreme cases. The execution or sacrifice of the offender was considered a much milder outcome.

Deprivation of status was enacted when the *ethnos* encountered something it could not integrate. We saw that in the case of the shamanic disease, where even the deviant behavior of the shaman was regarded as entirely natural and organic. What is more, his "strangeness" before and after initiation served as the main axis of norm-maintenance and the healing of all possible deviations from the norm within the *ethnos*.

The number of unintegrated deviations was not large. Feeble-minded, crippled and mentally defective people had their place in the *ethnos* on its periphery, which signified status, albeit a weak one. Only something absolutely incompatible with the norms of ethnic being, the properly "new," that which had never been before, which did not have a name and place in the ethnocentrum, was subject to banishment. The *ethnos* represses only that which manifestly does not fit into its structure. This, the *ethnos* considers "needless," "dangerous," "evil."

It is significant that in archaic *ethnoses* twins (which were considered anomalies, since they doubled the "mask," bore the principle of the mirror and reflection) were often killed, as were children who were born feet or hands first or with obvious anatomical anomalies. Such children were regarded as "substitutes," i.e. "spirits," who could bring misfortune to the entire tribe.

In this stubborn rejection of everything "new" that cannot be interpreted as old, i.e. eternal, the opposite site of ethnosocialization shows itself.

SECTION THREE

The Economy of the Gift: Ethnodynamics and Exchange

The Economic Balance of Archaic Economy

In his studies of archaic societies, the sociologist Marcel Mauss came to an extremely important conclusion about the character of archaic economy, which he called "the economy of the gift."[13] The meaning of the economy of the gift is that the global exchange of goods, which can be conducted in rather broad intertribal systems, has as its goal the preservation of a strict equivalence of possessions. In other words, in the process of economic exchange in archaic *ethnoses*, the principle of equilibrium dominates: as a result of economic operations, each should receive exactly as much as he gives or else change in the balance in one or another direction (loss or gain) was considered a negative result, a failure, "dangerous," "risky." Thus, according to Mauss, archaic economy proves to be a system of exchange of material and immaterial articles, which normatively aims not at gain (and also, as is obvious, not at loss) but at the preservation of an equivalent balance. That is how the principle of ethnodynamics expresses itself in the economic sphere: the *ethnos* exerts tremendous effort to preserve its static, constant structure, meticulously taking care neither to incur losses

---

13   Marcel Mauss, *The Gift: Forms and Functions of Exchange in Archaic Societies* (London: Cohen & West, 1966).

nor to receive gains. "The new" in any form—in the forms of both "loss" and "gain"—is "evil," "erroneous" and needs correction.

Here we can adduce the example of the etymology of the words "surplus" ["izlishek"], "superfluous" ["lishnii"], and "interest" ["likhva"]. They are all formed from the root "likho," which means "evil" and "lack" ("deprivation") but can also relate to the excessive, the "superfluous."[14]

Mauss carefully studies the structures of archaic societies and shows that in them everything "superfluous," both "deprivation" and "surplus," are "evil."

The Potlatch

Following the idea of equivalent exchange led Mauss to the "potlatch" ritual, during which the possessor of some item with a status value knowingly destroys it to show other members of the *ethnos* his power and the scope of his freedom. At the root of the potlatch ritual lies not so much a demonstration of the status of the possessor as the idea of a negative attitude towards surplus in the *ethnos* in general. The potlatch is the radical form of the destruction of surplus underlying "offerings," according to Mauss.[15] If we leave this "surplus" as something numerically "new," it will bring misfortune, since it will undo the integrity of the ethnocentrum. So it is necessary to get rid of "surplus" if it accrues. And since "danger" has a holy character, threatening the whole *ethnos*, then the destruction of "surplus," too, should have a holy character, expressed in religious rituals, offerings or magic mysteries.

Mauss himself defines the potlatch as follows:

14   Georges Bataille, *The Accursed Share: An Essay on General Economy* (New York: Zone Books, 1988).

15   Henri Hubert and Marcel Mauss, *Sacrifice: Its Nature and Functions* (Chicago: University of Chicago Press, 1964).

We propose to leave the term 'potlatch' for the kind of institution that can more carefully and precisely, though too much lengthier, be called '*total prestations of an agonistic type*.'[16]

The term "agonistic" is formed from the Greek αγον, which means "combative," "militant." Destroying his own property during the potlatch, the owner does this with an aggressive aim: demonstrating his will and power to someone else, who must either respond with a symmetrical potlatch or acknowledge the status superiority of the one who carried out the potlatch. The "prestation" in this case is done for conquest, domination, and the establishment of superiority over the one to whom the potlatch is addressed.

Total Prestations

The term "total prestations," introduced by Mauss, describes the very essence of ethnodynamics in its economic dimension. Mauss describes this phenomenon as follows:

> What they exchange is not exclusively goods and wealth, real and personal property and things of economic value. They exchange rather courtesies, entertainments, ritual, military assistance, women, children, dances and feasts; and fairs in which the market is but one element and the circulation of wealth but one part of a wide and enduring contract. Finally, although the prestations and counter-prestations take place under a voluntary guise they are in essence strictly obligatory and their sanction is private or open warfare. We propose to call this the system of *total prestations*. Such institutions seem to us to be best represented in the alliance of pairs of phratries in Australian and North American tribes, where ritual, marriages, succession to wealth, community of right and interest, military and religious rank and even games all form part of one system.[17]

According to Mauss, the "system of total prestations" is a process of continual exchange, thanks to which the *ethnos* is constituted. It is important

---

16   Mauss, *The Gift*.

17   Mauss, *The Gift*.

to note that the gift and gift-giving in return, the receipt of gifts ("total prestations") and return of gifts are not voluntary but obligatory. Having received something as a gift, the member of the tribe is *obligated* to carry out a symmetrical, reciprocal act. Under the threat of a loss of status, he cannot accept something and give nothing in return. But the principle of "equivalence" has a socio-symbolic dimension. The value of the thing exchanged is not practical but social.

Thus, archaic tribes most often exchange articles that in the eyes of the contemporary European have no value. Richard Thurnwald shows that most often the objects of exchange are dog teeth and wild boar teeth. People constantly trade them among kin groups, kin and distant groups. This exchange has tremendous significance, as it is a constant stream of the circulation of articles imbued with affective qualities. What the members of the *ethnos* exchange is a sign, a name, a mask; personifications of psychic power.

Taonga and the Hau Force

Mauss studied the system of exchange among the Polynesian Maori. The Maori tribes exchange in their economic activity what they call "taonga," a general equivalent of exchange.

Mauss tried to find out how the Maori themselves explain and describe the logic of exchange. To explain to anthropologists what seemed to themselves obvious, the communicants from the tribes of the Maori introduced the term "hau." They explained hau as a kind of force inherent in any thing, phenomenon or person. Forest, boat, individual, tribe, rivers, sun — they all have hau.

When the Maori tried to explain why after receiving a gift of taonga they had to give something in return, they had recourse to the following explanatory construction:

> The obligation attached to a gift itself is not inert. Even when abandoned by the giver, it still forms a part of him. Through it he has a hold over the recipient, just as he had, while its owner, a hold over anyone who stole it. For the taonga is animated with the hau of its forest, its soil, its homeland, and the hau pursues

him who holds it. The thing given is not inert. It is alive and often personified and strives to bring to its original clan and homeland some equivalent to take its place.[18]

The motionless structure of the same is produced from this complex model of the circulation of things. The whole dynamic of the circulation of hau serves to ensure that nothing in the *ethnos* changes, that none of its members acquires more than he had or suffers some loss. The circulation of hau is a form of the ethnocentrum's care for its own stability and immobility, the work of securing static balance. And if this balance is disrupted, the destructive aspects of the hau force come into play.

Generalizing this economic regularity to all aspects of the *ethnos*, Mauss writes:

> *All* these institutions reveal the same kind of social and psychological pattern. Food, women, children, possessions, charms, land, labor, services, religious offices, rank — everything is *stuff to be given away and repaid.*[19]

In certain situations, the structure of economic activity appeals directly to a supra-individual factor, which can be called "the ethnocentrum itself" but which can as a certain approximation also be designated "the sphere of the gods." The taonga that people exchange do not belong to them. They are borrowed as signs and symbols of status, as psychic, affective values, from the "whole," i.e. "the gods." Mauss writes about this:

> People believe that they have to buy from the gods and that the gods know how to repay the price. This is expressed typically by the Toradja of the Celebes. Kruyt tells us that the 'owner' can 'buy' from the spirits the right to do certain things with his or rather 'their' property. Before he cuts wood or digs 'his' garden or stakes out 'his' house he must make a payment to the gods.[20]

Here it is important to interpret accurately what is meant by "his" and by "belonging to the gods, spirits." The hau force belongs to no one, not to

---

18   Ibid.
19   Ibid.
20   Ibid.

people, spirits or animals. It is common to the ethnocentrum and permeates everything with its complete presence. When an individual receives or takes for use some point of the ethnocentrum (a thing, tree, trophy, instrument, artefact, game caught in a hunt, edible fruit, etc.) he enters a system of new obligations: his situation-point (mask, personality) comes into contact with another situation-point (mask, personality), and an existential knot is formed, which carries certain obligations. The individual can use this knot, but he is obligated eventually to untie it, i.e. to distribute the points to their places, to "return the hau" to the place from which it was taken. That is what it means to "repay the gods," i.e. to reestablish the invariable, static structure of the ethnocentrum in its integrity.

Thus, the economy of the gift is a vividly expressed process of maintaining the invariable balance of ethnostatics, for which the gigantic power and economic potential of the *ethnos'* labor is activated. Acting, working, exchanging and moving, the members of the *ethnos* first of all strive for the assertion, maintenance and protection of the invariable conservative complex.

Sacrifice and the Accursed Share

Mauss devoted a separate text to the study of the social function of sacrifice, *Sacrifice: Its Nature and Functions*.[21] Mauss considered the meaning of sacrifice in light of the social function of the potlatch, as an action that "changes the status of the person performing this act."[22] Through sacrifice, the member of the *ethnos* proves that he belongs to the tribe (following its arrangements and showing fidelity to its traditions) and secures his personal positions, evincing his might.

Relying on Mauss' ideas about sacrifice, the sociologist Georges Bataille (1897–1962), who set himself the task of studying irrational facts in the organization of society and learning in detail about the phenomenon of the holy in archaic societies, developed on the basis of those ideas

---

21 Henri Hubert and Marcel Mauss, *Sacrifice: Its Nature and Functions* (Chicago: University of Chicago Press, 1964).

22 Ibid.

the concept of "the accursed share."[23] Bataille thought that archaic society, the *ethnos*, is founded on the basic idea of the balance of opposites, a shift of which in any direction was considered a "threat." An expression of this threat was the "accursed share" of any of the *ethnos*' products or acquisitions, that very "excess" or "surplus" that was subject to destruction in the potlatch. Bataille thought that the purpose of sacrifice and the festivities accompanying it (often bearing an orgiastic character and temporarily breaking taboos usually strictly observed in normal times) is to express the irrational side of life, to compensate for the rationality of ordinary social life. At a certain moment, the normal functioning of the *ethnos* leads to the appearance of "surplus product" in both direct (food resources, instruments) and figurative (new technologies, more effective social and economic institutes and practices) senses. Marx saw in precisely the manipulations of "surplus product," its accumulation and appropriation by separate groups, the sources of class division in ancient societies. According to Bataille, the *ethnos* possesses a clear intuition about the "danger" inherent in "surplus product," in its accumulation and in the process of the rationalization of social and economic practices. Gradually, quantity transforms into quality and a critical mass of the "new," the "superfluous," leads to a change in the *ethnos*' social model.[24] Sacrifice serves to artificially prevent this process and to ritually destroy "surplus product" on all levels through giving away food, valuable articles and instruments of labor, war, and hunting to the "gods," "spirits," and "ancestors," and through irrational, thoughtless behavior during orgiastic festivals, accompanying or following the sacrificial rites.

Through sacrifice and orgy, through the emancipation of the irrational, the *ethnos* admits chaos into order, night into day, madness into reason, expenditure into accumulation, reproducing thereby the balance of world and social oppositions. Thus, the structures of the ethnocentrum and time are returned to their indivisible, integral sources, to the primordial

---

23   Bataille, *The Accursed Share.*

24   Natalia Melentyeva, "Obshchaya teoriya vosstaniya Gerda Bergfleta," *Elementy* no. 5 (1994).

unity in which chaotic cohesion and homogeneity precedes the appearance of regulated elements distributed in space, time, society and nature. The structure of society is directed to its indivisible roots, compensating thereby for the process of its fortification through the continuous process of ethnosocialization.

Sacrifice is then a crucial moment of ethnic being: the collective initiation of the whole society occurs in it, the descent to indivisible unity and a new ascent to ordered ethnic structure. During this operation, the "accursed share" is destroyed, spent, lost. The *ethnos* remains within the limits of invariable and symmetrical balance. The ritual destruction of excess through sacrifice removes the accumulation of surplus. Orgies periodically cancel the accumulation of psychoanalytically repressed "desires." Ecstatic dances and intoxication temporarily interrupt the functioning of reason. Sometimes technical materials, wealth, instruments of labor, weapons, etc., are destroyed, which slows "technical progress" and returns the *ethnos* to naked being in its pure, unalienated form.

Summary

Ethnodynamics is a broad, continuous spectrum of kinds of *ethnos* work, aiming at the constant, cyclical production of the general static picture of the ethnocentrum. On the static level, the *ethnos* appears to us as an invariable structure, organized such that the very possibility of social change is excluded. But to preserve this condition, it is necessary to exert tremendous efforts, to expend energy and power, constantly supporting, reproducing, renovating and reestablishing the structures of the ethnocentrum, which is subject to the influence of "entropy" internally and externally. Externally, natural conditions change. Internally, "excess" accumulates, threatening to transmute into a new quality and to change the social model. The gigantic work of the *ethnos*, often little noticed by outside observers, is directed against these "challenges."

The *ethnos* works not only when its members procure food, produce instruments of labor and war, prepare meals, raise children and conduct social and religious rites. The *ethnos* works always and extremely intensely:

it works through speech, which affirms language as the sign-structure of the ethnocentrum, and through games, which constitute the binary axes of sociality. The *ethnos* works through festivals and orgies, periodically descending into chaos and ascending again, refreshed, to order (destroying excess along the way). The *ethnos* works when its members give each other gifts, ensuring the circulation of forces (hau). The *ethnos* works by the fact that it is and that it is the way it is. This existential work of the *ethnos* can be called "the process of ethnic being."

CHAPTER THREE

Ethnokinetics

The Figure of the "Other"

The Definition of Ethnokinetics

Let us now consider the special situation when the ethnocentrum, the static picture of the *ethnos*, enters the phase of irreversible changes. In ethnostatics, the *ethnos* is thought of as a constant social form. In ethnodynamics, we start to distinguish the processes, efforts and work that ensure the constancy of the *ethnos'* structure. Ethnostatics and ethnodynamics together comprise the area of study of the *ethnos* as koineme, the condition in which society is strictly identical to ethnic society. This domain embraces the changes (fluctuations) that, affecting the general structure, do not lead to irreversible consequences or provoke full-fledged social changes.

In ethnostatics and ethnodynamics, the *ethnos* remains essentially itself. It does not move and does not change with regard to its fundamental bases. Ethnostatics and ethnodynamics are defined by the formula: "society = *ethnos*." At the same time, ethnostatics postulates the *ethnos* as a norm, while ethnodynamics considers how this norm is realized in practice.

Ethnokinetics is the part of sociology that studies those states of society in which the processes of the qualitative change of the ethnic structure or ethnocentrum begin. In ethnokinetics, the *ethnos* ceases to be self-identical. It begins to change its structure qualitatively; i.e. it moves towards being *ethnos* + *something more*. In ethnokinetics, the structure of the ethnocentrum fundamentally changes and, correspondingly, the whole algorithm of ethnic being changes, including ethnic intentionality, ethnic space, ethnic time, ethnic anthropology, etc. Ethnokinetics describes the transition phase from ethnic society to post-ethnic society. However, the specific character of ethnokinetics consists in the fact that this process is described from the perspective of the *ethnos*. The *ethnos* and its structures are taken as a norm that alters during ethnokinetic transformations.

The correlations between ethnostatics, ethnodynamics and ethnokinetics can be described as follows: ethnostatics describes a mechanism (for instance, an automobile) in its fundamentally static state — it is the diagram of a car, a draft sketch of one. Ethnodynamics can be likened to a started car, in which all the details are working and which, in working, expends a certain amount of energy to remain in place. Ethnokinetics relates to the state in which the car moves; i.e. the mechanism is brought into action and its location in space changes. But if we do not know what a car is at all and how its separate elements function, we will never understand why and where it moves. In order to understand ethnokinetics, we must first know ethnostatics and ethnodynamics.

In ethnokinetics, the *ethnos* begins to change. This change should be regarded as an irreversible process, since it presumes the fracture and breach of the main ethnic structures. True, at any moment of ethnokinetics a reverse movement back towards the *ethnos* can occur. However, after the *ethnos* has entered the ethnokinetic phase, a return to the *ethnos* produces a new *ethnos*, since the structure of the old *ethnos* will have been irreversibly destroyed. Ethnokinetics signifies the irreversible social change of a given, concrete *ethnos* but not the *ethnos* as such, as a sociological and ethnosociological paradigm.

Ethnokinetics describes the first transition phase from simple ethnic society to post-ethnic society, to the first derivative from the *ethnos*, the *narod* (*laos*). Inasmuch as this transition is a principal moment of qualitative social change, it can be considered separately and separated out into its own category. A separate chapter will be devoted to the examination of the *narod*. But the phase of ethnokinetics, when the *ethnos* enters the area of irreversible (by itself) and fundamental qualitative changes, transgressing the main model and structure of ethnostatics and transforming the ethnocentrum, can be taken in a separate direction, the specific character of which will consist in examining the processes occurring within the *ethnos* and its own structures during movement toward the next, post-ethnic phase of society.

The *Ethnos* and the Other

It is convenient to consider the meaning of ethnokinetics through the figure of the "other." In ethnostatics, there is no "other" in the structure of the ethnocentrum, neither within nor without.

The ethnocentrum includes everything: far and near, inner and outer, cultural and natural. That is why there is nothing beyond the borders of the ethnocentrum. The ethnocentrum is totally inclusive. The same thing can be said slightly differently. Beyond the ethnocentrum, the *ethnos* does not see something "other" but "nothing." At the same time, this "nothing" has a positive character. It is a kind of "good nothing," which does not frighten or evoke horror and which is also regarded as something included in the ethnocentrum.

In the ethnocentrum, all temporal cycles and spatial paths are fundamentally closed, so there is no "other" either in time or in space. Everything is "this." This is easy to see through the example of the *ethnos'* attitude towards death. Death is not an end, disappearance or transition into "nothing." Death is regarded as an immanent aspect of life and in dying, a member of the *ethnos* does not go far but is dispatched to ancestors and progeny, i.e. he is immersed in the nearest and most intimate circle of being, in which the *ethnos* itself reposes. In the *ethnos*, the domain of death is a tender homeland, populated by darling "ancestors" and kindred people. Kindred in two senses: they lived in the tribe and they will live in the tribe through new generations of infants. So death is an initiation, a rite, a ceremony. It is a "good death" by definition, since it is included in the absolutely plenitude of the ethnocentrum.

In ethnodynamics, the "other" acquires more distinct features.[1] It acts as "that towards the overcoming of which the gigantic work of the *ethnos* is directed." The "other" here is "danger," "risk," "threat," consisting in the possibility of "changes," the appearance of the "new," the accumulation of "excess." While there is no "other" for ethnostatics, there is partly an "other" for ethnodynamics and it is "evil." As before, it is indistinct and formless and can be regarded as "nothing" but this is now a different "nothing," an "evil" nothing, "nothing" as threatening. However, ethnodynamics is based on the fact that the "other" in it is quickly and successfully *overcome* and the structure of the ethnocentrum — in its invariability and total inclusiveness — is triumphantly consolidated.

Sacrifices, potlatches, initiations, marriage ceremonies, the circulation of gifts, burial rites and mythologies of rebirth, economic activity, linguistic intercourse, myths and rituals — the entire life of the *ethnos* is an overcoming of the "other," the inclusion of the excluded, the reestablishment of totality, the overcoming of the threat of the "new," the assimilation of "nothing" and its transformation into "good nothing." *The "other" is equivalent to social change, active, persistent, powerful resistance against which comprises the essence of the work of the ethnos.*

The "other" and "nothing" act entirely differently in ethnokinetics. In this phase, the "other" acquires autonomy, "substantiality," and it proves to be comparable with and isometric to the ethnocentrum. From now on, the victory of ethnodynamics over the challenge of social changes is no longer guaranteed; the constancy of the structure of the ethnocentrum is seriously called into question; "nothing" takes on the character of concrete, clearly discernable and powerful "evil."

Ethnostatics in principle does not know of an "other." Ethnodynamics (relatively) easily overcomes the "other" and makes it so that it no longer exists. Ethnokinetics for the first time encounters an "other" face to face, constitutes evil as a serious and imposing challenge — victory over which

---

1   Iver B. Neumann, *Uses of the Other: "The East" in European Identity* (Minneapolis: University of Minnesota Press, 1999).

is possible but problematic — that is in its main characteristics comparable (in force and might) with the *ethnos* itself.

Henceforth, "nothing" becomes aggressive and dense. The "new" clearly appears on the horizon of the ethnocentrum. And all of this radically changes the structure of ethnic society.

The "Other" as an Autonomous Ethnosociological Phenomenon

In ethnosociology, the figure of the "other" is a fundamental and independent category. This figure does not arise from conflict with a phenomenon outside the ethnic world — with natural catastrophes, the invasion of enemies, an epidemic, or exhaustion of subsistence. Such phenomena can and do occur at all stages of ethnic life. But while the *ethnos* remains in the framework of ethnostatics and ethnodynamics, it quickly integrates these events into the integral picture of the ethnocentrum, regarding them as a "test," "sacrifice" and "initiation," which only serve the movement of the *ethnos* along its closed spatio-temporal paths in the boundaries of the continuous, integral ethnocentrum.

Encountering an "other" as a challenge, as the "new," the *ethnos* can act in accordance with three paradigms, through which it evaluates that which it encounters. It can ignore the "other," not discovering in it anything "other," interpreting the "other" as "this." This is characteristic of ethnostatics. The *ethnos* can acknowledge it as a hindrance, easily overcome through a series of rituals avowing that the matter concerns "this" and not an "other"; i.e. it can include the "other" as "not other," excising the "accursed part." This is the case in ethnodynamics. Finally, the *ethnos* can acknowledge it as something equal to it, a reality alongside itself; i.e. it can constitute the "other" as an "other" proper.

When we observe different archaic societies, we see that the paradigm the *ethnos* selects in its encounter with the "new" depends not so much on the scale and scope of the "new" as on the inner condition of the *ethnos* itself. Some *ethnoses* can "not notice" their total enslavement and conquest by other *ethnoses*, ignore radical changes of climate and the environment, "easily" cope with deadly epidemics and the death of a large part of its members. At the same time, they still do not change their structure, do not recognize the "new" and do not constitute the figure of the "other."

In other cases, the *ethnos* can come across an "other" under the influence of rather harmless factors which, at first glance, are even difficult to notice. Changes in the behavior of animals, slight climatic shifts, series of insignificant microsocial facts perceived as anomalous, bad predictions made by fortune-tellers — these can lead to panic, horror, the experience of catastrophe, and entry into the ethnokinetic state.

So the figure of the "other" and the ethnokinetic phase are independent ethnosociological facts, at the basis of which lie deep social conditions in the *ethnos*. The transition from ethnodynamics to ethnokinetics is thus conditional on internal reasons, rooted in the structure of the *ethnos* and not in circumstances external to the *ethnos*.

The *ethnos* constitutes the "other," the "new," the "evil nothing" in a strictly defined phase of the breakdown and splitting of the ethnocentrum.

The "Other" and the Splitting of the Ethnocentrum

What is most important in the figure of the "other" is not its concrete embodiment but its general sociological meaning. If the figure appears in the *ethnos*, the ethnocentrum's whole paradigmatic model of interpretation breaks down.

Serious and real catastrophes, like merciless wars with a neighboring *ethnos*, epidemics, lack of game, drought or bad harvest, starvation, natural catastrophes (floods, volcanic eruptions, earthquakes, etc.) and at first glance insignificant or "fictitious" events, like bad omens, unfavorable oracles, the attacks of "evil spirits," a series of bad dreams, the death of the shaman, etc. can both be evaluated as incursions of the "other."

If the *ethnos* can integrate these "challenges" through ethnodynamic processes, then they will lead to the appearance of an "other." Only if this does not occur is the figure of the "other" firmly fixed on the horizon of the ethnocentrum. Then the ethnocentrum splinters, splits, and begins to change its structure and symmetry, repelling the "other."

The most important thing is the splitting of the ethnocentrum, the transgression of its temporally and spatially closed character. Ethnokinetics represents the breaking open of the ethnic map, the circulation of forces, souls, shadows and articles (taonga). The deceased cannot find the land of their ancestors; the souls foreordained for birth flit about in search of the corresponding bodies but do not find them. Evil spirits enter the territory of the tribe and begin to break open the habitual closed chains of behavior, hunting and intertribal and interphratrial relations. The shaman loses his power to heal and reestablish balance. Animals begin to oppose people. Everywhere, lines of division and interstices in the ethnocentrum appear.

Thus, in the process of ethnokinetics, new kinds of binary oppositions and a new symmetry of society are formed: in it, there first arises the non-integrated pole, oppositions that are not removed and not overcome dialectically in the integral and balanced structure of the *ethnos*.

The symmetry of a fully enclosed holomorphy with a center and periphery is replaced by a *dual symmetry of "this" and "other."* Only here are those dual notions that Sumner studied formed: the "we-group" and "they-group."[2] Auto and hetereo-stereotypes are also constituted here.

In ethnokinetics, the very foundation of ethnic intentionality changes. For the first time, the border is felt between the ethnonoema as an endopsychic (in the collective sense) notion of the thing and the thing itself, which is constituted as an "other" and with the "quality" of an "other." The *ethnos* encounters something that rejects and denies its being and its thought, and it begins to fortify its defensive positions, to transform the ethnocentrum, previously open in all directions, into a fortress with defensive installations and clear borders.

Drawing a border between "this" and "other" is the main feature of ethnokinetics.

---

2   William Sumner, *Folkways: A Study of the Sociological Importance of Usages, Manners, Customs, Mores, and Morals* (New York: New American Library, 1960).

SECTION TWO

The Ethnosociology of War and the Figure of the "Slave"

The Sources of War and the Antitype

The appearance of borders and a new symmetry produces a new map. From now on, the ethnocentrum is not thought of as an endless and all-inclusive field, at the core of which the *ethnos* dwells, while it is on the periphery, too, only in an expanded, extended scale — the *ethnos* of kindred stars, lights, mountains, forests, gods and spirits. Beyond the borders of *this ethnos* there is now found *another ethnos*. *Other* means radically *not-this*. The *other* cannot be integrated and is thus a challenge to the entire *ethnos*. With an "other" as the expression of "evil nothing" or "evil death" there can only be a relationship of war.

Ethnostatics also knows military conflict. But in the context of the preservation of the ethnostatic paradigm, conflict with another *ethnos* is thought of in the category of game, exchange or hunt. Since death itself is nothing unordinary or irreversible but only a moment in the circulation of life, murder does not have an obviously taboo character. In games and contests within and among phratries, and also during initiation, people can die from the hands of members of their own tribe. So "head-hunting" or cannibalism, practiced by diverse archaic *ethnoses*, is not a sign of war. This can still be regarded as a continuation of competition or economic exchange (parts of the body of the dead opponent act here as taonga). Cannibalism adds elements of the hunt.

Anthropologists describe many situations when enmity of tribes in archaic societies suddenly and imperceptibly transforms into common dances or celebrations, translating aggression and hatred into a culture of benevolent competition and the peaceful exchange of canine teeth, shells, beads or tusks.

Those killed violently by the hand of an opponent are also integrated into the *ethnos* and return to the circle of life, as do those who died in normal circumstances. And if the war of another *ethnos* takes their "force," it returns again to the tribe if people from the other tribe are set upon and killed.

If the balance of the ethnocentrum is preserved, then all violent acts remain fluctuations of peace and do not properly become war. Ethnostatics does not know war, even if the *ethnos* has to fight. Peace here includes war, which is thought of as another form of peace, as a game, a ritual, a sacrifice, an initiation.

War as such begins only in ethnokinetics. Here, a situation is constituted in which it becomes possible to fall out of the ethnic cycle forever, irreversibly. This terrible possibility for the *ethnos* is visualized in the "other." Thus, the model of the "they-group," radically opposed to the "we-group," arises.

The German psychologist Erich Jaensch (1883–1940) called this the "antitype" (*Gegentypus*).[3] The meaning of "antitype" consists in the fact that it is formed in reverse symmetry with the auto-stereotype. It considers the "other" as "opposite," "reverse," "counter." If in the static ethnocentrum the *ethnos* projects onto everything the integrating principle of similarity, holography, in ethnokinetics the "antitype" begins to prevail. There is a consolidation of the auto-stereotype on one pole and beyond it the antitype is formed as a figure of the "other," understood as "evil," "threatening," "dangerous," "evil nothing," and "evil death" ("kakothanatos").

Here, *the ethnocentrum transforms into ethnocentrism*, i.e. into the consolidation of one's own (auto-stereotype) and the demonization of the other (hetereo-stereotype).

Hence, for the sources of wars of groups, tribes and societies as social phenomena, one should always look for a "war of stereotypes," "antitypes" and the radicalization of binary oppositions.

The German jurist, sociologist, and philosopher Carl Schmitt (1888–1985) defined the sphere of the Political as the appearance of the

---

3   Eric R. Jaensch, *Der Gegentypus: Psychologischanthropologische Grundlagen deutscher Kulturphilosophie ausgehend von dem was wir überwinden wollen* (Leipzig: Ambrosius Barth, 1938).

pair "friend-enemy."[4] If we accept this definition, then we must search for the sources of the Political precisely in the ethnokinetic phase. In ethnostatics and ethnodynamics, there is no Political since there is no "other"; the "other" is interpreted as one's own and war is thought of as the continuation of a game, hunt, ritual or exchange. Only in ethnokinetics does war acquire its political and ontological dimension. War becomes part of social being, acquiring autonomous and independent significance.

Defense/Attack and the "Secret Societies of Warriors"

The phenomenon of the "antitype" and the appearance of a radical binary opposition provoke a dual complex in the *ethnos*: "defense-attack." Danger as an antivalue, as a challenge, constitutes security as a value. But in the symmetry of the "antitype," in order to ensure security for oneself, it is necessary to create danger for the "other." An important consequence follows from this: having constituted a source of danger, the external "other," the *ethnos* admits this "other" into itself. Since there is "evil," there must be something to defend the *ethnos* from evil and at the same time to do "evil" to the other *ethnos*, the "enemy." Defense and attack are bound together into a single phenomenon. The "other" without provokes the "other" within.

The institute of "secret societies" of a military type has its origin here. At first, in ethnostatics, the art of war is regarded as one of the aspects of the "male union," where the initiated youth is taught hunting, myths, rites, the production of instruments and how to attack "enemies." War is not distinguished as a separate domain, since it is thought of as an elementary, integrated part of peaceful being. Only in the ethnokinetic phase do separate, purely military organizations sometimes form on the basis of the "male unions." These organizations gradually concentrate in themselves the principle of the "other" and become in turn an "other" for the *ethnos*. They are called on to defend the tribe from the "antitype" and "evil" but

---

4   Carl Schmitt, *The Concept of the Political* (Chicago: University of Chicago Press, 2007).

to do this, they must have contact with "evil," interact with it directly and, consequently, they themselves become dangerous for their tribe. Wars are called to fight to the death and so they carry death in themselves; this time not the "good death" of the ethnic circulation of souls and forces along the closed path of the ethnocentrum but "evil death," a gaping ontological wound, a split in being.

In the "military union," the "other" proves to be located in the structure of the *ethnos* itself, acting as the first, or more precisely as a preliminary, stage of social differentiation and stratification. In stasis, the *ethnos* does not know any fundamental internal distinctions. It distinguishes neither social groups (differentiated along the sociological X-axis) nor social strata (differentiated along the sociological Y-axis). So in stasis, the *ethnos* is a *koineme*, a society with null (or near-null) differentiation along its axes. The whole *ethnos* is indivisible. In ethnokinetics, together with the separation of pure "military unions" — the transformation of ordinary "male" initiatory societies into military ones — the preconditions for vertical and horizontal social differentiation are laid down. It is enough to introduce the "other" into the *ethnos* for differentiation to begin to develop according to its autonomous logic in every direction. Ethnodynamics can no longer stave off division; the work of the *ethnos* gives way to the force of the "new." The *ethnos* enters the area of "social changes."

The creation of military unions is a clear sign of this process.

The New Ethics of Military Unions

As anthropology shows, the secret society of warriors is based on relations that differ fundamentally from ordinary relations in the *ethnos*.

The unit of the male society is not the kin, phratry or family but the warrior-individual. He has an individual military name and an individual mask. Military unions are the first type of society that, in contrast with the *ethnos*, is built on the basis of the individual.

Further, the individual character of the member of the military union transforms him into a unit demanding formal regulation, i.e. a special system of behavior. If in the *ethnos* facts about the structure of the ethnocentrum, the entire system of the life of the *ethnos*, are conveyed constantly and totally, then military unions dealing with death are outside of what is ordinary for the *ethnos* and are developed and formed as an isolated, discrete, differentiated order. The military union, in contrast with the ordinary male union, is a group aside from the tribe, not a group in the secret center of the tribe (like a regular initiatory male union).

The association of warriors is an artificial association, built along special rules, different from those common to the *ethnos*. These rules are much simpler than the rules of the *ethnos*. They do not at all include the entire structure of being but only the separately taken sphere of war. As a result, relations in the military union are not built on consensus but on orders. The union is not guided by *tradition* in the broad sense but by *regulations*.

Propp detects descriptions of military male unions in fairy tales.[5] As a rule, these unions were held in "big houses," built far from the main settlement. Young warriors lived in them according to special rules. Sometimes, conflicts would arise between the members of these unions and the *ethnos*, based on the dualism of ethnic structures and social arrangements in both groups. The male warrior homes were often ornamented with trophies in the form of the heads, skulls, teeth and other parts of the bodies of the vanquished.

Propp connects with the development of *military unions* from the older, integral *initiatory male unions* the change in structure of monster-slaying myths and corresponding initiatory plots associated with monsters. In the archaic unions of hunters, combat had an ambivalent character. The killer was the killed, the swallower the swallowed. Monster slaying bore an integrating character. During battle, man and monster (beast) exchanged their symbolic elements and thereby established a union of center and periphery, culture and nature, man and beast, life and death.[6]

In the initiations of military unions, this complementarity is lost. The monster becomes an absolute enemy and the aim of the battle is its

---

5   Propp, *Istoricheskiye korni volshebnoy skazki.*

6   Ibid.

complete and irreversible annihilation. This semantic shift in fairy tales corresponds strictly to the transition from ethnostatics to ethnokinetics.

The Social Code of War

Where war becomes an autonomous social phenomenon and a special intra-ethnic group of warriors arises, certain "laws of war" or "rules of conduct in war" form, the warrior code. It is a radically new phenomenon, unknown to the ethnocentrum. It is developed on the basis of the symmetry of the "antitype"; on "war as war" and not as the continuation of the game, hunt, exchange or ritual. Behavior directly opposed to customary ethnic behavior is prescribed as normative. Here, warriors deal with an "inverted world" and hence must act in accordance with "inverted rules." In war, one can and must do that which is categorically forbidden within the ethnocentrum. Warriors are ordered to kill enemies without warning and without the formulae that precede the killing of animals; to rape women without marriage ceremonies; to plunder surpluses of material articles and foodstuffs and not to destroy them as sacrificial offerings; to steal the "force" of the enemies and accumulate it more and more without expending it, in order to become "the most powerful warriors," etc.

The warrior does what is unacceptable and precisely the unacceptable and objectionable become his standard. Thus, within the *ethnos* an area of the inner "antitype" gradually forms. Part of the *ethnos* begins to live by special rules that are the reverse of the common rules. This forms the basis of differentiation.

At some point, the "male association" is constituted as a separate parallel society, partially opposed to its own tribe. To a certain extent, this opposition is regarded as necessary: someone has to deal with "evil" to defend the *ethnos* against it. But entrance into the zone of "evil" and the "other" brings with it irreversible consequences. Male warrior unions are acquainted with two contrasting norms: direct and reverse, peaceful and military. This duality weakens their energy for fortifying the ethnocentrum and changes the quality of their ethnic work. Warriors often form their own "secret language," a parallel language; i.e. they create the core of "another *ethnos*" in society. And this "new" thing influences the entire *ethnos*, this time splitting its structure irreversibly.

Slavery and Its Significance

The phenomenon of slavery is a turning point in the process of the eth-nocentrum's decomposition. The ethnics of the "antitype" suggests that the "other" as "enemy," a "living nothing," "evil" and "death," should be annihilated without a trace. The meaning of "antitype" consists in the imperative to annihilate its bearer. Not only the people of the hostile tribe are annihilated but also its fetishes, religious sites and sacred objects. The enemy's ethnocentrum as such is annihilated. So the purest archaic codes of war forbid the taking of captives. The enemy is anti-human, an antipode, a representative of "the other side," an "evil spirit." He must be wiped off the face of the earth, dispatched to non-being. Women, children and articles can be seized and included in the sphere of the *ethnos*-victor but through repressive measures of *adoption*, including rites, language, ceremonies, etc. They are subjected to exorcism; freed from the "evil" dwelling in them. But the warriors of the inimical tribe are just "evil" in its pure guise. If they were to attack a tribe, the same result would follow: the men would be massacred without distinction, sacred objects would be utterly destroyed and women and children would be assimilated. Neither living, nor dead, nor shamans, nor rivers of "eternal return" would be left of the tribe. They would bring to ruin the settlements of the ancestors and souls not yet born. Thus, they are forces of non-being and must be completely annihilated, without exception.

In this way, the murder of all men of the inimical tribe follows from the sociology of the "other" in the ethnokinetic phase. But in certain, clearly exceptional cases, the warrior-victors begin to preserve the lives of captives and transform them into slaves. The status of slave and the use of slaves in the *ethnos* are fundamental features of the transition from the *ethnos* as *koineme* to a more complex and stratified social structure.

The slave is not only not fully human or an object; he is a visible ex-pression of "evil," an "anti-human," an "antitype." He should be destroyed but he is not destroyed, rather he is brought into the *ethnos* as a visible expression of the "other," separate from everything, like death itself. It is significant that in ancient Egypt slaves were called the "living dead." They should have died like warriors of the inimical tribe, like the "antitype," but they did not. Having died in principle, they preserved only the appearance of life. Thus, the slave is sociologically a "specter," a "necromantic" shadow, the demonic simulacrum of a human.

Evolutionistic anthropologists and Marxists thought that the slave was used as a "soulless technical instrument" and that this equating of man to a dead implement of labor formed the basis of early class-structured societies. This perspective is mistaken, since all instruments and implements of labor in the *ethnos* were personified, animated and considered "relatives," carriers of holy forces and integral parts of the living and indivisible ethnocentrum.

As former warriors of an inimical tribe, slaves were regarded as something radically different from instruments. They were concentrated expressions of "evil death" and thus had a special status, which was altogether absent from the *ethnostatic* and *ethnodynamic* phases, and which appeared as something socially "new" only in *ethnokinetics*. That is the status of the "living dead," the "other" located in the "this" but not included in the "this."

"Slave" is the fundamental notion for describing the transition phase from the *ethnos* to the *narod*, from the *koineme* to more complex societies. The instruments of labor themselves, Marx notwithstanding, do not lead to alienation between man and the external world. There are no preconditions for such alienation in the context of the *ethnocentrum*: world, man and instrument are all included in a global, multidimensional circle of circulation of time, acts, and the permanence of living space. In destroying the "accursed part," which could include instruments of labor, the *ethnos* removes the preconditions for alienation. Only the appearance of the slave in the *ethnos* radically challenges this picture. *Real alienation* enters with him but not because the slave becomes an important source of economic production. Today, historians show that in practically all societies, even those in which slavery was widely developed, slave labor was a small part of production, while the main producers were free or semi-free peasants and hunters. The issue is that along with the slave, society affirms an irreversible and asymmetrical *distance*, not included in the cycle. This distance is embodied in the fact that the element of "evil death" is present *within* the *ethnos* in the person of the slave. The slave is an un-integrated "other," so in relation to him a distance is constantly consolidated between living and dead, "this" and "that." This gives rise to an entirely new, post-ethnic type of society, based on the widening and complication of this distance.

In relation to implements of labor, the following occurs: it is not that slaves are compared with them but that they themselves in some moment of social transformation begin to be taken as equivalents of slaves. The living hoe, living bow or living stone, personified, kindred to the *ethnos*, holy, endowed with force (hau, among the Maori) begins to be perceived as just as alienated, dead and instrumental, just as distanced, as the slave. Things and nature die through slaves. Slaves are the first step toward the appearance of the "object" opposed to a "subject."

If the economic institution of slavery is not decisive and has little effect on the general structure of production in archaic societies, sociologically it is decisive and definitive, since with it social stratification, differentiation and the complication of the structures of society begin.

Hegel (1770–1831) considered the pairing "master-slave" fundamental for any society.[7] He defined the function of this pair through their attitudes toward death. According to Hegel, the master is the one who does not fear death and is ready to die. In this fearlessness, he receives for his reward not immortality but the slave. The slave is the one who fears death and surrenders before it. In return, he gets a slavish life. Hegel has in mind more complex societies but what is important is his linking of the slave with death. The slave is the "living dead." He is death and he lives only because he is "dead," "dead" in the sense of his ethnic status. If he insists on his right to an ethnic status, he will be destroyed. In the face of this threat, he, a former warrior, sheepishly acknowledges his existence as

---

7   Hegel, *Phenomenology of Spirit*.

social non-being. [Стоит только ему предъявить право на этнический статус, его уничтожат. Перед лицом этой угрозы он, бывший воин, признает покорно свое существование как социальное небытие].

SECTION THREE
Lev Gumilev: The Start of Ethnogenesis. Passionarity

Terminological Correspondences between Gumilev's Theory and Ethnosociology

The examination of *ethnokinetics* as a special phase of the *ethnos'* transformation overlaps with what in Gumilev's theory is called "ethnogenesis."[8] We have already spoken of the difficulties in Gumilev's terminology which, on one hand, understands "*ethnos*" biologically and materialistically and, on the other, calls more complex social systems (like the "*narod*") "*ethnos*." Ethnosociology examines the *ethnos* as society in its simplest form, as a *koineme*, without any biological connotations whatsoever. It examines more complex forms, derived from the *ethnos*, as other, post-ethnic sociological constructions. After making these corrections, we can apply Gumilev's methodology to the stages of ethnokinetics we have been considering. What ethnosociology understands by "*ethnos*," Gumilev calls "homeostasis," i.e. the balanced and invariable existence of the *ethnos* in harmony with its environment, in the absence of any social changes. Homeostasis is ethnostatics and ethnodynamics. Ethnokinetics relates to the phase that Gumilev calls "ethnogenesis" or the "passionary impulse." That which Gumilev calls "ethnogenesis" should in our terminology be determined as "laogenesis," i.e. "the origination of the *narod* (*laos*)" from the *ethnos*.

Thus, we get the following table of terminological correspondences:

---

8   Lev N. Gumilev, *Etnogenez i biosfera Zemli* (Moskva: *Progress*, 1990).

TERMS / THEORIES	GUMILEV'S THEORY OF PASSIONARITY	ETHNOSOCIOLOGY
Ethnos	Sociobiological Organic System	The simplest society, *koineme*
Ethnogenesis (only in Gumilev)	The cycle of the rise and fall of passionarity in an *ethnos*	Laogenesis, transition from the simplest social form (*Ethnos*) to more complex forms (the *narod*, first of all)
Homeostasis	The stagnant existence of the *ethnos* under the prevalence of harmonious personalities (passionarity is equal to the survival instinct)	The *ethnos* as such in its ethnostatic and ethnodynamic phases
The beginning of ethnogenesis (only in Gumilev)	The passionary impetus	Ethnokinetics
Superethnos (only in Gumilev)	An *ethnos* that integrates a few ethnoses into itself	The maximum scale of the *narod* (civilization, religion, empire)

Figure 4. Table of Terminological Correspondences.

This table helps us understand that when Gumilev describes the start of "ethnogenesis" (in his terminology), he gives us a picture of what ethnosociology calls "ethnokinetics." The *ethnos* begins to "move"; it changes its qualitative proportions. This is precisely what Gumilev describes in his theory of "passionarity." As a researcher, he is little interested in the *ethnos* in homeostasis (which, by contrast, ethnosociologists and cultural anthropologists do as a priority, striving to understand thoroughly and describe correctly the simplest form of human society, the *koineme*); he devotes a few scanty paragraphs in his works to that phase. Gumilev begins to come alive when he encounters "passionarity," the start of social changes in society, its movement. This explains his whole theory: Gumilev is interested in the development and changes of post-ethnic structures under the influence of the energy of passionarity. Hence, his taxonomy of elements of the *ethnos*: *convicinities, consortia, subethnos, ethnos, superethnos*. Since he understands by "*ethnos*" more likely "*narod*," "*laos*" as a complex structure built over the ethnocentrum, active, aggressive, spreading, and expanding, he identifies the moving force of the *ethnos* in the artificial association of individuals (convicinities or consortia), which clearly recalls precisely the male military union and not the ethnocentrum in its static or dynamic phases. For Gumilev, everything interesting begins in the moment of ethnokinetics, which is where he sets passionarity and where all further changes of the *ethnos* begin. Ethnokinetics is the process during which the *ethnos* leaves the condition of closed eternity and enters into history, into the open element of constant dialog with death.

Passionarity and Ethnokinetics

Now we can understand the term "passionarity" more precisely. From a sociological viewpoint, it describes the special condition of parallel sociality, characteristic of the secret male union inside the *ethnos*. The meaning of passionarity in Gumilev is its energetic superiority over the ordinary existential energies of the balanced, homeostatic *ethnos*. But these "energies" can be explained (without appealing to matter, solar flares, etc.) through the opening of the closed structure of the ethnocentrum and the freeing up of the gigantic potential of non-equilibrium, which comes to the surface during this opening. The element of war, taken as an autonomous sociological reality, opens up before the warriors, separated out as a distinct group, new traumatic horizons. Death throws down a challenge, to which they are ready to respond not by its integration into the eternal life of the *ethnos* but by encountering it face to face.[9] For the *ethnos*, this is a fatal deviation, a divergence from the norm, but psychologically it opens up a reservoir of new possibilities. The criterion of passionarity is well suited to describe the special being of tribal warriors who have become a professional group.

Passionarity manifests itself only and exclusively in *war* and in *the will to power*.[10] All its other actions are arranged exclusively along this martial volitional axis. The passionary man wars in the name of power and exerts power in the name of war. No other attributes are of principal importance to him.

---

9   Alexander Dugin, *Smert' i yeye aspekty, Radikal'nyy sub'yekt i yego dubl,' Yevraziyskoye Dvizheniye*, (Moskva, 2009).

10   Friedrich Nietzche, *The Will to Power* (New York: Vintage Books, 1968).

The passionary man builds a postethnic structure. The passionary impulse is the moment of the fateful splitting of the ethnocentrum. The passionary man is a breach in the ethnocentrum. His energy is the energy of destruction, the establishment of distance and division. The passionary man smashes and dismembers society and the world, producing differentiation in the *ethnos* in every direction — along the lines of the division of labor, the formation of separate social groups and along the line of social stratification. In his power-impulse, the passionary man expresses the vertical, absent in the *ethnos*, and he begins to build up social strata along this vertical.

The passionary man simultaneously simplifies and complicates the *ethnos*. He simplifies it in that he discards the many ties that unite diverse points of the ethnocentrum. But he complicates it in that he dissolves the unity and integrity of the ethnocentrum.

The passionary man leads the *ethnos* to movement (ethnokinetics) and he himself embodies its movement.

In this sense, "passionarity" can be regarded as an ethnosociological phenomenon.

Shaman, Warrior, and Deviation

In the simplest societies (the *ethnos* in its pure guise) we almost always meet with the figure of the shaman and never with male military unions. That is, in the simplest ethnic society there is the shaman but not the warrior. The shaman prevails where ethnostatics (homeostasis) is preserved. The shaman shows signs of deviation and anomaly but this deviation has a propaedeutic character, as a kind of inoculation against social anomie, necessary to transform poison into medicine, to have the possibility of self-healing (through rites of shamanic initiation) and, as a result, healing others — the living, the dead, spirits, etc. The shaman encounters the challenge but he removes it through ethnodynamic efforts of integration, restoring and supporting balance. The shaman and his work are a concentration of the work of the *ethnos*. The shaman is thus the hardest working personality in the *ethnos*.

The *ethnos* lacks separate warriors and all men of the tribe (peasants or hunters) become warriors when the need for defense or attack arises. The secret male union is not at first comprised of specific warriors and all its members are engaged as a first priority with ordinary labor in the structure of the *ethnos*. Their encounter with deviation and "evil" is exhausted by their personal initiation, in which they are raised.

The appearance of a separate, purely military group represents a more serious deviation. This is "passionary deviation." "Warrior-passionarity" is too attracted to the pole of "evil nothing" to overcome it. It is not satisfied by initiation and the restoration of balance, and in this it differs fundamentally from the shaman and the ordinary men of the tribe. Passionarity pushes the warrior to take another step forward, into the element from which the threat arises. He is captivated and enticed by the irreversibility of the "new" that he is called on to fight and oppose. He enters into certain relations (deviant for the ethnic majority) with the forces of "evil death" and begins to gradually concentrate destructive energies in himself.

These energies can serve the *ethnos* for defense from precisely such passionary neighboring *ethnoses* but the passionary man never stops where he is and seeks encounter with death, the element of risk, even where it is not immediately close. If it is not there, the passionary man sets off to look for it.

Thus, a binary model of principal and fundamental types is gradually consolidated: the shaman and the warrior (chief). The shaman ensures the integrity of the ethnocentrum, its harmony. This comprises his main function and is the source of his authority. The warrior (chief) is also exceptional and is also sometimes endowed with holy, magical power but this power and authority have an entirely different quality: they are based on personal and direct contact with the element of death in open and risky dialog, which is not removed by the restoration of harmony (as in the case of the shaman).

The charisma of the shaman consists in overcoming deviation through reintegration. The charisma of the warrior-chief consists in risking the accumulation in himself of surplus existential energies connected with the element of "evil death."

Where we see a detached group of warriors or a strikingly expressed model of the peculiar power of the warrior (with the accompanying stratification), all the signs of ethnokinetics are present. At any moment, the *ethnos* can enter a series of social transformations. The "new" is already within it and further everything depends on the concentration of passionarity in the group of warriors or the chief.

At the same time, ethnokinetics still preserves a connection with the *ethnos*. Exit beyond the *ethnos* is possible and probable but it has not yet occurred as an irreversible fact. All the preconditions for it are there but the passionary impulse has not yet occurred. The balance between the shaman and chief symbolizes this. The shaman restrains the chief from the passionary burst; he tries to preserve the ethnocentrum. The warrior-chief and secret male union of warriors pull the *ethnos* in another direction but often their passionarity is not enough to overcome the integrating will of the shaman. So the shaman-chief dualism has a stable position in the most diverse societies and in the most complex and contemporary societies we see its reflection in the balance between the dual-power of priests and kings, Merlin and Arthur.

Summary

Ethnokinetics is the last phase in the examination of the *ethnos* as the simplest form of society, the *koineme*. In this phase, the main sociological preconditions are formed for movement beyond the limits of the *ethnos* and for the appearance of a new, more complex and complicated form of society, the *narod*. The dissolution of the ethnocentrum, the ethnosociology of war, the formation of sociological groups of passionary men — all these are phenomena that will become the basis for the *narod* as the next sociological category, as the first derivation from the *ethnos*. In ethnokinetics, the *ethnos* transitions to the state of readiness to lose some of its principal features.

But at the same time, ethnokinetics remains in the domain of the *ethnos*, since these phenomena are not yet fully realized. The preconditions for change are assembled but they have not yet produced their effect. The *ethnos* can "congeal" in an ethnokinetic state and ethnokinetic energies, processes and unfolding chains of logical consequence can be contained through the defensive mechanisms of the ethnocentrum. The ceaseless work of the *ethnos* in reproducing its static construction can in certain cases slow down the process of ethnokinetics, freezing the moment and keeping society on the verge of irreversible changes, for which everything, it would seem, had long been ready.

In some cases, ethnokinetics can last for very long periods, while the accumulation of passionarity proves insufficient each time to impart a final and irreversible character to the social changes. So it is possible to regard the ethnokinetic phase as an independent, although also a border-line, model of the *ethnos*.

Moreover, in certain circumstances ethnokinetics can be turned back, reversed. The *ethnos* begins to move towards irreversibility and the split-ting of the ethnocentrum but for some reason it stops and again enters an ethnostatic condition. In this case, efforts to carry out an irreversible gesture and enter into the open element of history can be preserved in the *ethnos* as a "memorial phase" (according to Gumilev) and live on the level not of the actual but of edifying myths.

At the same time, from the position of laogenesis, i.e. the sociological processes of the becoming of the *narod*, ethnokinetics can be regarded as its initial phase, as its prelude. We will see this in the next part.

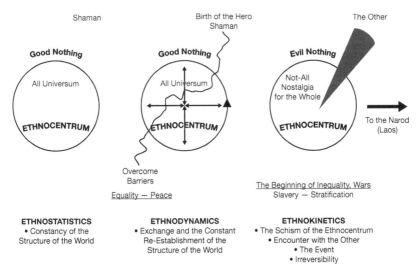

Figure 6. The Three Stages of Being of the *Ethnos*.

2

The *Ethnos* in Complex Societies:
Derivatives of the *Ethnos*

CHAPTER FOUR

Narod (*Laos*)

SECTION ONE

Narod as an Ethnosociological Category

The Importance of the Concept "*Narod*" for Ethnosociology

The introduction of the concept "*narod*" ("*laos*") into the ethnosociological taxonomy is explained by the necessity of distinguishing as a separate category the type of society that would simultaneously preserve certain traits of the *ethnos* and represent a much more complex and differentiated structure than purely ethnic societies. In sociology and history, attempts were repeatedly made to divide ancient societies, differing from one another qualitatively, through numerous essential characteristics. Thus, Marxism distinguished a number of political-economic formations: the primitive-communal, slave-owning society, feudalism, capitalism, socialism and (in the future) communism. Morgan spoke of "savagery, barbarism and civilization." In some cases, they distinguish "archaic society," "traditional society," "contemporary society" and "post-contemporary society." Other authors and schools offer other classifications.

The concept of *narod* as an ethnosociological structure is necessary to separate out into a distinct domain the examination of an intermediary type of society between the *ethnos*, with its simple and self-enclosed structure (the *koineme*, ethnocentrum) and contemporary society, in which division in nation-states predominates. Between the *ethnos* and the nation is located an independent, complex and multi-dimensional sociological and ethnological domain, which includes a huge spectrum of variations, where the *ethnos* undergoes the most complex transformations, social structures change qualitatively and society acquires entirely new traits, absent from the *ethnos* but not yet present in the nation and civil society. This intermediate sphere between the *ethnos* and the nation includes centuries and millennia of human history, comprises the principal content of historical processes and gives us a wide array of religions, states (*gosudarstva*)[1] and civilizations, differing sharply from archaic ethnic cultures and contemporary Western civilization.

Ethnosociology and the Taxonomies of Other Scientific Disciplines

Different disciplines—history, economics, philosophy, political science, cultural studies, religious studies, art history, etc.—single out from this vast sphere of major actors the main regularities and priority processes in accordance with their specific approach and, correspondingly, refer to the studied object with their own special terms.

Ethnosociology, proceeding from its own special scientific and methodological character, defines this manifold as a specific type of society, which is the first derivative from the *ethnos*. This means that the main features of the *ethnos* in its pure, static condition change during the transformation to the *narod*. But the character of this change allows us to clearly trace the connections with the preceding ethnosociological structure, i.e. to detect rather easily in the *narod* the *koinemes* and their combinations. These *koinemes* (i.e. *ethnoses*) are partially preserved in the *narod* but no longer in a pure form, rather in the composition of a complex polyethnic structure. This comprises the peculiar character of the *narod*: it necessarily consists of two or more *ethnoses*, i.e. it is a polyethnic structure.

---

1   Dugin uses the term state "*gosudarstvo*" to refer specifically to the modern understanding and definition of what a state is.

For convenience, we can correlate the different types of taxonomies of society with the model used by ethnosociology (see Figure 7).

Culturology, Paradigmal Analysis	Pre-Modern			Modern		
History	Pre-History		History	Modernity		
Sociology	Archaic Society		Traditional Society	Modern Society		
Economy	Pre-Industrial (Agrarian)			Industrial	Post-Industrial, Information Society	
Anthropology	Hunters/Gatherers	Peasants and Cattle-Breeders		States	Contemporary Complex Societies	
History of Religion	Natural Religions	Polytheism	Monotheism	Deism	Atheism	
Marxism	Primitive Communal System	Slave-Holding System	Feudal System	Capitalistic System	Socialism	
Morgan	Savagery	Barbarism	Civilization			
Tönnies	Gemeinschaft			Gesellschaft		
Lévi-Bruhl		Primitives		Civilized Peoples		
Comte	?	Theology	Metaphysics	Positive Science		
Attali	?	The Order of Force	The Order of Faith	The Order of Money		
Ethnosociology	Ethnos	Narod		Nation	Civil Society	Global Society

Figure 7. Summary Table of Classifications of Types of Society in Various Disciplines and Among Various Authors.

In this figure, we see how different types of classification correspond to each other. The transition from the *ethnos* to the *narod* is fundamental, since this line corresponds to a definite period, also clearly distinguished by other disciplines. In sociology, it corresponds to the transition from archaic society to traditional society and in historical science to the transition from prehistory to history. According to Morgan, the watershed between "savagery" and "barbarism" occurs precisely here. In the history of religion, the line between "natural religions" and "polytheism" is drawn here. These clearly established parallels with the taxonomies of other scientific disciplines allow us to get a better understanding of the ethnosociological category *narod*.

In sociology, we see a line drawn between the archaic and the traditional, which we can interpret as follows. The *ethnos* is based on organic integrity, i.e. on the principle of integrality. This integrality is ensured by the *ethnos'* ethnodynamic work but it is taken as something already possessed and present, which must only be supported. This comprises the essence of the archaic: integrity given from the beginning ("αρχη" — "beginning"). Traditional society, corresponding to the *narod*, sees integrity not as a given but as a goal, as that which is still to be realized, something problematic and demanding great efforts. Tradition presumes not integrality but integration; not wholeness [or integrity, as translated above] but its conquest. Tradition reproduces the archaic model of wholeness [integrity] as a memory of the past and a goal in the future. In the present, the *narod* finds itself between these two normative conditions and is called on to strive toward two horizons — the past ("the golden age") and the future ("the return of great times") — embodied in Tradition.

The *narod's* position between two normative states (paradise in the past and eschatology in the future) is expressed in its stepping into History. The *narod* is an *ethnos* that has stepped into History. Historical science [historiography] fixes this moment sharply, since precisely then the model of time is first broken open and a certain distance is established between past and present. Thus originates unidirectional and irreversible historical time.

In the history of religion this transition to the *narod* is expressed in the transition to polytheistic and later monotheistic theories, where the holy is present not as an immediate given (as in magic and natural religions) but through a system of theological constructs with a clear personification of separate gods and their functions. This rational theology reaches its culmination in monotheism. And it is no accident that precisely monotheism, in the form of the Judaic religion, unambiguously formulates for the first time the concept of unidirectional historical time. Historical time corresponds to the *narod* but is unknown to the *ethnos*.

In the problem of the differentiation of *ethnos* and *narod*, we should note the parallel between ethnosociology and Marxism, which considers slave ownership as a special case. And if from the economic and historical perspective the significance of the institution of slavery for the economic activity of archaic tribes was repeatedly (and rather convincingly) disputed, from the ethnosociological perspective the appearance in the *ethnos* of slaves is indeed a principal factor in the dissolution of the ethnocentrum and, accordingly, extremely important for the transition from the *ethnos* to the *narod*.

Morgan's classification (which today almost everyone rejects), differentiating "savagery" and "barbarism," also points to the ethnosociological division that interests us.[2]

If we look at certain classifications in which this division is not taken into account (for instance, in cultural studies or economics and also in the conceptions of separate authors), then it becomes clear why the concept *narod* is not at all given due attention in all cultural-anthropological and ethnosociological theories. However, if it is not critical for other disciplines to neglect the concept of the *narod*, for ethnosociology its absence leads automatically to insoluble conceptual contradictions and confused ideas. If we do not distinguish *narod* as a separate ethnosociological category, we inevitably confuse *ethnos* and nation. This results in numerous conceptual obstacles and errors, leading to naïve primordialism, an unfounded constructivism, or a baseless [неправомочно] generalized instrumentalism.

---

2   Lewis H. Morgan, *Ancient Society* (Tucson: University of Arizona Press, 1995).

The Inner and Outer "Other"

From an ethnosociological viewpoint, the *narod* is that sociological structure that logically completes ethnokinetics, if the social changes in it gain the upper hand over the conservative work of ethnodynamics, which strives to reestablish the structure of the ethnocentrum in its static, invariable form.

That means that in the *narod* the figure of the "other" dominates and precisely it explains the main characteristics of the *narod*. The *narod* irreversibly constitutes the "other" outside and inside itself and is built on the process of this constitution.

The *narod* is a traumatic phenomenon. It is a split ethnocentrum, which cannot reestablish the lost integrity by the *ethnos'* usual means. The *narod* knows of wholeness [integrity] and gives it a decisively significant value. But this wholeness [integrity] henceforth becomes an aim, an imperative, a moral task, a distant horizon. As a good, this wholeness [integrity] (the ethnocentrum) was formerly a fact and its reestablishment is a goal for the *narod*, its fate. Precisely for this reason the *narod* is an ethnosociological category: in it, the *ethnos* and the ethnocentrum play the main constitutive role. The *narod* is a society that wants to be but cannot be an *ethnos*; that wants to but cannot reestablish the ethnic model of a closed spatial and temporal cycle. Both sides of this statement— "wants to but cannot"—have tremendous ethnosociological significance. The *narod* is not an *ethnos* and this manifests in the fact that it "cannot" be one. However, the *narod* sees its value norm in ethnic parameters, i.e. it "wants" to be an *ethnos*.

Thus, the situation in which the *narod* dwells is characterized by the following duality: now it is the *narod*, not the *ethnos*, and that is tragic; but earlier it was the *ethnos* (and that was good) and later it must again become like an *ethnos* (this is its mission). Let us pay attention to the expression "become like an *ethnos*." The *narod* cannot become an *ethnos*, since it no longer has that "innocence," that ignorance about the "other" that characterizes ethnic being. The *narod* knows that the "other" is an "other." And this knowledge is the essence of the *narod's* being. But this knowledge is deeply tragic. It makes the present insufficient, barren, "damned." That is why the *narod* cannot simply return to ignorance about the "other"; it is called on to defeat the "other," to overcome it, to include it in itself not as "this" but as "other," or to exclude it such that nothing of it remains and this "nothing" no longer disturbs the *narod's* being. But this means to become not the *ethnos* but "like the *ethnos.*" Overall, the *narod* cannot be an *ethnos*. It only strives toward reproducing by will and historic action the irretrievably lost unity (in the form in which it once was).

The *narod's* being is imbalanced, asymmetrical, traumatic and dramatic. The *narod* is a restless society, moved by its whole social structure towards a series of social changes, since its present condition is always insufficient. The *narod* is not content with what is; it strives to realize something "other." This is its sociological nature.

The "other" predetermines the structure of the *narod*, its laocentrism. Outside, the "other" is constituted in the figure of the enemy. The *narod* necessarily has an external enemy. In the absence of one, it will create one. This is an existential condition of its existence. The *narod* must fear and hate an enemy and must strive toward combat with it. Precisely the "enemy" (Sumner's "they-group," Jaensch's "antitype," etc.) embodies that from which the *narod* "suffers." It is its projection. The *narod* needs it to explain internal pain. The *narod* identifies the "reason" for its discomfort, asymmetry and the open condition of the ethnocentrum with the figure of the enemy. Here, the sociology of war, outlined in the ethnokinetic phase, acquires its sociological significance. The *narod* is always and necessarily a warring *narod*. It is created by the male warrior union group and is represented by precisely that group.

The *narod* cannot be peaceful. Even if it does not wage war, it is always only for the time being, temporarily. In this, it differs fundamentally from the *ethnos*. The *ethnos* is always peaceful and remains peaceful even in the conduct of war. "To defeat the enemy" is a way and means to overcome inner pain, to extrapolate suffering. The *narod* sees the restoration of integrity only in the destruction of the "other" as an external enemy (see Figure 8).

The *narod* has an "other" within. This is expressed in an obligatory social stratification and class (in the sociological sense) differentiation. In the *narod* there are always necessarily elites and masses, upper and lower classes. They are "other" for each other. The elites suffer from the immobility of the masses; the masses from the mobility of the elite. They extrapolate onto each other the figure of the "other," thereby relieving themselves of the oppressive feeling of the dissolution of the ethnocentrum. So the structure of the *laos* is always hierarchical and vertically dual. It is built along the axis of the will to power, which organizes the energies of great dissatisfaction. The masses experience it as suffering, the elites as malice.

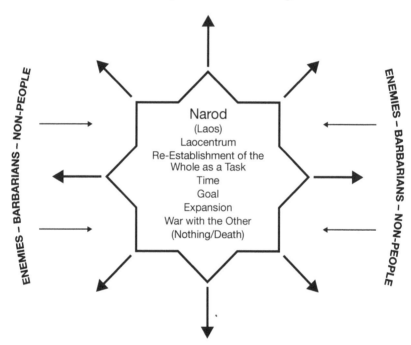

Figure 8. The Structure of the *Narod* / Laocentrum.

The balance between the inner and outer "other" determines the cycle of wars. The majority of *narods* in history wage war continuously, so it is difficult to say how long they would hold out with only internal contradictions.

War is a constitutive element of the *narod*.

The "Other" and Religion: The Exclusion of the Gods

A specific type of religion is formed in the *narod*. In contrast to the all-permeating holiness or numinosity of archaic cults, a theologically developed form of religion most often distinguishes the *narod*. This reveals another aspect of the "other." Gods or God become "others" for the *narod*. Gods were "one's own" or "kindred" for the ethnocentrum; they were "included." In the *narod*, gods and God are excluded, exceptional; they are again an "antitype" to humans but this time taken positively. Gods are good and perfect; humans are evil and imperfect. This gives rise to a specific form of religion, based on a positive understanding of the "transcendent" and a negative interpretation of the "immanent." For humans, gods are "other" but humans are also "other" for gods. This is a tragic state of affairs. It must be corrected and the moral imperative of differentiated religion consists in this. The *narod* is called on to be not like humans but like gods. That is the meaning of "sublimation." Religiously, the *narod's* status quo is perceived as "flawed" and "damaging." It is necessary to arrive at a completely different order and as an institute of battle against the real state of affairs in favor of the ideal or normative model, religion aims at precisely this end.

Archaic forms of ethnic religions are radically reconceived in the *narod*. Distance is established between humans and gods. Gods are set apart on inaccessible heights, producing a second layer of being: "heaven," the "otherworldly," the "distant horizon." This purely religious layer is in opposition to the land of humans. Here, the sharp opposition of radical binaries that distinguish the *narod* as such acquires a religious form.

The Anthropology of the *Narod*: The Hero

The central figure in the *narod* is now finally and irreversibly (in contrast to the ethnocentrum) the hero. This is the generalized archetype of the warrior as the solitary individual, encountering death, "evil," "nothing," the "other" face to face. The hero is man as a problem, confronted with everything else as a problem and opposed to everything and to himself.

As a sociological and ethnosociological type, the hero is an entirely new figure for the *ethnos*, a postethnic figure to a significant extent. There is no place in the *ethnos* for the hero. The shaman takes upon himself the main functions of confronting the problematic side of being and in a certain sense he makes this known of himself in prophylactic doses in initiation. But each time, the problem is "closed" and the integrity of the ethnocentrum is restored.

The hero deals with the incomplete procedure of restoration. He is involved in the process of "mending" the ethnocentrum but at some point "something goes wrong" and he must search out decisions and paths that are not anticipated in the ethnodynamic scenario. So the hero himself becomes an "other" for his society, embodying the problem he is solving but has not yet solved.

The figure of the hero is a sociologically generalized type of warrior, separated out into a distinct group and orientated exclusively toward war. But if the warrior is exhausted by war, the hero is something more than just a warrior (although the most usual and characteristic expression of heroism consists in feats of war). The hero is the one who deals professionally with "others" in every sense. War against an adversary is only one projection of the "other." The "other" is also present in society (social strata, elites and masses); so the hero is an expression of "the will to power," i.e. a "tsar," "leader" or "avenger of the *narod*," "ringleader of the rebellion," "revolutionary." The "other" enters the center of the religious faiths of developed theologies, polytheistic and especially monotheistic. Thus, the hero becomes the anthropological archetype of the *narod*. In this, he replaces the shaman, the archetype of the *ethnos*.

The characteristic feature of the hero is his individuality. If the shaman is a function, the hero is a fate. The hero transforms personality (as sociological status) into individuality and ritual into history. The hero is not status at all but something entirely unknown to the *ethnos*, a fundamental anomaly, a schism, a risk, the embodiment of the imbalanced and dramatic, comprising the essence of historical being.

The hero divides the *narod* into a few pairs of new oppositions: the heroic and the unheroic, the individual and the ritual, the historical and the cyclical. The laocentrum necessarily has two poles, between which there is a tension constitutive for all ethnosociology. Everything inclined toward differentiation gravitates toward the pole of heroism. Everything inclined toward harmony and the ethnocentrum in its static condition gravitates toward the other pole. In the *narod*, the heroic pole prevails qualitatively, although quantitatively the masses practically always outnumber the elites.

The hero is distinguished by his passionarity, his contempt for death and his drive to test fate. The hero lives at risk and sees this as his calling.

The Ethnic Duality of the *Narod*

Since the *narod* contains differentiation and schism, it is entirely logical that it is built on a principle directly opposed to ethnic homogeneity. The *narod* begins where the *ethnos* ends and splits. Historically, this corresponds to the formation of complex, polyethnic (bi-ethnic, at least) societies.

The most frequent case of the appearance of a *narod* in history is the fact of one *ethnos'* conquest by another. At the same time, what is important is not the fact itself but the ethnic processes that occur within the *ethnos*-conqueror. No ethnic conquest leads to the appearance of a *narod* if there are no preconditions for the social formation of figure of the "other" in the *ethnos*-conqueror (the "leading *ethnos*," in Shirokogorov's terminology).[3] Most often, this entails the formation of special secret warrior societies. Precisely this group of professional warriors is able to organize interethnic relations between the victors and the vanquished in accordance with a vertical, hierarchical principle and without the direct assimilation on equal conditions that the integral ethnocentrum would tend toward. The warrior-victors can take the vanquished *ethnos* as a "space of slaves," establishing aloof rule over it, formulated as "superiority." This "superiority" is conceived of simultaneously as "ethnic" and "polyethnic," and the *ethnos*-victor is constituted as an elite, as a master caste. With this, we get a dual picture, where the ethnic dichotomy is transformed into a

---

3   Shirokogorov, *Etnos*, 108.

caste and estate hierarchy. Ancient states were formed in precisely this way, according to many sociologists (Gumplowicz, Ratzel, Oppenheimer, Thurnwald, etc.). Social stratification within a separately taken *ethnos* has no internal reasons. The ethnocentrum is too closed and stable a model to allow in itself so high a degree of social differentiation as is required for the creation of a stratified society. Anthropologists who thought that social differentiation has endogenous causes and occurs from the gradual rise of the role of kin group elders in the tribe or from the accumulation of "surplus product" among the tribal nobility (as Marxists think) did not take into consideration empirical facts and the massive material of folklore and mythology, which even among the most archaic *narods* contains references or at least allusions to the ethnic dualism lying at the basis of social stratification.

Before Gumplowicz, who popularized the theory of the ethnic origin of political elites,[4] the French historian Henri de Boulainvilliers (1658–1722) formulated these ideas, demonstrating on the basis of France the general model of the formation of differentiated society on through the imposition of the German elite of Franks on the autochthonous Gallic population.[5] Gumplowicz showed the general character of this regularity on the basis of hundreds of historical examples.

The *Koine* and Polyglossia

The stratified polarity of the *narod* occasions many of its typical features. In the linguistic sphere, it gives us the *koine* and polyglossia.

The *koine*, from the Greek for "common," is directly analogous in the *narod* to what was language in the *ethnos*. The main difference between the *koine* and language is that in the *narod*, consisting of two or more ethnic groups, the "*koine*" is an organic language for only one group, while the remaining ethnic groups use it as a "language of interethnic

---

4   Ludwig Gumplowicz, *Der Rassenkampf* (Saarbrücken: VDM Verlag Dr. Müller, 2007).

5   Henri de Boulainvilliers, *Histoire de l'ancien gouvernement de la France*, vols. 1–3 (La Haye et Amsterdam, 1727).

relations" but not in their own, familiar intercourse. This substantially affects the structure of the *koine*. It is used by both those for whom the internal structure and system of associations and implications of the language are self-evident and obvious without comment (i.e. the work of the *ethnos* in preserving the stasis of the ethnocentrum) and those for whom this system is entirely foreign, who see it as a cold instrument for the reduced transmission of necessary information for practical aims, and who have a different language for the support of their ethnocentrum. So the *koine* ceases to be an organic language of one *narod* without becoming the organic language of the other *narod*. The fact that people who do not "understand" the structures of the "koine" speak it, influences those for whom the "koine" was earlier the native language. The structure of language is torn down and transformed. It more and more becomes a technical means, losing its holy ethnic dimension. Thus, a language gradually forms that is known to all but native to none. Naturally, its fundamental function changes together with this transformation.

At the same time, the *narod* most often preserves polylinguism or polyglossia, since the different *ethnoses* continue to use their native language along with the *koine*. This complicates the general picture, because there occurs not only the borrowing of terms of different ethnic glossia by other *ethnoses* and their saturation of the *koine* but also the mixing up of holy-associative sets, torn away from the structure of name-places that grounded their place in the ethnocentrum and in turn constantly reconstituted the ethnocentrum in the process of verbal intercourse.

Even those *ethnoses* that preserve their ethnic languages and rites when integrating into the *narod* are seriously impacted by the new linguistic reality with which they must reckon in one way or another.

Thought in the *Narod*

In comparison with the *ethnos*, the structure of thought also changes fundamentally in the *narod*. The introduction of the figure of the "other" radically changes the structure of ethnic intentionality. In the framework of thought, a space arises for "doubt," for distance from careless ethnic certainty in the identity of noemata and things, in magic power and the autonomous being of names. In the thinking of the *narod*, "that which cannot be named" appears, the "ineffable."[6] "That which cannot be named" (the "other") constitutes the second horizon of meanings, opposite "words," which means that it makes possible and institutes an extra-linguistic reality, unknown to the ethnocentrum. The *ethnos* knows all things; all things have a name in the *ethnos*. To be and to be named are the same thing there. The meaning of speech in the *ethnos* coincides with context and context, in turn, is something spoken. The myths of the tribe are the paradigmatic context of speech.

The appearance of the "other" in language and thought engenders a split in the closed contextual tissue of the ethnocentrum. Beyond the ethnonoemata becomes "something" not identical with the noema, something that escapes it, threatens it. This is the death of the name.

The death of the name has two sides, which extend the process of ethnoesis in both directions beyond the ethnic limit: outside ("to") and inside ("from"). Thus arise the first seeds of that which contemporary logicians call "intentionality" and "extensionality," or "sense" and "reference." In the *ethnos*, the name is sense and reference; it is auto-referential and contextual, since it indicates itself in a context. It does not have a separate sense and it does not indicate anything or mean anything in the extra-linguistic world, as this world does not exist for the *ethnos*.

In the *narod's* "split" thought, the troubled conjecture arises that *the name is a sign*. So on both sides, two horizons begin to glimmer: the inner horizon of sense (intensional) and the outer horizon of the signified, i.e. the article, the thing (extensional).

The narod begins to doubt. This doubt is evoked by the figure of the "other." This figure, admitted into the process of consciousness, engenders the triad "sense-sign-reference" and produces the preconditions for later birth of the subject and object.

Not all historical *narods* come to formulate this logical rule fully; but, in contrast to ethnic intentionality, which is the sole way of thought in the

---

6   Mirce Eliade, *The Sacred and the Profane: The Nature of Religion* (New York: Harper and Row, 1959).

ethnos, the preconditions for a differential relation toward the problem of language and consciousness are found among many entirely archaic *narods*.

In the *narod*, thought changes qualitatively. At the same time, it is important that the change of the regime of thought occurs instantly. There is no gradualness here, nor accumulation of separate social qualities. While there is an *ethnos* as *ethnos*, it itself destroys the preconditions for the appearance of the "other" through the sacrifice and the potlatch. And this safeguarding is the *ethnos'* principal feature. But as soon as an "other" appears, the whole model of thought abruptly transitions to a new regime.

The Poles of the *Narod* and Forms of Thought

Strictly speaking, thought in the *narod* does not change radically throughout the entire social space in comparison with the *ethnos*. The structure of the *narod* (*laos*) as a derivative of the *ethnos* is qualitatively more complex than the structure of the *ethnos*. So we should always distinguish two poles in the *narod*, two social zones that commune with one another, exchanging certain socio-cultural, political and economic impulses but simultaneously preserving a certain degree of autonomy. These two poles can be described as social strata (or classes). In Pareto's (1848–1923) terms, we can speak of the dualism of the "elite" and the "masses."[7]

According to Gumplowicz's law and the theory of "superposition" (*Überlagerung* — Ratzel, Thurnwald, etc.), the elite and masses have at root the distinction of two *ethnoses*, their "imposition." The differentiation of sociological strata characteristic of the *narod* and the presence between them of qualitative differences are connected with this fact. In the *narod* as a sociological concept, we can speak of the differences of the two types of mentality on its poles. The structure of thought of the higher strata (the elite) differs qualitatively from the thought of the lower strata (the masses). Since nominally the elite represents the *narod*, we can take the heroic type of thought, characteristic of precisely the elite, as the normative

---

7   Vilfredo Pareto, *Compendium of General Sociology* (Minneapolis: University of Minnesota Press, 1980).

and constitutive element of the *narod* as a form of society. In this case, everything said about the figure of the "other," "doubt," "distance," the preconditions of the "subject-object" dualism, the approach to logic and the sign (which has sense and reference), will be entirely accurate. But we should add that this corresponds to the thought of the elite, of the sociological pole where the higher strata are concentrated.

The second pole of the *narod*, the masses, continues to remain in a zone of thought based on uncritical ethnointentionality. The model of the ethnocentrum and ethnodynamics operates in this thought.

If we consider the structure of the *narod* in its pure guise, in abstraction, we can identify in it an elite, heroic pole, for which "rational," "logical" thought is characteristic and the pole of the masses, where ethnointentionality predominates. So we can speak full well of gnoseological dualism, of the coexistence in the *narod* of two normative types of thought. The *narod* is gnoseologically dual.

But such a strict division remains only a sociological model. In practice, we do not always see a clear, unambiguous division; as a rule, we encounter it in rigidly caste-based, hierarchized societies. Most often there is an exchange of gnoseological perspectives between the two poles of the *narod*. The masses project thought in the algorithm of the ethnocentrum onto the elite and the elites turn the structure of their consciousness toward the masses. This softens the rigid dualism of rational, logical thought (often through separate religious and mythological plots, reconciling contradictions) and disturbs the cycles of "eternal return" in the consciousness of the masses, introducing into it elements of "tragedy," "expectation," "nostalgia," i.e. "linear time."

Thus, the structure of thought in the *narod* overall can be described through two relatively autonomous types of consciousness (the thought of the elite and the thought of the masses), which interact with each other, producing mixed types. Altogether, both types of thought and the intermediate variations, projected onto a plane, produce a model of the consciousness of the *narod*, which, carefully considered, displays a dual structure.

Correct ethnosociological analysis requires, then, a few operations at once:

- Explication of the mental structure of the elite;
- Explication of the mental structure of the masses;
- Tracing their interactions;
- Studying the process of the emergence of mixed forms.

Social Changes in the *Narod*

In contrast to the *ethnos*, the *narod* is a kinetic system; its structures change constantly. The *narod* is organized around the disequilibrium of the differential, which opens the possibility for social changes. Moving in the moment of its emergence from the static and dynamic structure of the *ethnos* to historical existence, the *narod* does not stop changing; at its basis lies the "event," the "*novum*," and its being, which consists of events and also comprises the content of its history. During the *narod's* historical being (lao-genesis), its ethnic model changes repeatedly. *Ethnoses* mix among themselves in both elite and masses, influencing each other's economic, social, technological and religious peculiarities. Each social change has a historical character, i.e. it is isolated and irreversible. Although the *narod* itself can at some point put an end to its historical existence and dissolve into numerous *ethnoses*, so long as it exists, everything that occurs in it has a "singular" character.

Of course, this affects the *narod* as a whole, as a system. On the level of separate, settled ethnic formations included in the *narod*, a completely different picture of time can exist. There, it is full well possible that nothing changes and the "event" is interpreted as a cyclical phenomenon, i.e. not as the "new" but as a return of the "same." So social changes in the *narod* have at a minimum a dual structure. On the level of the elite and certain intermediate layers between elite and masses, the logic of history operates; in the depths, in the masses, the "eternal return" continues to dominate, and the unchanging ethnocentrum is preserved.

Thus, the *narod* requires a twofold sociological approach, which would simultaneously study the processes of change at its upper level and their cyclical interpretation (in the spirit of the "eternal return") among the masses.

The *narod* constantly changes on the surface and at the heights, and it remains invariable in the depths and in the *narodni* masses. This predetermines the specific character of its historical existence, which, on one hand, is indeed historical and, on the other, is non-historical and synchronic.

As a result of such an imposition, we can extract the main vector of the historical being of the *narod* and the orientation of the social changes occurring within it. The *narod* is based on the fact of the "splitting of the ethnocentrum" as primordial integrality, integrity. This predetermines its identity. But at the same time, it is still closely connected with that integrality and, lacking it in fact, it erects it as a moral imperative, as a value that must be attained. Thus, the main vector of social changes in the *narod* is the attainment of non-historical unity by historical means: the restoration of the split integrity with the help of instruments that were born in the moment of splitting. The aim of change in the *narod* is to attain a condition of invariability.

Instead of the integrality of the *ethnos*, the *narod* is moved by the will to integration. It strives to realize the integration of the whole. If the shaman could restore the world, the hero only strives to do so and in contrast to the shaman, his victory is not guaranteed; it is called into question and problematic.

Thus, we can distinguish three horizons in the *narod* (*laos*):

- The masses (*ethnoses*), dwelling in "dynamic invariability";

- The elite, the main carriers of social differentiation and, consequently, social change;

- The aim toward which the *narod* strives, formulated as the attainment of a supra-historical ideal (mission).

This produces the complex dialectic of social changes, since in the being of the *narod* there are simultaneously present three times, three levels of process, influencing each other.

The Role of Nomads in Laogenesis

The emergence of the *narod* from the *ethnos* in the historical perspective can be reduced to a simplified model, to a general scenario that repeats in various historical periods and in various geographical areas. Supporters of the theory of "superimposition" (*Überlagerung*) describe this typical case as follows.

At the basis of the transition from the ethnos to the narod there most often lie martial, patriarchic tribes of breeder-nomads who have mastered the domestication of cattle.

Such *ethnoses* are formed in certain conditions on the basis of a non-migratory peasant settlement. In agrarian societies, the simplest type of the gender division of labor between hunters and gatherers is transformed into the dualism of female agricultural work and the male breeding of cattle. This gender specialization does not upset the balance of the agrarian ethnocentrum and does not lead by itself to fundamental changes in the *ethnos*. This agrarian form of ethnic being differs substantially from the society of hunter-gatherers but it does not go beyond the limits of ethnodynamics.

At a certain point, the men breeding cattle begin to move far away enough from the settlement to come into contact with other *ethnoses* and to have likely conflict with them. This moment often coincides with the creation of male military unions. Another critical point is the domestication of large cattle: oxen, horses, camels, llamas, deer, etc. From these elements, *ethnoses* of a certain type are formed, with clearly expressed patriarchal, masculine features: mobile, dynamic, aggressive, belligerent and inclined to transfer their skills in dealing with large cattle to the conquest of *narods*. That is why many archaic kings were symbolically called "pastors," "shepherds"; it is connected with all the metaphors of the "*narod*" as "flock," etc.

In precisely such masculine, stock-raising *ethnoses*, the conditions are produced for the split of the ethnocentrum and the transition to a new ethnosociological type. The *narod* is created under the influence of masculine *nomads*.

Laogenesis (the becoming of the narod) can be described in the simplest case as the conquest by a nomadic, martial tribe of a settled, agrarian ethnos. In certain cases, instead of conquest, there can be softer forms of interethnic alliance, the sociological essence of which nevertheless remains the same. Nomads form the upper strata in the *narod*, the aristocracy, the nobility; the settled farmers, accordingly, form the lower strata. The *narod* become the elite; the peasants the masses. Hunters and gatherers are most often found on the lowest level and are either subordinate to the agrarian layer or are displaced to the periphery, where they preserve relative autonomy. Thus occurs the structuring of the *narod*. The martial nomads convert their ethnocultural type into the higher strata, caste, estate, class. The ethnicity of the settled peasant population becomes the social paradigm of the lower strata, caste, estate, class.

Thus, a hierarchized society is produced, which just is the *narod*. Warriors are at the top, peasants at the bottom. Together, they form a single sociological system in which ethnic dualism gradually transforms into the political differentiation of castes and estates. From the perspective of economic practices, the symbol of this synthesis is the cultivation of the land with the help of plow and cattle (oxen, horses, etc.) by plowmen. Livestock are an attribute of aggressive-masculine nomads. Agriculture as such is a matter for peaceful, female peasants. The figure of the plowman with a plow driven by a yoked ox or horse is a figure of the *narod* as a special ethnosociological category.

In the sphere of food, a "synonym" for this synthesis is the meat (from the meat of cattle) or cheese tart. Meat and milk products (especially cheese) are the main food for nomads. At the same time, many archaic nomadic tribes have a taboo on the use of plant foods, since "animals eat them." Hence the extreme forms of the nomadic identification of peasants with "animals" and the justification of the "right" of their conquest. The combination of meat or milk food, sacred and exclusive for nomads, with dough from cereals, expresses the sociological essence of the *narod*. Meat (cheese) is a stuffing (upper strata); dough is the crust (lower strata).

We can consider as the origin of the *narod* the distance introduced by nomads into a settled society. This distance is expressed in the borders the *narod* establishes around itself and within itself. This distance has ethnic roots and makes itself known in culture, society and thought.

The nomad-conquerors have in relation to the conquered settled *narods* the same distance that is natural for them in relation to their own herds or to the conquered soldiers of the other *ethnos*, who have been transformed into slaves. Here, the vertical power axis of social organization, lying at the basis of all political systems, forms. The *ethnos* by itself is not political; it lacks the vertical stratification necessary for politics. The *narod* necessarily has a political dimension. Historically, this dimension most often dates back to the concrete moment of the birth of the *narod*. This is the moment of the establishment of power by aggressive, nomadic warrior herdsmen or other types of aggressive male groups over a settled *ethnos* of cultivators. The *ethnos* enters history at precisely that moment.

SECTION TWO

The Sociological Forms of the *Narod's* Historical Creations

The *Narod's* Creations: State, Religion, Civilization

"*Narod*" is an ethnosociological category and describes the first derivative from the *ethnos*, in which there occurs a fundamental social change of the basic ethnic structure. The *narod* (*laos*) is distinguished by the method of sociological analysis as that social form which is closest to the ethnic model but is at the same time on an order more complex and not directly drawn from the *ethnos*. Just as when we were dealing with the *ethnos* we needed at a minimum two genera, phratries, or clans, so in dealing with the *narod* (*laos*) we need at a minimum two *ethnoses*. But the correlations between the *ethnoses* in the *narod* are not based on a system of kinship and property, on marriage relations, but on the power and political relations of "Master" and "Slave" (according to Hegel). Therefore, just as it was impossible to come to the *ethnos* from one genus, so it is impossible to build a *narod* from one *ethnos*. The *narod* is thus necessarily polyethnic. And this comprises its qualitative difference.

The *narod*, appearing in history, necessarily produces one of three forms (sometimes all three or two of them at once and sometimes moving from one to the other in sequence):

State–Civilization–Religion

The *narod* cannot exist outside one or a few of these forms. Where we meet with a *narod*, we meet either with a state, a civilization or a religion. At the same time, it can well be that showing itself through a state, the *narod* can simultaneously produce or accept from without a highly differentiated religion and produce its own civilization. Or the reverse: without producing a full-fledged state, the *narod* can express itself only through religion or only through a civilization. In some cases the *narod* simultaneously produces a state, accepts a religion and develops a special civilization. In other cases, starting with religion, it produces a state and civilization. In a third case, starting with a state, it constitutes a religion and civilization. In a fourth, starting with civilization, it then produces a religion and state. Historically, we see all possible variations. In some cases, the sequence can repeat in cycles, and not just once. So in the most general form we can correlate the *narod* with all three forms at once as immanent possibilities of the *narod* as an ethnosociological phenomenon. At a minimum, one of these possibilities must be realized in each concrete historical moment, while others can exist latently.

Thus, we can draw the following conclusion: there is a *narod* only where there is a state, religion or civilization, or any combination of them. We cannot speak of the presence of a *narod* if we do not observe at least one of these. The reverse is also true: if any of these three elements are present, the *narod* as a special ethnosociological category necessarily stands behind them and only remains to be discovered and described.

Sociological Versions of the Hero-Type

The hero is the main sociological type, the "basic personality," of the *narod*.[8] In this figure, the *narod* typifies itself. The concretization of the hero changes depending on the form the *narod* takes.

In the state type, the hero is expressed in the figure of the tsar, chief, king, prince and more broadly as the military hero or military elite. The individual personification of the hero is the tsar; the collective is the military elite.

Since the creation of a state by the *narod* is the most widespread and most widely encountered historical phenomenon, the figure of the tsar is the most usual and widespread case of the sociological expression of heroism. The tsar or prince is the personality synonymous with the *narod* itself. That is why everywhere in historical chronicles and even in contemporary political journalism the *narod* is represented through the metonym of its tsar, leader, president, etc.

The ruling elite, the princely house and even the retinue are thought of as a continuation of the tsar, a collective hero. They also act as bearers of the heroic type.

The figures of the hero and soldier are almost always identical. So in the majority of cases tsars are military leaders or generals of the army or militia. Historically, the founders of the majority of princely dynasties are the leaders of military detachments, commanders; i.e. soldiers and their leaders.

In the state, all society is structured accordingly: military service and virtue are the norm.

In religion, the figure of the hero is expressed through the special phenomenon of prophetism. The prophet type is very specific and differs substantially from priestly (shamanic in archaic *narods*) functions.[9] The prophet deals with a transcendent deity, located at an "infinite" distance

---

8   Henri Hubert, *Culte de l'heros*, in Henri Hubert and Marcel Mauss, *Mélanges d'histoire des religions* (Paris: Librairie Félix, 1929), 266.

9   Geydar Dzhemal, *The Revolution of the Prophets* (Moskva: Ultra Kultura, 2003).

from human society and the world. Thus, he is a carrier of a differentiating principle. The prophet testifies to the distant, to the goal, to what must be, to the moral and ethical dimension. He does not heal the world and society, like the shaman. He points to a deep, open wound in the world and he interprets it as a trace of the existence of a threatening, impartial divine principle. The prophet prophesizes about a "distant God" in the name of a "distant God." This is not one of the kindred "gods" of the tribe; it is an all-powerful tsar, with whom the faithful are connected not by ties of kinship and property but by ties of subordination and obedience. On the religious level, the prophet reproduces the transition to a political system of power relations along the Master-Slave axis, which characterizes the transition phase from the *ethnos* to the *narod* in general.

Like the soldier, the prophet is a figure of war, not peace. He depicts the horizon of final victory as a task, related to the sphere of moral duty. In the present, he indicates the imperfection of the world and society, and exhorts others to "heed the ways of the Lord."

In civilization, the philosopher, the wise man, performs the role of the hero. He acts as an individual who brings into correlation diverse forms of split ensembles, bringing to the unity of logos the multiplicity of phenomena in the surrounding world. But this bringing to logos is not a reestablishment of harmony, merely the project of such reestablishment. The logos around which civilization is built is an intellectual imperative, demanding to be grasped and embodied in life. It is not the givenness of being, which, on the contrary, consists everywhere of fragments; it is the task of realizing the violent alteration of the world, which is done most often with the help of techne. And the primary techne with which civilization operates is philosophical techne. The philosopher is a hero because he goes into the unknown. He challenges settled systems of thought, casting doubt on ethnointentionality and working out new horizons of dual, split ontologies, where the worlds of causes, patterns and ends oppose the worlds of consequences and copies. In this distance between the way the world should be and the way it is, the philosopher dwells in constant contradiction, which comprises the impulse of his being and the structure of his activity. The philosopher makes the world problematic; he thematizes it; calls it into question. He disturbs thereby the usual views of the ethnocentrum and opens up the "other" side everywhere, in the simplest, at first glance, things.

Like the soldier and the prophet, the philosopher establishes a hierarchized symmetry along the vertical axis of power. At the top, he places the one, the model, Logos; below, plurality, copies, the things themselves. In this sense, philosophy is primordially and necessarily political.

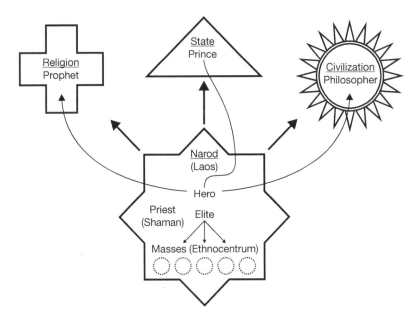

Figure 9. The *Narod* and the Three Forms Generated By It.

Traditional State: Mission and Violence

The state the *narod* creates when it steps into history is in the usual case a traditional state. The adjective "traditional" indicates that we are dealing with a sociocultural model relating to traditional society. In sociology, "traditional society" is opposed to contemporary society, the society of modernity. So we refer to traditional state as premodern state.

Traditional statehood is distinguished by the following fundamental features:

- It is organized vertically along an axis of power;

- Social strata are clearly distinguished in it: elite and masses, higher and lower, "masters" and "slaves";

- Social inequality can take a caste (invariable kin group membership) and estate (kin group membership combined with the possibility of increasing status on the basis of personal merit) system;

- The state has an integrating mission;

- The state has a *dispositif* of force, which is legitimately used outside and inside.

The traditional state strives to establish an order where there is none or where it is insufficient (or where it does not recognize what is there as "order"). This determines its main function. The state integrates a split social and geographical space; it asserts a certain model of power-economic relations and preserves it.

All historically known states were created by soldiers and arose in the process of wars. As the peak of the power hierarchy, the tsar is a warrior-conqueror or the descendent of one. The elements of war and victory are decisive for the legitimization of the power of the elite in the state. States are created through war and guarded through the maintenance and expansion of a *dispositif* of force (army, police, etc.).

A state necessarily has those who rule and dominate, and those who submit and pay tribute. The lower strata are as necessary for a state as the higher are.

State, the Phenomenon of the City and the Birth of the Demos

A state necessarily has a strategic center. It can be fixed or mobile but in either case the center is in the first place a military headquarters, the dwelling place of the tsar, the prince and his retinue. Precisely this sociological function lies at the basis of the ancient city. The purpose of the city is to be the center of power and the dwelling place of the tsar. This is characteristic for both city state and state territories. In the case of nomadic state, the mobile camp of the tsar can serve as this center. But since according to the theory of "superposition" practically all states are founded by mobile, aggressive, militant nomadic elites, we should examine the phenomenon of the city as the development or fixation of the mobile camp of mobile nomadic troops. The city is a camp, station, place from which soldiers launch raids and where they take defense from enemies. Resources from surrounding areas, necessary for military affairs, flow there.

The city is not an expanded village or borough with a predominance of peasants. Villages are integrated into the city depending on their growth rate but the cities proper are founded according to a completely different logic, as autonomous military-political centers, located at strategic points, convenient for defense or attack. The city as a phenomenon is an expression of the sociology of war.

We should see in this function of the city a typical sign of precisely the *narod*, most often of a *narod* that has created and secured a state.

Thus, in the context of the village and settlements, cities have an entirely special status from a sociological perspective. The city is created around the male warrior union, lead by a chief or tsar. The military detachment develops around itself a subsidiary social group, representing an entirely new (in comparison with the *ethnos*) sociological phenomenon. This social group is the serving staff of the soldiers. As a rule, it consisted of slaves, taken into the tribe after the defeat of an opponent or taken by force or some other means from settled agrarian ethnic societies. This social group of "servants" is exceptionally significant, since it is the embryo of a specific sociological or historical phenomenon: the resident of the city, the city-dweller. The Greeks called the city-dwellers *"demos"* ("δῆμος"), which can be translated as "population." The term "city limits" was used in ancient Rus with this same meaning.

The *demos* emerges together with cities, the state, and the *narod* as its unique sociological sub-product. The *"demos"* does not relate to the *ethnos* (since its representatives are torn out from the ethnic milieu), nor to the aristocracy in the structure of the *"laos."* This is an entirely special phenomenon, the full meaning of which for ethnosociology we will see later, when examining the nation and the role in it of the "third estate."

SECTION THREE

The State as a Typical Creation of the *Narod*

Recognizing the *Narod* behind the State

The state is the most typical expression of the *narod* in history. Most often, once it appears, the *narod* creates precisely a state, a traditional state. This is so general a phenomenon that many historians and sociologists consider the state an independent and autonomous socio-historical phenomenon. In the majority of historical reconstructions, the *narod* is entirely concealed behind the façade of the state and is not distinguished. Only an ethnosociological approach helps us distinguish the stratum of the *laos* in the general structure of the state, to describe its ethnic and sociological peculiarities and to notice that in some cases the *narod* can also manifest itself outside state forms. So one of the most important aims of ethnosociology is the ability to distinguish the *narod* in the state, to separate one from the other and to examine their mutual structures, comparing them in what they have in common and determining their particular characteristics.

We will mention a few examples of settled states known to us from history. Their settled quality shows us that we are dealing with the settled structure of the *narod*, in which nomadic newcomers, forming at the moment of its inception the higher caste of the *narod*, settled firmly in city centers, which are the capitals of the whole socio-political system or regional outposts of power. We will also take note of those instances when statehood is combined with the presence of religion or civilization.

The Egyptian Kingdom

The Kingdom of Egypt is a vivid example of a strictly hierarchized ancient state, combining in itself both a specific religious form and a developed civilization.[10] It was created at the end of the sixth century BCE, i.e. at the time of the political unification of Upper and Lower Egypt under the rule of the first pharaohs. Egyptians thought of the pharaohs as "others," i.e. as "gods," beings of an immeasurable higher nature than regular people. The pharaohs were military leaders and almost always, with rare exceptions, led their lives in constant battles. It is significant that the "otherness" of the pharaohs went so far that incestuous marriages were not only permitted but were mandated, whereas they were categorically forbidden for all others in Egypt. This was a manifestation of the endeavor to preserve the "otherness" of the pharaohs' blood from mixing with other layers. It also underscored the "antitype" on which were based the ancient structures of the *narod*, which rigidly demarcated higher and lower, as rigidly as one *narod* was demarcated from a neighboring one.

The Kingdom of Egypt lasted over three centuries, during which a few stable regimes alternated with periods of relative instability, known as transitional periods. Ancient Egypt reached its highest flourishing in the time of the New Kingdom, after which a gradual decline set in.

The state, religion and civilization of the Egyptians represent three variations of one and the same general hierarchical structure, manifest in political institutions of power and the territorial organization of the state space, in a developed polytheistic religious system and in a special civilizational type, which also influenced societies outside Egypt.

10 *Istoriya Drevnego Vostoka*, ed. Kuzishchin (Moskva, 1988), 270.

The ancient Egyptians were precisely a *narod*. The Egyptian *koine* was the official language, which had various periods of written history, from linear pre-dynastic script to hieroglyphic script, while at the same time the dialects and separate languages of ethnic minorities were developed, especially those spread throughout Upper Egypt (polyglossia). In the caste dualism of the kin of pharaohs (and at one time the leading dynasties of new nomads, the Hyksos) and the local population, we see a trace of fundamental ethnic dualism. The presence of slaves in Egpytian society underscores its highly differentiated character and is directly connected with the technical development. At the same time, despite popular notions, slaves did not play a decisive role in the Egyptian economy, as contemporary historians show. The majority of products were produced by the relatively autonomous peasant population, charged with the necessity of providing food products for the pharaohs, nobility and multitudinous priests.

The Babylonian-Akkadian Kingdom

The Babylonian Kingdom is another example of an ancient state, also with its own religious system and civilizational features.[11]

The Sumerians were newcomers in Mesopotamia from a mysterious "island" (Dilmun), spoken of in legends. Most likely, this was a martial nomadic tribe that conquered the even more ancient layers of the autochthonous population. The Sumerians founded one of the most ancient cities, Eridu, in southern Mesopotamia. The later Amorites were a Semitic tribe, arriving from the West (Am-uru, a *narod* of the West).

In the Sumerian period, the ethnodualism of nobility and commoner is difficult to distinguish. But after the conquest of the Sumer by the Amorites, the new wave of martial newcomers became the military elite, while the masses, it seems, remained Sumerian. The Amorites brought with them the Amorite tongue, which became the *koine* in the Akkadian period. But the polyglossia of small ethnic groups was also preserved.

---

11   Ibid.

The switch from the Sumer to Akkadian *koine* altered the cuneiform but certain Sumerian aspects remained.

The religious system of the ancient Sumerians differed from the Egyptian one. It was a developed cosmological and theological construction, in which the gods were considered global archetypes, models for the cosmos, society and state.

It is significant that the very ancient epic of Gilgamesh was composed in Sumeria. King Gilgamesh is a figure of a heroic type, who sees the world's dividedness and performs feats with the aim of overcoming the trauma of being. The epic as such is a vivid example of precisely the *narod* as an ethnosociological form of society.

Elam

Elam, with its capital of Susa, was an ancient state east of Mesopotamia.[12] It was an independent and original political formation but from a religious and civilizational perspective it was significantly influenced by the Sumerian culture.

The Elam language was peculiar and there are arguments over its correct classification in the family of languages. Elam lost its political independence and won it back often. The *ethnos* of the ruling elite also changed a few times.

The Elam kings practiced incestuous marriage (on a principle analogous to that of the Egyptian pharaohs) and levirate (the brother's marrying the wife of the other brother in the event of his death). The Elam religion was close to the Sumerian one. The cult facilities were also similar, ziggurats. In the case of the Elam, we have a developed state, which should be categorized as Mesopotamian in its religion and civilization.

The Persian Kingdom

The history of ancient Iran gives us an even more obvious illustration of the algorithm of the emergence of a state.[13]

---

12   Ibid.

13   Ibid.

The martial, nomadic, cattle-breeding Aryans, formerly related to proto-Vedic Aryans, invade northern Iran and settle there. It is clear that these territories were inhabited by non-migratory *ethnoses* over the course of a few thousand years BC, while the newly arrived Indo-European nomads from the Eurasian steppes became the ruling strata over the more ancient settled *ethnoses*.

In the eighth century BCE, the Median dynasty is formed, when Median soldiers subjugate Persia, right up to Elam. Later, another tribe, the Persians, take power in the Median Empire.

Wave after wave of nomads from the Great Steppe descend south to the territory of contemporary Iran and organize a hierarchized political space there. A new wave replaced the preceding one in the function of "ruling *ethnos*." The Persians seize Elam. Later, they also added the weakened Assyrian empire.

Different Indo-European nomadic *ethnoses* — the Cimmerii, the Medes, the Hephthalite, the Halani, the Pahlavani, the Sarmatians, the Baloch, the Persians, etc. — were carriers of a specific martial culture with a vividly expressed patriarchal, cattle-rearing orientation. In their inner arrangements, these *ethnoses* were wonderfully fit for the creation of political structures and differentiated societies, i.e. states, which emerged everywhere nomads subjugated ample territories populated by settled farmers, capable of ensuring material support and the resources necessary for life. Such political zones arose on both sides of the Great Steppe: to the north (in the area originally settled by the Finno-Ugric and later by Slavs and Balts) and to the south (from Mongolia to the pre-Caspian zone and Anatolia).

Setting themselves over against agrarian societies, Aryan nomads from Eurasia created differentiated religious systems, vivid examples of which are Iranian Mazdaism and Zoroastrianism.

The Persian Empire was an example of an "Aryan state" (the name "Iran" comes from the expression "*arya*," which the aristocracy of these nomadic tribes used in reference to themselves) with an original religious system and a specific civilization, comprised of certain autochthonous elements mixed with aspects of Elam and Mesopotamian culture.

It is significant that in ancient Iran the maintenance of the ethnic "purity" of the ruling strata was made a religious and sociocultural principle, while dualism became the basis for the both the political system and the religious worldview. Iranian culture took dualism to extreme forms, opposing a "light god" (Ahura-Mazda) to a "dark" one (Ahriman).[14] At the same time, the "*arya*" distinguished themselves as aristocracy from the lower strata, right up to the sacred prescription of incestuous marriage (the preservation of "holy blood"). In the sphere of sacred geography, the Iranians opposed Iran, "the country of Arya," and the domain of "the god Ahura-Mazda" to Turan, the areas populated by the nomadic *ethnoses* of the Great Steppe. Turan was regarded as the domain of the dark god Ahriman. Here, we see radical forms of the *narod*: a rigid division into "these" and "those" inside and outside the state. This dualism was also extended to the religious sphere.

In Iran, we have the model of a heroic culture. The kings and padishahs of Iran express the hero-warrior type. Zarathustra is the archetypical model of the prophet, who reforms archaic religion in accordance with the new sociocultural conditions of the *laos*. The totality of cultural peculiarities produces the entirely specific Iranian civilization, whose influence spread throughout Greece, India, the Great Steppe, all the way to Tibet and the northern areas of Eurasia, where in the archaic folklore of the Finno-Ugric and Slavs one often meets with typically Iranian motifs, plots and symbols. Lev Gumilev thought that the origins of the Tibetan religion Bonpo should be sought in Iranian Mithraism.[15]

Rome

Rome has long been a universal symbol of empire, i.e. of a traditional state of maximum scale.

In its history, we find all the classic attributes of the emergence of the *narod* (*laos*). According to legend, emigrants from Troy, escorted by

---

14   Mary Boyce, *Zoroastrians, Their Religious Beliefs and Practices* (London: Routledge & Kegan Paul, 1979).

15   Lev N. Gumilev. Drevnemongol'skaya religiya (Doklady VGO no. 5, 1968).

the hero Aeneas, founded Rome. Aeneas and his companions have no women (the women of Troy remained in Sicily). They get their women from the local *ethnos*, ruled by King Latinus. The history of the theft by Romulus' soldiers of the Sabine women describes an archetypal storyline of the shortage of women in the *ethnos* of the aggressive, male, martial type ("newcomers," "nomads of the sea") and their encounter with an autochthonous, settled, agrarian population (the Sabines of Titus Tatius). The battle between the newcomers and the autochthonous population is resolved, according to legend, by the Roman women, who threw themselves into the crowed of slaying men, fathers and brothers, and stopped the battle. Here begins the history of the Roman *narod*, called "Quirites" (from the name of the god Quirinus). The Roman *narod* originally consisted of two clearly distinguished layers: the descendants of Romulus (the upper castes) and the descendants of Titus Tatius, i.e. the autochthonous Sabines. Georges Dumézil thinks that the ancient Roman society had three layers, to which there corresponded three gods: Jupiter (priests), Mars (soldiers), Quirinus (peasants).[16] We can suppose that the figures of Jupiter and Mars were brought or reinterpreted by the "descendants of Romulus," while Quirinus (and this has been proven) is an autochthonous god of the local population of Latium, the Sabines.

The style of the Roman state is forged on the basis of pure military ethics and is a model of a highly developed and extremely historically successful heroic society.

In Rome, the archetype of the hero-soldier dominates, embodied in the personality of the Caesar and in the aristocracy. Moreover, this archetype was spread throughout the soldiers of the Roman cohort, who had the possibility of raising their social position through participation in the heroic practice of war.

The Roman religion was rather syncretistic and open to external influences, among which the Greek religion was decisive. Roman civilization was also built around the political principle of Empire. And in this question the Greek influence was tremendous. Rome's uniqueness consisted in

---

16 Georges Dumézil, *Jupiter Mars, Quirinus*, 4 vols. (Paris: Gallimard, 1941–1948), 274.

the fact that it expressed the universality of the political principle of state, brought to its apogee.

Latin was the *koine* in the Roman Empire. After the conquest of Greece, Greek became the second *koine* of the empire. In addition, there lived on the territory of the Roman Empire hundreds of *ethnoses* with their own languages and even some *narods* (laoses), with a distinct religious identity (Jews) and semi-autonomous statehood. The Roman Empire became the model for world government, which embraced the most diverse types of society, from the most archaic to the most highly differentiated and possessing their own statehood, religion and culture (Greece, Egypt, Phoenicia, etc.).

The example of Rome shows how in certain instances there can be a universality of the principle of the *narod* following its mission of integrating all humanity and including into its area of order everything that its members — the Romans, in this case — see as lying outside it.

So in the ancient Roman era, precisely statehood was the axis around which there occurred the crystallization of the Roman *narod*, which realized so widely the sociological vector laid up in the *narod* that it fully merged with its political-sociological expression. Rome shows us the example of a *narod* that fully and practically without any remainder became a state, identified with it.

The adoption of Christianity in the fourth century CE put an end to this triumphal path of Roman heroism and imparted to the empire a unitary and universal religious dimension.

The Scythian Kingdom

We will enumerate states of a nomadic type, which have left far fewer memorials and chronicles but not played a smaller role in the political history and laogenesis of many historical *narods*. Moreover, precisely nomadic states were the ferment for all other historical forms of statehood. The male military unions of a heroic type produced, on top of settled cultures, practically all state known to us. The Scythians did not create a single, integrated empire but nevertheless, precisely their nomadic states united politically the vast areas of the Pontic, the Trans-Caspia and southern Siberia. Fragments of Scythian culture that have come down to us allow us to establish that the Scythians knew a tripartite hierarchy, common to the majority of Indo-European *narods*, in which the priestly, military and peasant castes were strictly distinct. At the same time, those whom the Greeks called Scythian agriculturalists were most likely settled *ethnoses* with a different origin. Thus, the scholar Rybakov thinks that between the Don and the Dnieper there entered into the composition of the Scythian society ancient Slavs, placed among Scythian herdsmen.[17] It is likely that the Scythian kingdoms with their center in the Steppes and a core of warrior-nomads, from which expressive artefacts of animal style and burial places were preserved, established control over the forest-steppe zones and near fertile areas in the pre-Caspian region, where non-migratory agrarian societies were settled. We cannot exclude the possibility that under the influence of the states of steppe nomads, hoe farming gave way to the use of horse and plow. Thus, the Scythians can full well be considered the most ancient *narod* (*laos*) of Eurasia.

The Hunnic Empire

In the second to the fourth century CE, the Steppe is united under the command of the Hunnic tribes — consisting of Mongols, Manchurians, the Finno-Ugric and Turks — which produced a gigantic nomadic empire, the expanses of which reached to Pannonia and Transylvania.[18] In the fifth century, Attila, king of the Huns, almost conquers the Western Roman Empire.

The Huns are a nomadic, cattle-rearing *narod* of polyethnic origin, organized as a single army with a clear political hierarchy and discipline.

The Hunnic Empire integrated the steppe areas of Eurasia, also seizing the agrarian regions of the north and south.

---

17 Boris A. Rybakov, *Gerodotova Skifiya* (Moskva, 1979).

18 Lev N. Gumilev, *Khunnu. Sredinnaya Aziya v drevniye vremenaSredinnaya Aziya v drevniye vremena* (Moskva, 1960), *Khunny v Kitaye* (Moskva, 1974).

Yuezhi and Tocharians

Representatives of the Indo-European *narods* of Yuezhi and Tocharians feuded (rather successfully) with the Huns and integrated huge territories from Bactria and Amu Darya to the Tarim in north-west China (contemporary Xinjiang).[19] The Tocharians settled in Xinjiang and produced a specific culture there. Later, this territory was conquered by Turk-Uyghur, who mixed with the local Tocharian population, which had most likely imposed itself on a more archaic autochthonous stratum.

The descendants of the Yuezhi Kushans created the Kushan kingdom.

The Turkic Khanate and Khazaria

In the sixth century CE, the Great Steppe was united under the control of the Göktürks, who established the Turkic Empire, known as the "Blue Horde." Their rule extended from the Altai, where their political history begins, to the Volga.[20]

The main vector of the Göktürks history, as in the case of the majority of other nomadic empires, unfolded around battles with surrounding nomadic *narods*, who either ceded their territory or else integrated into the "Blue Horde." All of this promoted active ethnic mixing, during which intense linguistic, cultural and social exchange occurred. New ethnic groups were formed and disappeared.

In the seventh century CE, the Turkhic Khanate is replaced by the Khazar kingdom, in which the Turkic *ethnoses* fulfill the function of the elite, while the name "khazar" is applied to the settled Indo-European *ethnoses* of the pre-Caspian region. With their subjugation and assimilation, the history of the Khazars as a Turkic-language *narod* begins. The Khazars create a powerful steppe empire, the distinctive feature of which is a politically fixed center (the city of Atil), located among fertile lands, which clearly predetermined the vividly expressed dual character of Khazar statehood: a military, nomadic elite imposed on a more ancient

---

19   Lev N. Gumilev, *Ot Rusi do Rossii. Ocherki etnicheskoy istorii* (St. Petersburgh, 1992).

20   Lev N. Gumilev, *Tysyacheletie vokrug Kaspiya* (Moskva: Iris Press, 2008).

and technically developed agricultural culture. The Khazars adopted Judaism from the Jews who had left Iran. It became the religion of the Khazar nobility, ethnically Turkic.

As the Huns, Scythians, Yeuzhi and others had done, the Khazars fought with other nomadic tribes and established control over agrarian regions of northern Eurasia. Thus, in one version, Khazars founded Kiev as a center for collecting tribute. In the ninth century, the Vyatichi and other eastern Slavic tribes paid tribute to the Khazars. The Khazars were finally defeated by the Russian prince in the tenth century.

Beginning with the "Blue Horde," the Turks become one of the most important ethnic elements in each subsequent phase of polyethnic *narods* in the Steppe that integrated or tried to integrate it into a single political system.

The Mongols of Genghis Khan

The Mongols of Genghis Khan became a *narod* that was able over a certain historical period to embody the plan of building a world empire, comparable only to Rome, but superseding it in the reach of the integrated territories.

Ghengis Khan reorganized a small Mongolian tribe, tending toward homeostasis with the surrounding environment, i.e. to existence in the ethnocentrum, into a military detachment and began a series of conquests which gradually brought him to rule over the vast space of Eurasia.[21]

Ghengis Khan created a new Eurasian *narod* through the simplest principle of the *narod*-army, into which there freely flowed, beside the Mongols, the passionary heroic types of all surrounding *ethnoses*. The Mongols professed various religions (Christianity, Nestorianism, Buddhism, Shamanism, etc.) but neither religion nor civilization were dominant for their laogenesis: Ghengis Khan focused exclusively on the establishment of a world empire and succeeded in establishing one.

---

21 Erendzhen Khara-Davan, *Rus' mongol'skaya: Chingis-khan i mongolosfera*. (Moskva: *Agraf*, 2002), 276.

Ghengis Khan's soldiers conquered Mongolia, Manchuria, China, Central Asia, Iran, the Cuman steppe and the territories of the Old Russian principalities. Almost all of north-east Eurasia was under the control of his empire. As in the case of Rome, the Mongols rapidly assembled into a *narod* and at the same time identified entirely with an imperial socio-political system. They laid the foundation for a new Mongolian dynasty across of a range of ancient states: China, Iran, etc., forming the skeleton of the "new aristocracy." During Ghengis Khan's life, the Mongols also comprised the ethnic core of a new *narod* but soon after his death the political stratification in each part of the empire, divided by Ghengis Khan among his descendants, became the main form of self-identification for the Mongols as a ruling class mixed with the military elite and the passionary ones of other *ethnoses*.

If Rome represents the historical maximum of empire building west of the Eurasian continent, Ghengis Khan's empire is the symmetrical formation in eastern Eurasia.

SECTION FOUR

Religion as an Ethnosociological Phenomenon

The Religiosity of the *Ethnos* and the Religiosity of the *Narod*

Religion, with a more or less developed transcendental theology, is a characteristic feature of the *narod*.

The ethnocentrum knows the holy and numinous, which are its main quality. In the *ethnos*, the highest form of holiness is the *ethnos* itself, its self-enclosed character, its auto-referentiality, its self-identity. The sacred is the *self-same*, the joyous, dizzying and simultaneously terrifying experience of the immanence of everything to everything. Spirits, gods, animals, people, ancestors, souls, shadows, stones, etc. — they are all sacred in practically the same measure, comprising a continuous and constant chain of sanctity, in which nothing is more distinguished than anything else. And if an article from without happens to be found in the ethnocentrum, it is sacralized, becomes holy, is endowed with a new, sacred meaning.

The religiosity of the *ethnos* is immanent. The religious characteristic of the *narod*, by contrast, is built around the dimension of transcendence. We can say that the typical quality of the *ethnos* is *religiosity* (as numinosity, all-sacredness) and that the typical quality of the *narod* is *religion* (as a construction, based on transcendence). The term "religion" stems from the Latin word "*religare*," i.e. "to bind," or more precisely "to bind again." In the *ethnos*, everything is already bound, so strictly speaking there is nothing there to bind; the task is only to maintain what is already bound in its present state. Thus, we speak of the religiosity, holiness, magicity, and mysticity (Levy-Bruhl) of ethnic consciousness. Religion as such, i.e. the necessity of "binding the split," only begins with the *narod* as a society at the center of which stands precisely a "split," "separation," "trauma," needing "restoration," the "binding" of its separate parts.

Religion separates the world into two parts: a "this side" and an "other side," a "temporal" and an "eternal," etc. In religion, the transcendental dimension, the notion of "another world," is fundamental. This is a distance separating "one" from "another."

The Priest and his Functions

The prophet stands at the center of religion in its pure form. The prophet is a figure that embodies the distance between "this" and "that."[22] In contrast to the shaman, who is the embodiment of the holiness of everything and the main figure maintaining this holiness, the prophet draws and preserves borders; he testifies to the lack of convergence of the world and God, of the human and the divine. Precisely the prophet as an expression of the hero in religion has a twofold mission: to indicate the presence of distance and to find a way to overcome it.

---

22 Dzhemal, *The Revolution of the Prophets.*

The duality of the prophet and shaman embodies the principal difference between religion and religiosity and, accordingly, between the *narod* and the *ethnos*. However, historically this dualism is sustained in full force only very rarely. Since the *narodni* and ethnic dimensions are present in the *narod* simultaneously, the spheres of religion and religiosity often mix. Thus arises a special synthetic figure: the figure of the *priest*.

As a rule, the prophet is regarded as the founder of the religion, its pioneer, the one who establishes new norms and compiles the first religious instructions. Later, religion moves to the authority of the priests, who are called on to maintain the distance between the "transcendent" and the "immanent," to act as guardians of precisely religion and its theological aims [or directives]. But this does not always happen. Quite often, the priestly functions acquire the character of shamanism. The accent begins to fall not on distance and ways to overcome it but on the universal holiness of the world, on the maintenance of "numinosity." Thus, a gradual and imperceptible transformation of *religion* into *religiosity* occurs and the priestly activity is functionally joined to the shamanic role of maintaining the harmony of the world and smoothing over the incurable wound on which the being of the *ethnos* and religion itself as knowledge of the "transcendental" are based. But the prophetic principle is also preserved in religion, so the priestly activity nevertheless differs fundamentally from shamanism dogmatically, stylistically and formally.

Hence, when encountering the phenomenon of priestly activity in various societies, the ethnosociologist should analyze each concrete case very carefully, since the institution of the priesthood can be the expression of a prophetic chain or it can be veiled shamanism. In the majority of cases it is both simultaneously and the distinction of types should be sought in more concrete situations and cases.[23]

---

23 Ibid.

The Structure of Religious Time

Religion has its distinct form of time.[24] This time defines the present as "evil," "deviation from the norm," the situation of the "fall." It is supposed that in the future there will only be further tests and catastrophes, corrected by episodic periods of relative improvement, connected with the activity of religious devotees or new prophets. The past is thought of as "heaven," "the golden age," a period for "imitation." Thus, time flows downward. The perfect, harmonious world belongs to the sacred past. The present is a fall and suffering, and ahead lie greater tragedies.

Religion sets in opposition to downward flowing time an alternate path, which we can call a "vertical path," a "path leading upward." This vector opposes the inertia of time and strives to change the direction of its flow. As a result, a specific time emerges: the time of salvation, soteriological time or messianic time.

The world moves toward the end through descent. The faithful must move contrary to time, along the axis of a "different time," which flows perpendicular to usual time or against it. Thus, alongside time as regression (a general feature of the world as such), religion asserts another heroic dimension, projected onto a particular future and comprising the sphere of religious eschatology (from the Greek "εσχατον," "end").

Eschatology is a distinctive feature of time in the society of the *narod* (*laos*). The characteristic quality of the *narod* appears in it: the project, the will, the lunge into the future, the dialog with the forces of fate. Religious time sees in the future the denouement of the heroes' battle against evil. This denouement is an end, an "eschaton." This end will be the ultimate concentration of "world evil," which the "final savior," the "messiah," will encounter face to face, along with his faithful, heroic followers. The being of the *narod* as a religio-messianic community is directed toward the eschatological denouement of religious time. Properly speaking, the eschatological perspective and the idea of regress comprise the meaning of "sacred history" and of history as such, inasmuch as the entire history

---

24 Gilles Pronovost, *Sociologie du temps* (Paris: De Boeck/Université, 1996), 278.

of the *narod* is sacred. However, this sacredness does not consist in the *narod's* experiencing itself as a deity (as happens in the case of the *ethnos*) but in the *narod's* striving to realize in its being the heroic act of self-overcoming, of healing the split of "transcendence," of accomplishing the "restoration of being" comprising the meaning of the historical process. In the eschatological era, the final battle is completed and the universal resurrection of the dead occurs as the end of history, the Last Judgment, salvation, the final note of the *narod's* being.

Such soteriological time lies at the basis of the religious cult.[25] Religion establishes the cult to actualize the "transcendent" dimension within the world, as special, exclusive conditions. That which is impossible for the world as such is possible for religion and its institutions. But this possibility does not guarantee automatic "salvation." The faithful has to exert heroic effort to acquire it. Religion shows the way but each must travel it independently. Thus, the personal, heroic principle is contained in the basis of religion. It demands high differentiation — in the comprehension of religious doctrines, in the education of the will, in overcoming the actually existing conditions and limitations that press on man. So religion, even though it is addressed to all, nevertheless remains an elite affair. To realize its norms, to bring one's life into accord with its ethics, to master religious dogmas and rules, it is necessary to radically go beyond the borders of everyday (ethnic) existence, to discover "another world" beyond the visible and immediately given one.

Because of this structure of religion and religious time, when applied to the *narod* (*laos*) as such, it necessarily splits into two parts: the *religion of the masses* and the *religion of the elite*. These religions can differ formally or they can appear identical. Even if the religion of the masses will not be distinguished in some special way, ethnic religiosity will prevail in it and the priestly function will approach the shamanic one. Religion as such, with all its theological and transcendental baggage, will, by contrast, be

25 Henri Hubert, *Étude sommaire de la représentation du temps dans la religion et la magie*, in Henri Hubert and Marcel Mauss, *Mélanges d'histoire des religions* (Paris: Librairie Félix, 1929).

concentrated in the elite, where its theological and heroic aspects will be especially appropriate.

Thus, in the layered society of the *narod* we encounter simultaneously two forms of time: the closed cycle of "eternal return" (the religious time of the masses) and the tragic pair of world regression and the heroic personality opposing to it soteriological and messianic time (the religious time of the elite).[26]

Examples of Religions

All the aforementioned features appear most distinctly in the world's monotheistic religions, although they are present in polytheistic religions too, especially in dualistic Iranian Mazdaism or Zoroastrianism. But monotheism — Judaism, Christianity and Islam — represents these tendencies in their pure guise. More than other forms of religion, monotheism accents the "transcendence" of God, his difference from the world. God creates the world as an "other," other than Him. All the acuity of monotheistic theology is contained in this idea. And this, of course, is a clear sign of the *narod* as an ethnosociological phenomenon.

We will now consider a few monotheistic religions from the ethnosociological perspective.

Judaism

Let us begin with Judaism. The ancient Jews became a *narod* that formed exclusively around the religious idea.[27] In Jewish history, there were various states that came and went and there were periods of existence without a state. But always, at any stage, the Jews were precisely a *narod*: a highly differentiated polyethnic society, stable, active and mobile, rallying around religion and religious forms.

---

26   Paul Ricoeur, Claude Larre, Riamundo Panikkar, Alexis Kagame, G.E.R. Lloyd, André Neher, Louis Gardet, Aron Gourevitch.

27   Baron Salo Wittmayer, *A Social and Religious History of the Jews*, 2nd edition, 18 vols. (New York: Columbia University Press, 1952), 280.

In Judaism we see all the characteristic features of religion:

- The transcendentalism of the One God;

- The idea of creation out of nothing;

- The radical dualism of Creator and created (world);

- An elaborate theology;

- The central role of the prophet;

- The dramatic character of moral choice;

- The ethics of the heroic overcoming of the regular conditions of existence;

- The idea of sacred history, leading from heaven to "the last days";

- Hope for the messianic restoration at the end of the world, the opposition to time;

- A sharp awareness of the opposition of the community of the faithful to all other surrounding *narods*;

- Extreme aggression and utmost sacrificiality.

It is significant that in Judaism the central concept is "am ha-kodesh" ("sacred *narod*"), i.e. the Jews themselves: they are conceived of as radically distinct from other *narods* and *ethnoses* in that only they know about the distance separating the world from its Creator.

The Jewish religion formed together with the Jewish *narod*; the history of the Jews and the history of Judaism are identical. The Jews lived among other *narods*, mixed with other *ethnoses*, in certain periods created statehoods with monarchic rule, were sent into dispersion and capture, and again gathered in Palestine, but they always understood themselves as carriers of a specific religious mission, equating their own history with the history of the salvation of the world, awaiting the arrival of the "moshiach."

Although in the history of the Jews there were periods of full-fledged statehood (the state of Israel as the "latest" [or last] form of Jewish statehood, according to the religious interpretation of contemporary rabbis, exists in our time), the Jewish *narod* cannot be equated with a state, since it preserved its identity for millennia without it, in the diaspora. At the same time, of course, there were many cases of ethnic mixing but the sociocultural type of the Jews, built around the idea of the "sacred *narod*" and its mission, was preserved unchanged.

Thus, Jews are a very vivid illustration of the way the *narod* can exist for centuries without a state, not assimilating and not transforming into a homeostatic *ethnos*.

Christianity

The Christian religion, starting from the fourth century CE, is a form of historical being of the Greco-Roman world, including Roman colonies in the Near East, which produced a kind of "Christian *narod*," a *narod* of the ecumene, spreading far beyond the borders of the Empire of the Romans into Europe, Rus, Asia, etc.[28] It is telling that in Greek Christians are called "ἱερός λαός," "hieros laos," i.e. literally "sacred *narod*," not using the terms "*ethnos*," "genos," or "*demos*," but precisely "*laos*," i.e "*narod*" as a specific ethnosociological category.

At the core of Christianity there stood precisely a monotheistic religion, with a developed theology, eschatology, dogma, soteriology and philosophy of history. Christianity adopted part of its dogmatic elements from Judaism and many others were altogether original. Overall, Christianity put forward a highly differentiated, tragic picture of a split world, with an abyss separating man from God, but saved thanks to the Sacrifice of the Son of God.

Christianity offered its faithful a heroic perspective of the complete overcoming of oneself, self-elevation, ascesis, rejecting the "world," martyrdom, and confessorship. The Christian cosmos differed radically from the ethnocentrum: in it, there prevailed a constant tension and strict separation of "the world, lying in evil," from which one must flee, and the "Heavenly kingdom," towards which one must strive. To unite them

---

28   Archpriest Petr Smirnov, *Istoriya Khristianskoy Pravoslavnoy Tserkvi* (St. Petersburgh, 1914).

was not in the power of man but God, Jesus Christ. The Christian was supposed to follow Christ along the difficult road: "God became man, so that man could become God" (in the words of Basil the Great).

All these characteristics of the Christian religion, the Christian world-view, facilitated the transition to the condition of *narod* of any *ethnos* adopting Christianity. From the fourth century, Christianity became the official religion of the Roman Empire and the *narod* of the Empire received a new impulse to historical being. Moreover, within the Empire, on its periphery, and in the territories abutting it, new *narods* rapidly formed, which significantly contributed to the spread of Christianity as a religion.

Catholicism and Orthodoxy

The disintegration of the Roman Empire into East and West brought to light again the existence on a new phase of two *narods*, the Roman (Latin) and Greek (Romaion) with their *ethnos*-satellites. The church schism was connected with the historical choice about the way to correlate the Christian religion with the historical challenges of two *narods*, Eastern Christians and Western Christians.[29]

The Latin world became the basis of the Western European *narod*, which existed for a short while in a single state (the Western Roman Empire) but formed into Western European civilization, bound together by the Catholic religion, with the supreme power of the Pope, the Latin mass, a celibate clergy and a specific sociocultural system. Some European philosophers, Husserl in particular, called this community "European humanity." From an ethnosociological perspective, it would be more precise to call this phenomenon the "European *laos*." Catholicism played the fundamental role in the formation of this "European *laos*," comprised, in turn, of a few self-sufficient *narods*.

The fate of the Eastern Roman Empire, Byzantium, proved entirely different. There, the state lasted almost a thousand years longer than it did in the Western Roman Empire. Byzantium became the form of the

---

29   Aleksey P. Lebedev, *Istoriya Razdeleniya Tserkvey v 9-kh, 10-kh, i 11-kh vekakh* (St. Petersburgh, 1999), 282.

historical being of Romaion *narod*, which also became the core for the diffusion of the Orthodox religion and the center of a special Eastern Christian civilization. *Narods* and states assembled in accordance with the Byzantine model: eastern Slavs and also Caucasian and Near-Eastern societies. If Western Europe was a civilization bound together by Catholicism, Byzantium was a religious center and civilization but also a state. That is, we see here all three forms of the *narod's* being at once.

Russian Orthodoxy

Kievan Rus' adoption of Orthodoxy almost coincides in time with the creation of the state and it is the most important impulse for the emergence of the Old Russian *narod*. The Orthodox religion became the basic state idea and the axis of the official worldview.[30] The general identity of the *narod* and its statehood were thereby fortified. Civilizationally, ancient Rus belongs to the Byzantine zone.

Later, after the fall of Constantinople to the Turks, Muscovite Rus assumed the function of being the core of the Orthodox world, which was expressed in the theory that "Moscow is the Third Rome." The Russian *narod* attained the culmination of its awareness of its place in history, regarding itself as god-bearing *narod* and Rus as Holy Rus, endowed with a special eschatological mission. The very existence of an independent Orthodox statehood was perceived as a sign of "chosenness." The identity of the Russian *narod*, precisely as a *narod*, as a historic community reached its apogee.

Protestantism

Protestantism was the form of historical expression of the German *narod*, which came together later than the other *narods* of Europe on the basis of a few Germanic *ethnoses* and weak, dependent feudal states.[31] It also

---

30   Yevgeny Golubinsky *Istoriya Russkoy Tserkvi* (Moskva: Direktmedia Publishing, 2008).

31   Elena V. Revunenkova, *Protestantism* (St. Petersburg, 2007).

exerted a large influence on the appearance of the Swiss confederacy, built on Protestant foundations. But Protestantism is a religious phenomenon on the border of modernity, when a new form of societies arose: the nation as the second derivative of the *ethnos*. So we will consider the sociological function of Protestantism in another chapter.

Islam and the Caliphate

The Islamic conquests—a vivid example of how the *narod*, the Arab *narod*, was in essence artificially produced by Mohammed, like the Mongolian *narod* by Ghengis Khan—put half the world into motion, creating a state and civilization under the aegis of a religion.[32] Here, we see the figure of the prophet at the center, Mohammed himself. Moreover, the specific character of Islamic monotheism consists in the fact that in this religion there is a total lack of priestly activity. There is only the prophet and the faithful who follow him and worship the "transcendental God," about whom he prophesizes.

The *narod* here, as in the case of the ancient Jews, is formed around religion but in contrast to the Jews it expresses its historical appearance in the blazing creation of a gigantic empire, the Islamic Caliphate.

At the core of the Islamic *narod*, coinciding with the Islamic religious community, the Ummah, were the ethnic Arabs of the Arabian Peninsula, the first associates and tribesmen of Mohammed. But very quickly, other Near Eastern, North African, and Asiatic *ethnoses* join the religion, melting into a new social system formed around the Islamic religion.

Arabization was sometimes rather superficial: the North African Berbers, to say nothing of Iranians, Hindus (Pakistanis), Pashtuns, Central Asians and Filipinos preserved their ethnic peculiarities.

When the caliphate weakened and fell apart, new states and new *narods* arose on its basis, which were either the Islamized versions of more ancient *narods* (Iran), or emerged under the influence of Islam as a highly

---

32   Konstantin P. Matveev, *Istoria Islama* (Moskva: ACT: Vostok-Zapad, 2005).

differentiated sociological religious environment and passionary impulse of the Arabian conquerors.

Overall, the general religious and civilizational space was preserved in the Islamic world after the fall of the Caliphate. That is, the original "Islamic *narod*" of the seventh and eighth centuries was transformed into a civilization and general sociocultural type, which long outlived its own state as such.

Later Islamic States

Within the framework of Islam, some *narods* tried to establish new models of religious civilizations. First and foremost, this is the Shiite Qarmatian Caliphate (in the tenth century in Bahrain, Syria, Iraq and western Iran, a huge, politically organized *narod* formed on the religious basis of Sevener Shia, which included Egpytians and Berbers), Shiite Iran (from the sixteenth century), the Khawarij state, supported by Berbers, etc.

The Ottoman Empire, announcing itself as the heir to the Caliphate, with the dominant religion of Islam, was to a large extent a reproduction of the nomadic empires of Eurasia. After seizing control over the weakened Mediterranean states, the martial Turk-Ottomans united the Eurasian style of organizing a large space with the instrumental conception of the restoration of the Caliphate. As a result, a unique cultural style and specific *narod* took shape, formed around the ethnic core of the Turks with a huge share of Greek, Slavic, Anatolian, Near-Eastern, and Asiatic elements. For the Ottomans, Islam played a big role but it was already a Turkified, Eurasian Islam, differing substantially from Arabic Islam.

SECTION FIVE

Civilization and Its Structure

Civilization and the Challenge of a Split World

It remains to consider a few examples of the case when the *narod*, appearing in history, begins with the creation not of a state or religion but a civilization.

A civilization is a highly differentiated culture, uniting diverse societies without direct political or religious (strictly regulated) ties. By its nature, civilization is also based on an imbalanced, tragic, split consciousness, for which the world is a conflictual, asymmetric, dramatic structure, a challenge that demands to be overcome heroically. But the peculiarity of civilization consists in the fact that it responds to this challenge through the elaboration of *complex cultural systems*; in the first place, philosophy but also technology, arts, sciences, etc. A civilization is a society of the heroic type, in which passionarity is embodied in the creation of philosophical, aesthetic or technical systems. This is a special means for society to cope with the drama of a divided world.

Civilizations quite often form within religious or stately structures as one of the manifestations of the historic being of the *narod*. But there are many cases when the *narod* expresses itself through civilization without creating a state or religion, although at a certain stage it might acquire both or one of them, or some consistent combination of these elements. So we are justified in considering civilization a direct creation of the *narod*.

Greek Civilization

We will mention a few examples of how *narods* appear in history through civilizations.

Here, the classic example is Ancient Greece.[33] It did not have a single statehood or general religion. Greece was a constellation of city states with

---

33   Andrje Bonnar, *Grecheskaya Civilizaciya v 3-h tomakh* (Moskva, 1958).

different political systems, weakly connected with or even hostile toward one another. At the same time, the Greeks actively contacted other ethnic groups living in the Mediterranean and the process of ethnic mixing proceeded on a full scale.

The unity of the ancient Greek world was based on a specific type of culture, which was shared somehow or other by all participants of Greek civilization, from the Pontus and Anatolia to the Near Eastern, North African, Western Mediterranean Hellenic or Hellenized societies. The general style of philosophy, culture, art, technology, life and outlook united the members of diverse political systems and adherents of diverse cults and sects.

We can call the core of this civilization poetry in the Homeric period and philosophy in later times, after Thales of Miletus and other pre-Socratics. Philosophy became the quintessential Greek way of relating to the world, in which spiritual concern for the problem of the world found its highest expression. This philosophy concentrated in itself the extreme differential that comprises the core of the *narod* as an ethnosociological phenomenon. The ancient Greeks were a *narod* formed around philosophy, around a certain type of critical thought, directed toward and distrustful of oneself, capable of taking the position of the other in regard to oneself.

Heraclitus of Ephesus' first fragment tells us about this: "Having harkened not to me but to the Word (Logos), it is wise to agree that all things are one."[34] This comprises the essence of philosophy as a phenomenon. If you listen to the perception of a human, he sees around himself many things. He does not see unity; he sees non-unity and, strictly speaking, can only testify to multiplicity and plurality. But Heraclitus summons one to perform a leap, to renounce that perception, to move to another structure of thought. This structure is not obvious and its very existence is problematic and difficult. He calls it "logos" or the "wise" (the principle). And nevertheless, only from the position of logos is it possible to grasp the essence of the world as a unity and to overcome the cleavage of ordinary human perception. This demands tremendous efforts of the spirit, a

---

34 *Fragmenty drevnegrecheskikh filosofov.* (Moskva: Nayka, 1989), 199.

series of dissections and unifications, troubles and delights. It demands a strained and incessant work of thought, constantly directed beyond its limits, toward the transcendental sphere of logos.

The very structure of Greek philosophy is exceedingly close to religion and after the spread of Christianity, religion and philosophy merge tightly in the phenomenon of theology. On the other hand, such a degree of differentiation is possible only in a stratified society, having, by definition, a political dimension. Let us recall that Heraclitus was a king who ceded his throne to his brother. This gesture can be considered a symbolic choice of ancient Greek as such: it selects not state but philosophy. Thus, it gives us an example of how the *narod* can enter on the path of historical being through philosophy and civilization, laying precisely logos as the cornerstone.

Later, Alexander the Great, a student of the philosopher Aristotle, created a gigantic state and conquered all of Asia up to India. At some point, civilization was converted into Empire. At another time, the Greeks proved to be above all the *narod* of another state: Byzantium. Moreover, precisely Greek civilization becomes the custodian of the Christian religion and the Greek *narod* comprises the core of the "sacred *narod*" of Christianity ("ἱερός λαός"). It is significant that the New Testament was written in Greek and Greek is considered a "holy tongue" by the Christian religion.

But as a historical unity and as a community of heroic spirit, the Greeks appeared in history before a state and before a unified religion.

Indian Civilization

The Indian *narod* is another example of a *narod* that first produces a civilization and then the other forms. Indian civilization was created by Indo-European nomads, Vedic Aryans who had conquered an innumerable number of autochthonous, mostly Dravidian *ethnoses*.

Indian civilization is based, first of all, on a highly differentiated philo-sophical system, on which all of society is built.[35] Even in its most archaic forms, this system gives rise to complexity, reflexivity, maturity of rational methodologies and refined gnoseological elaborations. Underlying this system is a fundamental dualism with a ceremonial-ritual and purely philosophical expression: the dualism between the "immanent" and "transcendent," between "subject" and "object," between "this" and that." The reflection of Indian thought is spread over the most diverse sectors of being — from the common to the mythological, the natural, the anthro-pological, etc.

Indian society takes as its normative type the solitary person, the her-mit, devoting his life to pure ascesis, self-overcoming, the heroic practice of working out the "absolute will." After carefully studying Indian society, the sociologist Dumont showed that the "individualism" of Indian culture is much more radical and extreme than the individualism of contempo-rary liberal Western society.

But the peculiarity of the Indian approach consists in the fact that dualism — established everywhere in the world, in man, among gods and demons — must be overcome. This is called the principle of "*advaita*" ("not-two"). The root of reality, this dualism is nevertheless an illusion. The power of this illusion (maya) is tremendous. But the power of the soul of the ascetic and the philosopher-hermit can defeat even this might. The result is becoming a god and liberation from the cosmos as the prison error and ignorance. The highest ideal is "*moksha*," "freedom."

Indian society is based on the caste principle. Brahmins are regarded as the highest caste, occupied principally with religious ceremonies and meditation, philosophy, contemplation. The second caste is the warriors, the Kshatriya. The third is the Vaishya, peasants and artisans. There is also a fourth caste, the Shudra (proletariat), and outlaws, pariahs, those altogether without a caste.

In this stratification, we clearly see traces of the conqueror *ethnos* — the Aryans (the higher caste) — and the autochtonous, settled *narods* (the

---

35   Louis Dumont, *Homo Hierarchicus: The Caste System and its Implications* (Chicago: University of Chicago Press, 1980).

Vaishya and especially the Shudra). A religious caste system exists in India not so much on the basis of political unity and a traditional government as on the basis of a general civilizational structure, which justifies a state of affairs that corresponds to a differentiated world structure.

There have been many attempts in India's history to create statehood. The newly arrived Moguls had the most success, since Indians themselves clearly did not give this aim enough attention: the political aspects of the application of their passionarity did not concern them much; the existing statehood was shaky and unstable.

Although many aspects of traditional Indian culture resemble religion, this culture is too diverse, multifaceted and all-encompassing to correspond to the criteria of a religion. Here there are no dogmas, no strict theology, no prophets, no soteriology, eschatology, etc. In different parts of India, different cults predominate and in little villages local rites and gods are often preserved that bear a trace of pre-Vedic cults. Different schools interpret differently the gods and myths, the Vedic texts and the meaning of rites. Hinduism includes the most diverse elements and does not lose its distinctive character. It is not a religion in the full sense of the word but a civilization, a tradition, a spiritual culture, possessing an unmistakably identifiable style but lacking all strict formalism.

If we add to this such detached religions as Buddhism and Jainism, as well as the Hindu-Islamic syncretism of the Sikhs, which also formed in India, then the religious palette of India will be even more variegated and contradictory.

Chinese Civilization

China can also be considered first of all a civilizational phenomenon and only then a state.[36]

China is a *narod*, formed historically in the eighteenth century BCE around the populations of the contemporary provinces of Shaanxi, Shanxi and Henan, usually called the "Yin (Shang) dynasty." These were settled, agricultural tribes. At the start of the eleventh century BCE, the Yin were

36   Marcel Granet, *La Civilization Chinoise* (Paris: La Renaissance du Livre, 1929).

conquered by kindred tribes, the Zhou, descendants of the western branch of the Yangshao tribes, who had strong cattle-rearing traditions. The core of the Chinese *narod* formed out of the superposition of settled Yin and nomadic Zhou. There were rather intensive interactions between the two tribes, which ultimately led to the formation in the seventh and eighth centuries CE of the new ethnic community of Huaxia, direct ancestors of the contemporary Chinese.

The Huaxia created a peculiar culture, of which the Confucian teaching and the Daoist school of a certain kind of paradoxical, mystical philosophy became vivid expressions.

Confucianism strictly regulated the civilizational and socio-cultural structure of Chinese society. It was based on a dualism of male and female, high and low, order and disorder. But these opposed principles were regarded as poles of cosmic harmony, which must be discovered, established and supported through laborious and constant cultural efforts. The heroic aspect of ancient Chinese culture consisted precisely in culture, ethnics, morality, aesthetics, rules of behavior, the rational organization of labor and mutual relations, which exerted a decisive influence on the cultures of neighboring *narods*: the Japanese, Koreans, Vietnamese, Taiwanese, etc.

Chinese history knows periods of harsh political states with a political character but also long periods of disorder, civil war and disintegration. Representatives of nomadic steppe tribes repeatedly seized power in China. But each time, after a few generations they assimilated to Chinese civilization, leaving no trace in culture, politics or social organization.

Confucianism and Daoism are not religions in the full sense of the word: they are rather philosophies and even codes of a cultural worldview. Buddhism, which had come from India and was more dogmatically formulated, transformed quickly in the context of Chinese society and also became a kind of mystical, paradoxical philosophy, known as Chan Buddhism, or Zen Buddhism in Japan.

The Chinese *narod* is very much polyethnic. Even today, the southern and northern Chinese pronounce the same hieroglyphs differently, to say nothing of the plurality of distinct *ethnoses* that preserve their languages.

CHAPTER FIVE

The Nation

SECTION ONE

Ethnosociological Analysis of the Nation: The Second Derivative from the *Ethnos*

The Contemporary State as a Sociological Phenomenon

Let us now consider the second derivative from the *ethnos*, the nation.

The appearance of the nation is possible only *after* the formation of the *narod* on the basis of the *ethnos*. Although in some cases, when the nation is formed artificially, this stage can be reduced to a minimum or be "nominal." The nation emerges when a *traditional* state (as one of the typical creations of the *narod*) becomes a *modern* state, i.e. radically changes its quality.

The modern state arose for the first time in Europe in the modern era and gradually became the "normative" [or standard] form of the state, together with the spread of European, Western influence worldwide. In our time, when we say "state," we implicitly mean "the modern state," since precisely it is taken as the generally accepted model. However, this picture has formed only in the past 400 years and the process of the formation of national states on the basis of either traditional states or former European colonies occurred during this whole time in diverse regions of the world with varying speed. Even at the start of the twentieth century, national states (France, Italy, Spain, Holland, England, etc.) existed in Europe and Eurasia alongside empires, i.e. traditional states (Austro-Hungary, Russia, the Ottoman Empire, etc.). Many European colonies became modern states only in the twentieth century. The modern state, in contrast to the traditional state, is usually called a "national state" or "nation state" ("*État-nation*," in French).

The modern nation state differs from the traditional state in the following features:

- The transition from a caste and estate to a class hierarchy (based on material possessions and the relation to means of production);

- Taking as a normative type the third estate, i.e. the bourgeoisie (the modern state is a bourgeois state);[1]

- The predominance of practical rationality and material interests over "ideals" and "mission" in forming and carrying out state politics;

- The transformation of society as a historic phenomenon (the state as a "community of fate") into society as a rational, artificially organized phenomenon (the state as a product of a "social contract");

- The appearance as the principal and fundamental socio-political unit of the individual citizen as basic carrier of political will and social rationality;

- The political equalization of the complex social and ethnic structure of the traditional state (or *narod*) into the uniform concept of citizenship;

- The presence of strictly defined borders, recognized by neighboring states;

---

1   The socialist state, which is a post-capitalist model, is a special example of the modern state.

- The complete integration of the economic system, the division of labor in the state and a single legal system for the economy throughout the territories of the state;

- A secular character;

- The presence of a formalized system of right, clearly fixing the structure of the legal and illegal;

- The presence in the state of one (rarely two) national languages, the knowledge and study of which are necessary for all citizens as the basis for all official state documents and statutes.

In each of these points, the modern state contrasts with the traditional state. In the modern nation state, stratification is based on class, whereas in a traditional state it is based on the estate or caste; in the modern state, the figure of the bourgeois stands at the fore; in the traditional state, the hereditary aristocracy (soldiers) or clergy (priests) does. The politics of the modern state are determined by calculation, profit and interests; the politics of the traditional state are determined by a mission, a fate, a religious or historical goal (often irrational). The modern state is created artificially as an expanded version of a commercial partnership (the "social contract"); the traditional state is based on the fact of the powerful domination of elites over masses and cannot be abolished by the will of the masses (except in the case of insurrection and the coming to power of a new elite, a contra-elite, as Pareto says). In the modern state, the main political actor is the citizen; in the traditional state, it is the estate and above all the highest estate. In the modern state, citizenship overrides ethnic and estate cultures; in the traditional state, by contrast, they possess a significant degree of autonomy. In the modern state, the principle of fixed borders prevails; in the traditional state, borders are most often not lines but areas, poles, the domination in which by one or another power is constantly contested, so borders themselves are mobile and change. The economy of the modern state is organized rationally and is a closed system of production and consumption; in the traditional state, the economy can be regionally differentiated, relying on small closed zones (a natural economy), while economic legislation is as a rule weakly developed and differs substantially from region to region. The modern state is most often secular; the traditional state can be entirely religious. In the modern state, right is distributed throughout all socio-political spheres and aims to encompass as broad a sphere of life as possible (a right-state); in the traditional state, right regulates only the fundamental questions of the political and religious order and the estate is granted broad privilege in deciding political and social questions discretionally. In the modern state there is strictly *one* (rarely two) definite national language (Gellner calls these "idioms");[2] in traditional society there is real polyglossia, and a shared language (*koine*) is used in fact and does not have rigidly defined normative rules, fixed on the basis of one or another dialect.

The Nation as a Special Type of Society

The nation is one side of the modern state. Citizenship states are a special type of society, called a "nation," a national society.

All the characteristics and distinct features of the nation have significance only in the context of the "modern state" and are immediately connected with it. Outside the modern state, the nation does not and cannot exist. The nation is the social content of the modern state, its "filling," the society that creates the modern state and is created by it. The nation most often arises together with the modern (national) state, simultaneously. Where there is a modern state, there is also necessarily a nation. Where there is a nation, there is also necessarily a modern state. It is not possible to imagine a nation without a modern state. If we assume that some kind of society is a nation, then that automatically means that society has the social structure of a modern state.

It is a different thing that in political practice one or another social group (having shared ethnic and historical, i.e. *narodni* roots, or lacking them) can announce itself as a "nation." But that will mean only this, that this group wants to effect a "social contract" for the establishment

---

2   Gellner, *Nations and Nationalism*.

a "modern state," regardless of whether others recognize the validity of this contract or not. Thus, one can get the impression that sometimes the formation of a nation precedes the creation of a modern state, or, on the other hand, that the modern state transforms its citizens into a nation after its emergence. This "temporal" gap does not have decisive significance. In the strict sense, we can only speak of a "nation" when dealing with a modern state (actual or only wished for). And if a modern state actually exists, a nation necessarily exists together with it as the aggregate of its citizens. If there is a state but not yet a "nation," then we are not dealing with the "modern state" but with some form of "traditional state," which allows for broader interpretations of its social structures.

The Political and Economic Character of the Nation. Power (*Vlast*) and the Bourgeoisie

An important feature of the nation follows from the direct and fundamental connection of the nation with the state: *the nation is a political formation, i.e. a society united by a political marker and formed around a state political system.*[3] This radically distinguishes the nation from the *ethnos* and the *narod*.

The ethnos is an organic and primordial phenomenon. It is the simplest form of society, the *koineme*. In the *ethnos*, there is no differentiation along the axis of either social groups or social strata.

The narod is a historic phenomenon. In the *narod*, there is both vertical and horizontal differentiation. The *narod* is simultaneously an organic (since the ethnic structure is preserved among the masses and in part among the elite) and a political phenomenon. The *narod* is most often realized through the creation of a traditional state but it can also manifest itself through religion and civilization.

The nation is purely political and modern. In the nation, the main form of social differentiation is the class (in the Marxist sense, i.e. on the basis of the relation to ownership of the means of production). The nation

---

3 Ibid.

exists only under capitalism. The nation is inseparably connected with the "modern state" and the ideology of modernity. The nation is a European phenomenon.

For precisely this reason, we speak of the nation as the second derivative from the *ethnos*. In the *narod*, the main characteristics of society change, since the *ethnos* enters history. The formation of the nation represents another fundamental structural shift. This time, the basic characteristics of the *narod* as society change. In the nation, the *narod* moves from history and its peripeteia to the sphere of the rational organization of collective life under entirely new circumstances. The meaning of the nation is not the hero's struggle with fate (as in the *narod*) but the rationalization and optimization of economic life. Hence, the nation is closely connected not only with politics but also with economics. The nation state is simultaneously a political and an economic formation.

The political dimension also exists in the traditional state but it touches only separate parts of life and is concentrated primarily in the higher estates. The masses are politicized only indirectly and to an insignificant extent, maintaining the social algorithms of the ethnocentrum. In the national state, politicization reaches the very bottom of society, since the nation is a political community that distributes political privileges (included in the concept of citizenship) to *all* its members.

The economic dimension of the nation is its distinct feature. The national state is above all a product of a constitutive agreement (most often in the form of a "Constitution"), on the basis of which the participants (citizens as members of a constitutive assembly or society of shareholders) *come to an agreement* to form a joint enterprise that ensures the economic interests of each. So the provision of the economic and household wants of the citizen is the basic task of the national state. Thus, the nation can full well be thought of as a voluntary union of economic subjects.

The degree of responsibility for all undertakings (the "national state" as a commercial and industrial company) is distributed throughout bourgeois society not equally but in accordance with class stratification. The rich and well-to-do members of the nation, who have the same amount of political rights and social possibilities as all others, play a bigger role in the economic sphere than the lower classes. In this way, economic inequality combined with political equality leads to a specific form of social stratification, expressed in the domination of the bourgeoisie. The rich have more stock in the nation as an economic enterprise and, consequently, their influence increases. Politics, open to all, "objectively" becomes an instrument in the hands of the well-to-do bourgeoisie, first and foremost of the richer among them.

The rationality of national life is based on precisely the balance of political equality and economic inequality. The ruling class is interested in the participation in the political process of all citizens but only so far as the general political and economic paradigm of capitalist domination is preserved. Attempts at political organization by the lower classes with the goal of overthrowing the economic model of the bourgeois nation (socialism, communism, anarchism) provoke a logical reaction.

All of these processes are studied in thorough detail in the Marxist tradition.

Ethnosociologically, it is only important to underscore the structure itself of the socio-economic arrangement of the nation as the second derivative from the *ethnos* or the first derivative from the *narod*.

The Ethnosociology of the City

From the ethnosociological perspective, the genesis of the nation and the modern state should be sought in the phenomenon of the city.[4]

If the domain of ethnokinetics is the transition phase from the *ethnos* to the *narod* and the start of laogenesis, the sociology of the city lies at the basis of the *second transition phase*, from *the narod to the nation*. At the same time, the city and its sociological structure can also exist in the structure of the *narod*, inasmuch as it already contains those tendencies that prevail in the emergence of the modern state and underlie the nation as an ethnosociological phenomenon. Similarly, ethnokinetics can

---

4   Max Weber, *The City* (New York: Simon & Schuster, 1958).

be observed even in those societies that still remain in the context of the *ethnos* and only encounter the preconditions that can bring about the start of the process of laogenesis.

We saw that the basis of the city is the military headquarters of the *narod's* political elite (often a nomadic camp), created for strategic reasons in an "empty space" (and not developed gradually through increasing the population of a traditional, populated point of settled farmers). The city is not a big, expanded village. The city is originally and principally created according to another logic and with entirely different aims. Military and political power are concentrated in the city, which is also a center for the collection of tribute by those who do not produce anything by agricultural methods but merely accumulate the resources, products and goods pro-duced elsewhere.

The village populated by the *ethnos* is a folk society.[5] The city is populated by a professional military elite and its serving staff. In this elite, the principal of heroic, personal (and not communal, as in the *ethnos*) identification prevails. The city is a purely political phenomenon. And it is no accident that the very word "politics" stems from the Greek word "πολις," "polis," "city." In the traditional state, the city is the political and military center of the entire country, the locality of the statewide elite. This comprises its main sociological function. The rest of the territory of the state is regarded as something supplementing the city, dependent on the city, subordinate to it. That is why many states are named for their capitals; for instance, the Babylonian Empire or Kievan Rus.

The Phenomenon of the *Demos*

Besides the political elite of soldiers and priests, another social type, with its own unique characteristics, forms in the city. In general, it can be called "servile" (from the Latin "*servus*," servant, meaning a servant to an aris-tocrat in the broadest sense). Besides household servants, a broad layer of additional social units attended to the nobility. In places where elites

---

5   Robert Redfield, *Peasant Society and Culture: An anthropological approach to civili-zation* (Chicago: University of Chicago Press, 1956).

gathered, i.e. in cities, a large part of the population consisted of tax collectors, builders, artisans, cooks, stablemen, kennel workers, laundresses, workers in religious institutions, produces of everyday goods and luxuries, etc. Precisely they became the majority of the population of ancient cities, while the elite proved to be the minority in these cities. The existence of so vast a servile sphere itself demanded a social infrastructure, i.e. social and professional institutions called on to provide for the "servants" themselves, to serve the servants — all the more so since many servants of the nobility often became independent.

Alongside servants and serfs, this system also included free people who had come to the city for some reason or other (often because of bad harvests or natural catastrophes; sometimes seeking refuge from enemy attack). These layers mixed with one another. Free men acted as servants, well-off servants received the status of freemen and so on. As a result, *a specific social phenomenon* formed in the city, differing in its basic parameters from both the *ethnos* and the political elite of the *narod* (the heroic type: soldier, prophet, philosopher).

This phenomenon is usually referred to by the Greek term "*demos*," i.e. the "inhabitants" of the city.

The *demos* differed from the *ethnos* in that it had been torn away from the environment of the ethnocentrum, separated from it and put in circumstances that contrasted sharply with the ethnic world, its structure, forms of time and thought (intentionality). In their origin, these were representatives of the *ethnos* who had fallen out of it, been torn away from it, and lost their connection with the organic integrity that is the essence of the *ethnos*.

At the same time, the *demos* also differed from the political elite, since the level of its differentiation was much lower, weaker and simpler than among the elite. In contrast to the soldiers, the *demos* was cowardly; in contrast to the philosophers, stupid; in contrast to the prophets, too down-to-earth and rationalistic. It embodied the character of being differentiated in earthly matters: in the organization of the economy, in the production of handicrafts and objects, and even more so in trade.

Precisely tradespeople became the general symbol of the city's servant-artisan infrastructure.

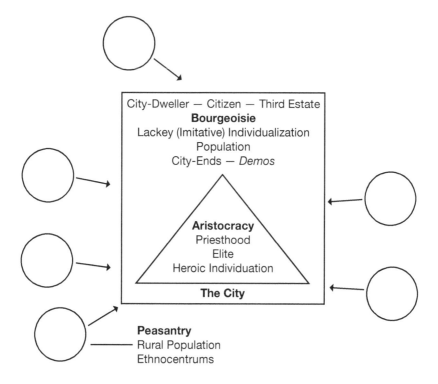

Figure 10. The Ethnosociological Structure of the City.

Labor had no significance for the aristocracy. From an economic perspective, they were consumers who purchased their consumption with their *traumatic existence*, expressed in war, violence, religious services or philosophizing.

For the *ethnos*, labor was an integral part of ethnodynamics, during which the invariability of the *ethnos* was constantly strengthened. Peasants probably regarded the exactions of the nobility as a form of "potlatch" or "sacrifice," i.e. they included them in an ethnic context.

Tradespeople (in the broad sense, including servants) organized contact between elites and masses; i.e. they satisfied the needs of the elite through requisitioning (most often by cunning, not force) the products produced by the *ethnos*. In the state, tax collectors, publicans, played an analogous role. They acted as intermediaries between the elite and the masses, between the heroic ranks and the *ethnos*. They ensured the social, cultural and economic connection among the various centers of the traditional state (cities), other countries and separate territories of the same country. The mobility of the tradespeople expresses on another, lower level the mobility of the military (previously nomadic) elite. What the elites of traditional society accomplished by force, the tradespeople acquired through cunning, calculation and rational strategies (i.e. relatively peacefully).

Tradespeople are a subproduct of laogenesis. As such, they were neither its cause nor its distinctive feature. They formed as a social group gradually, according to the extent of the concentration of the power elite (military, religious, and intellectual) in the cities. Territorially, this entire layer, represented primarily by tradespeople as a general function, was concentrated in one place and formed the *ethnos*. If the hero is the general social type of the *narod* (especially in its elite, ruling pole), then the tradesperson symbolizes the *demos*, the generalized social group of grand lackeys, "jacks," armor-bearers, etc., and free citizens, functionally united through the service of the ruling elite.

The *demos* is the origin of the bourgeoisie as a class.

The Bourgeoisie and Its Ethnosociological Characteristics

We should pay attention to the etymology of the word "bourgeois," from the French "*bourgeois*." It stems from the German word "*Burg*," i.e. "city," and originally meant "city-dweller." At the same time, the term "city-dweller" is equivalent to the word "citizen" not only in Russian but in Latin, where the word "*civitas*" means "city," and "*civis*," which is derived from it, means "city-dweller," from which we get "citizen."

In fact, the third estate, together with the first (priests), the second (soldiers) and the fourth (peasants, servants), consists of precisely "city-dwellers," citizens in the sociological and sociopolitical sense.

In this way, we get a semantic chain that helps us understand the ethnosociological essence of the phenomenon of the nation: "*city — citizenship — bourgeoisie — politics* (since the city is a "polis") — *demos* (= inhabitants of the city; the term "*demos*" is inapplicable to the inhabitants of a village and is only applicable to the those of a city).

The nation is the kind of political society in which the norm is not the *ethnos* (as in archaic society) or the *narod* (in the face of it elite, as in the traditional state, religion or civilization) but the "*demos*" as city-dweller, as citizen of a city and member of the third estate (the bourgeoisie).

Precisely this makes the nation the second derivative from the *ethnos*.

It is important to pay attention to the fact that we can hardly speak of some principally "new" character in the phenomenon of the "*demos*" that lies at the basis of the nation. Everything "new" that could be brought into the ethnocentrum was already contained in the *narod*. Through its differentiation, the *narod* opens the maximum scope for encountering the "new" and embodies it in the hero. Qualitatively, the *narod* is the most complicated society, turned toward the most distant horizons of this complexity. The drama on which the being of the *narod* is based simultaneously faces every direction: inside (social division, psychological implosion, the inner explosion of passionarity), outside (the aggression of interminable military campaigns), upward (the distant horizon of the "invisible" God), downward (horror of the abyss of a possible fall and death that constantly accompanies the historic being of the hero and the *narod* overall). The *narod* gives birth to the most complex empires, philosophies, theologies and works of art. Precisely the creations of the *narod* constitute everything that we consider human culture today.

But the *narod* builds its maximally complex forms on the basis of the maximum simplicity of the *ethnos*, drawing energy from the split of this simplicity. The *narod* splits the *koineme*, like physics splits the atom, receiving from its splitting gigantic energy, which comprises the content of human history. The spirit is born from the split of the ethnocentrum.

The dialectic of the *ethnos* and the *narod*, as the dialectic of the maximally simple and the maximally complex, exhausts the theoretical possibilities of human society. For precisely that reason, Richard Thurnwald's five-volume *The Ethno-Sociological Foundations of Human Society* ends on the stage of traditional states.[6] And Lévi-Strauss simply limits himself to the meticulous study of the ethnocentrum, the depths of which predetermine the basic vectors of what, by negation, will became the content of the *narod*.

In any case, the *ethnos* and the *narod* together give us two fundamental axes of human thought: intentionality and logos, and, accordingly, two relations to being: the ontic and the ontological. This is a complete, exhaustive, full model into which the "*demos*" and its constructions cannot bring anything fundamentally new.

This determines the essence of the *demos*. Its social possibilities are enclosed between the simplicity of the *ethnos* (the fourth estate) and the radical exertion of the elite's heroic will (the first and second estates). But the *demos* cannot and does not want to be either one or the other. It is too torn away from the *ethnos*, uprooted from it, but the passionary horizon of heroism is inaccessible to it. The *demos* is closest to the type that Gumilev called "sub-passionary."[7] The sub-passionary person is the typical representative of the *demos*. As a lackey, he imitates his master without being a master and he relates arrogantly toward the *ethnos* from which he came and which he despises as "simple."

The *demos*, i.e. the citizen, is much more complex than the peasant, and all the more so the hunter, but he is also much simpler than any aristocrat. The culture the *demos* creates is more differentiated than village culture but less differentiated than the culture of aristocracy.

But here there is another fundamental point: the simplicity of the *demos* in comparison with caste society is not a return to the *ethnos*. Of course, in certain cases the collapse of the state leads to the desolation of cities and their transformation into villages, which means the transition of the city-dweller into the village. This is also a likely scenario historically

---

6   Richard Thurnwald, *Die menschliche Gesellschaft in ihren ethno-soziologischen Grundlagen*, 5 vols. (Berlin: De Gruyter, 1931–1934).

7   Lev N. Gumilev, *Etnogenez i biosfera Zemli* (Moskva: *Progress*, 1990).

and cannot be excluded. Many small cities today, having once been political centers, represent precisely such an ethnicization of the *demos*. In this process, the prevalence of sub-passionary types, according to Gumilev, is replaced by a prevalence of the harmonious personality type.

But the essence of the *demos* as such, as a specific society, consists in something else: in being neither aristocratic, nor ethnic; i.e. neither passionary, nor harmonic. That is the specific characteristic of the sub-passionary type.

The Nation and the Proletariat

Herein lies the key to understanding the sociology of modernity and, accordingly, to understanding the nation. The nation inclines toward taking the *demos* as the normative social type, building society on the basis of the figure of the "trader," which means "not peasant" and "not hero."[8] The nation is always a community of sub-passionary people, who elevate their type to the norm and base their politico-social system on it. The nation is an association of traders, bourgeois and citizens, and, what's more, of precisely those citizens who do not relate to the higher estate. First of all, Ethnosociologically the bourgeoisie is a result of the insurrection of yesterday's servants, lackeys and jacks against their masters but organized to replace them in the structure of social stratification and to rule over the masses (the *ethnos*), although primarily in an economic sense.

The urbanization of the peasants, the relocation of the masses into the city, moves the problem of the *bourgeoisie (citizen)/ethnos (villager, peasant)* to a purely social plane: *bourgeoisie/proletariat*. And here there begins in full measure the excellently described sequence of Marxist sociological processes. The proletariat, relocated to the city, becomes international and loses its ethnic roots, as the bourgeoisie had earlier lost them. The nation transforms economic criteria into the dominant, supra-political ones. That is why the class problematic can be taken as sociologically general and as removing the theme of the *ethnos* (and the *narod*) from the agenda.

---

8   Werner Sombart, *Handler und Helden* (Munich, 1915).

When the (bourgeois) nation becomes the prevailing form of social being, the *ethnos* is concealed behind the horizon, it disappears from view. Thus, Weber's sociology in particular, which examined first and foremost bourgeois democratic societies and their prototypes in earlier stages of history (including the ancient world), does not pay much attention to the *ethnos*. In bourgeois societies, the ethnic factor is discarded. Herein lies the specific character of the ethnosociological analysis of the *ethnos*.

As we noted, the nation is something completely different from the *ethnos*, something extremely distant from it and in some aspects directly opposed to it. Already at the stage of the *narod* (*laos*) we exit beyond the borders of the *ethnos*, overcome it, and encounter its derivative. Already in the *narod*, the *ethnos* moves into the background and is partially concealed behind the concept of the "lower estate," "caste," "masses." But here, ethnic characteristics are not difficult to discern and the ethnosociological analysis of the lower (and in some cases the higher) strata of society is relatively easy to carry out.

In the nation, the ethnic factor recedes even deeper, while on the surface only class, economic, and political contradictions remain, and it becomes rather difficult to discover the ethnic layer beneath them. Nevertheless, ethnosociology allows us to do this, since the phenomenon of the bourgeoisie (the city-dweller, the citizen) can be analyzed from the perspective of its relation to the *ethnos*: in its origin, the bourgeois is a bondman, torn out of the *ethnos* and imitating the nobility. Ethnic characteristics are preserved in the proletariat to an even greater extent, inasmuch as he is torn out of the ethnic environment later and maintains its residue in himself for a long time, even in the city.

The bourgeoisie consists of lackeys, who are a simulacrum of masters (heroes): hence the idea of economic competition as a variation of military battles. The proletariat is a simulacrum of the *ethnos*, which introduces into its class nature elements of the worldview of the ethnocentrum: hence, it is easy to transition to an analysis of socialistic and communistic theories, which have numerous parallels with the structure of the ethnocentrum, transferred into new historical, social and political conditions. It is particularly significant that Marx himself uses the expression "primitive communism" in relation to the primordial social system; i.e. he clearly recognizes that the communist ideal in the future has an analog in archaic society.

The sociologist Bataille and the structuralists drew far-reaching conclusions from this terminological correspondence.[9]

From an ethnosociological perspective, communism is a peculiar projection of ethnic (archaic, "primitive," "primordial") consciousness onto the sphere of the bourgeois world. The internationalism of the proletariat differs qualitatively from the internationalism of capital precisely in that the proletariat base themselves on living ethnic archetypes, raised to a general, pan-ethnic matrix ("communism" as the formula of the meta-language of the *ethnos*), while the bourgeoisie base themselves on the overcoming of these archetypes but without achieving the authentic distance from the *ethnos* that is characteristic of the military aristocracy of estate societies. The internationalism of the bourgeoisie is conjoined with precisely the nation as the special instrument on the basis of which the bourgeoisie of one society arranges its relations with the bourgeoisie of another society. The nation acts here as a supplement to economics, an additional moment in a competition war. Thus, the internationalism (cosmopolitanism) of the bourgeoisie does not contradict its nationalism and the internationalism of the proletariat does not contradict its generalized pan-ethnicism, which it raises into a principle.

---

9   Georges Bataille, *The Accursed Share: An Essay on General Economy* (New York: Zone Books, 1988).

Nationalism as an Instrument in the Creation of a Nation

It is helpful in examining the complex dialectical particularities of the second derivative from the *ethnos* to turn to the constructivist method of Gellner,[10] Anderson[11] and other ethnosociologists[12] who focused on studying the phenomenon of the nation and nationalism. Gellner shows that the nation as a phenomenon was created in modernity by the third estate, the bourgeoisie, who had seized power in many European states.[13] Since the estate structure of these societies, i.e. the model of the *narod*, had been destroyed, the bourgeoisie were faced with the practical task of preserving the social cohesion of society in new conditions in the absence of feudal and religious restraints and to mobilize it for industrial and commercial economic aims. The bourgeois revolutions destroyed the estate-based social structures, while the ethnic structure had broken down even earlier and was preserved by inertia only among the rural masses. The city bourgeoisie erected itself as the normative social ideal and adjusted political institutions to sui itself. Here are the roots of the phenomenon of democracy, literally "the rule of the *demos*." "*Demos*," as we saw, is the general name for the city population that is not directly related to the feudal estate of the nobility. Essentially, the *demos* and the bourgeoisie are closely related, if not identical.

10 Ernst Gellner, *Nations and Nationalism* (Ithaca: Cornell University Press, 1983).

11 Benedict Anderson, *Imagined Communities: Reflections on the Origin and Spread of Nationalism* (London: Verso, 1991).

12 For instance Breuilly, *Nationalism, Power and Modernity in Nineteenth-Century Germany* (London: German Historical Institute, 2007); John Breuilly, *Nationalism and the State,* 2nd ed. (Chicago: Chicago University Press, 1994); Craig Calhoun, *Nationalism* (Minneapolis: University of Minnesota Press, 1997; Anthony Smith, *Myths and Memories of the Nation* (Oxford: Oxford University Press, 1999); Anthony Smith, *Nationalism and Modernism: A Critical Survey of Recent Theories of Nations and Nationalism* (London: Routledge, 1998). Elie Kedourie, *Nationalism* (London: Hutchinson, 1960); etc.

13 Ernst Gellner, *Nations and Nationalism* (Ithaca: Cornell University Press, 1983).

However, the principle of the individual civic person engaged in free business undertakings, applied to society as a whole and especially to rural society, which, on the eve of modernity, comprised a significant percentage of all Europe, was a threat to this society. At issue is the prematurity of the individual principle and its slippage "back into the *ethnos*," isolation in archaic rural societies or the atomization of such society into individual units pursuing their personal goals without taking into account the interests of their class. The conscientious members of the bourgeoisie could and did unite into parties and clubs but the rest of society (predominantly rural) proved to be in a suspended condition. For the artificial consolidation of societies in these new historical conditions, the European bourgeoisie invented the "nation" and the "nationalism" that accompanies it.

Gellner emphasizes that the "nation" was an artificial, mechanical model, created for purely pragmatic ends. The bourgeois state, having been atomized into individual citizens not united by anything, invented a social concept called upon to postulate unity, integrity and commonality where they did not and could not exist: the concept of the "nation." Benedict Anderson calls the nation an "imagined community."[14] "Community" is a characteristic of ethnic being, of "folk-society." In natural conditions, the *ethnos* is a real, not an invented, imagined community. And although *ethnoses* are often based only on belief in a common origin, this belief is organic and sincere, not subject to doubt. It is so deep that it is entirely identical with reality. There is no gap between reality and the object in the *ethnos*.

The "nation" is an entirely different matter. Here, the creators of the concept themselves do not believe in a community of origin. It is invented and inculcated in the masses for concrete, pragmatic aims: regulating the socium in new historical conditions of increased entropy, mobilizing labor activity and keeping society within strictly determined limits.

---

14 Benedict Anderson, *Imagined Communities: Reflections on the Origin and Spread of Nationalism* (London: Verso, 1991).

Gellner insists that nationalism is not a consequence of the existence of a nation but that nations themselves emerge from the development of the idea of nationalism.

It is nationalism which engenders nations, and not the other way round. Admittedly, nationalism uses the pre-existing, historically inherited proliferation of cultures or cultural wealth, though it uses them very selectively and most often it transforms them radically. Dead languages can be revived, traditions invented, quite fictitious pristine purities restored.[15]

Nationalism is a means of creating a nation as a specific industrial social culture. It spreads the city principle of bourgeois capitalistic society to all other areas of the state, which earlier, in the feudal period, were left to themselves and preserved an ethnic style of being. Gellner writes:

[N]ationalism is, essentially, the general imposition of a high culture on society, where previously low cultures had taken up the lives of the majority, and in some cases of the totality, of the population. It means that generalized diffusion of a school-mediated, academy-supervised idiom, codified for the requirements of reasonably precise bureaucratic and technological communication. It is the establishment of an anonymous, impersonal society, with mutually substitutable atomized individuals, held together above all by a shared culture of this kind, in place of a previous complex structure of local groups, sustained by folk cultures reproduced locally and idiosyncratically by the micro-groups themselves. That is what *really* happens.[16]

What Gellner calls "high" and "low" cultures are more accurately called "complex society" and "constellation of *koinemes*." But the essence of the process of the creation of a nation is described surprisingly precisely.

Nationalism invents the nation, i.e. a society that never existed but uses elements taken from the real historical experience of concrete groups (*ethnoses* and the history of the *narod*), torn from their context, deprived of their meaning and transformed into a compulsory sociocultural dogma, imposed with the help of the full force of the state apparatus.

---

15   Gellner, *Nations and Nationalism*, 55–56.

16   Ibid., 57.

Gellner emphasizes that the nation consists of a mechanical assortment of anonymous and atomic citizens alienated from one another but tries to pass itself off as a peaceful rural village community, cozy and familiar, where all know each other and share common habits and a synchronism of reactions. To accomplish this, the state machine is brought into play: education, a codified language, art productions and the glorification of the glorious deeds of the nation, some of which are real and some of which are invented.

The *ethnos* is an organic unity; the *narod* is a historic unity; the nation is not a unity at all, it is an artificial, mechanical simulacrum, a dummy, a counterfeit. The nation is based on a false genealogy: nationalism tries to pass it off as a direct continuation of the *ethnos* and the *narod*, failing to note that there is a fundamental sociological and conceptual shift from between the *ethnos* itself and the *narod,* and that the relations between the *narod* and the nation are as contradictory as those between the traditional and modern state. In the *narod*, the *ethnos* is problematic, though present. In the nation, it becomes doubly problematic and the *narod* itself also becomes problematic. That is why we should speak of the "imagined" character of the nation. Through nationalism, the bourgeoisie creates an artificial object, composed of real sociological components.

Two Forms of Ethnosociological Analysis of the Nation

In ethnosociology, the nation as society can be examined from two per-spectives. Earlier, we called these two approaches "ethnoanalysis" and "the analysis of post-ethnic societies."

The nation is a post-ethnic society and in analyzing the nation, the ethnosociologist must first of all perform the operation of clarifying when and under what circumstances a given nation arose; to what contempo-rary state it relates; what historical "myths" and artificial reconstructions it uses for the justification of its existence; what the character of the gap is between this nation and its "reconstructed past" and the real types of society — *narod* and *ethnos* (*ethnoses*) — that preceded it; and so on. This

is post-ethnic analysis and it must show in the first place the difference
between the nation and its pretensions to historicity and organicity; i.e.
it must demonstrate the distance between the declarations and postula-
tions of basic bourgeois nationalism (in Gellner's sense) and the authentic
ethnosociological reconstruction of previous stages. In other words, this
phase of study consists in showing in what way a concrete nation differs
from the *ethnos* and from the *narod*, with which it claims a "natural" and
"historic" bond. To perform this operation, it is necessary to trace in sequence the periods of history of the given nation and correspondingly of
the given modern state, paying special attention to the circumstances of
its emergence and the historical, political, economic and class conditions
that then prevailed. During this phase, it is necessary to reconstruct the
ethnoses on the basis of which the process of laogenesis occurred (if it occurred) and to trace this process. It is especially important to concentrate
on transition phases: from the *ethnos* to its first derivative, the *narod*, and
from the *narod* to the nation. In the transition to the second derivative
from the *ethnos*, analysis should focus on the problem of the city and the
third estate.

Only after performing all of these operations can one speak seriously
about the extent to which the "myths" and pretensions of the given nation
are well founded and sound, and how great its distance is from the *ethnos*
and the *narod*. The method of the constructivists (Gellner, Anderson,
Breuilly, Calhoun, Neumann, etc.)[17] can be applied here in full measure.
This approach must answer the questions: to what extent is the given
nation "imagined" and to what extent does its official genealogy correspond to something; who, when, why and under what conditions was this
"imagined community" "imagined"?

The second approach, ethnoanalysis, is called upon, for its part, to
show of what kind the actual situation of the *ethnos* or *ethnoses* is in a

---

17 Gellner, *Nations and Nationalism*; Anderson, *Imagined Communities*; John Breuilly,
    Nationalism and the State, 2nd ed. (Chicago: Chicago University Press, 1994);
    Craig Calhoun, *Nationalism* (Minneapolis: University of Minnesota Press, 1997);
    Iver B. Neumann, *Uses of the Other: "The East" in European Identity* (Minneapolis:
    University of Minnesota Press, 1999).

national society and how the *narod* is manifested in it as a historic community. After performing a series of strict delimitations and distinctions that determine why and to what extent the nation is neither the *ethnos* nor the *narod* but their second and first derivative (respectively), ethnoanalysis must now seek the ethnic layer of society and the influence of the *narod* on the nation (apart from the "nationalistic" mythology). The *ethnos* is preserved in the *narod*. The *ethnos* is also preserved in the nation. But it is much more difficult to identify and describe it in the nation than to do the same for the *narod*. If in a traditional state (less frequently in a religion or civilization) the *narod* is obvious, in the nation it is concealed, becomes invisible and shows itself only indirectly.

Classic sociologists have carefully studied the influence of the estates, religions and socio-cultural arrangements of traditional society on the bourgeois class society of modernity. Weber's masterpiece *The Protestant Ethic and the Spirit of Capitalism*[18] is an example of such a work.

The ethnoanalysis of the nation must find in the nation that which strictly speaking is not in it but that of which it is a simulacrum or "dummy." At the same time, ethnoanalysis aims to find on the lower layers of the nation not only the *ethnos* but also the *narod*, i.e. traces of traditional society, hidden behind the façade of "modernity." Methodologically, Smith's theory of "ethnosymbolism" fits best of all here.[19] The *ethnos* and the *narod* are not present in the nation in themselves but lie at the historical bases of society, continuing to abide in the sphere of the "social unconscious" and acting "symbolically."

Smith's "ethnosymbolism" as ethnoanalysis supplements Gellner's constructivism as a form of postethnic analysis perfectly. Bringing them together, we get a three-dimensional and complete picture of the ethnosociological analysis of the nation.

---

18   Max Weber, *The Protestant Ethic and the Spirit of Capitalism* (New York: Scribner, 1958).

19   Anthony Smith, *Myths and Memories of the Nation* (Oxford: Oxford University Press, 1999).

SECTION TWO
Nationalism

The Peculiarities of Nationalism and its Difference from Analogous Forms in Other Types of Society

As we saw, Gellner understands by "nationalism" the artificial initiative of the bourgeois to create a nation. This is a specific understanding of "nationalism" and we can use it only in studying the first, national stage of the formation of a nation. When the modern state has been created and the society within its borders has been formed as a nation, nationalism changes its functions and meaning somewhat.

In all cases, nationalism should be understood as a purely political phenomenon. As the nation is inseparably connected with the state and politics, so nationalism in all its forms and under all circumstances is necessarily joined together with the state and politics; like the nation itself, nationalism is a purely modern phenomenon and belongs to modernity. Nationalism emerges in the modern era and is one of its characteristic features.[20] Neither the ethnocentrum of the *ethnos*, nor the strict, conflictual differentialism of the *narod* with its "we-group" and "they-group" ("anti-type") should be confused with nationalism.

The fact that the *ethnos* does not see an "other" and considers itself "all" has nothing in common with nationalism. The *ethnos* does not know politics and cannot impart a political significance to anything. The *ethnos* does not know social stratification and cannot use representations and outlooks as socio-political instruments (ideology) in whosever interests. The *ethnos* believes that there is only it and "not-it" is also it, or is nothing. Nationalism knows perfectly well that alongside a given nation there is another nation but it artificially provokes an emphasized exaltation of the "auto-stereotype" and "hetero-stereotype" among an artificially

---

20 Anthony Smith, *Nationalism and Modernism: A Critical Survey of Recent Theories of Nations and Nationalism* (London: Routledge, 1998).

constructed collective (the nation) for entirely concrete political and economic interests.

Ethnism cannot by itself be nationalism but nationalism can use appeal to the *ethnos* (imagined or real) for the realization of its concrete political goals.

Despite all of its aggressiveness and bellicosity (with regard to the "other"), the *narod* is based on the political elite's sincere belief that war with the "other" has a "sacred" character. At its basis lies a "mission," a fate. It is necessary to destroy and be victorious over the "other" not for some concrete material aim but according to the existential nature of the hero himself. For that reason, traditional states often fight bloody wars whose rationality and benefit are doubtful. Many times, the places and objects of a religious cult (in the Crusades, for instance), lacking economic significance, are the objects of war.

The political elites of a traditional state do not use the figure of the "other" for the mobilization of the masses; they themselves are constitutively grounded in the asymmetric and dramatic striving to confrontation with an "other," who is a fundamental figure for them, determining their being. This too is not at all nationalism, since here there is no "nation," no "rational" goal, no manipulation and striving to artificially formulate an economic strategy. This is the difference between the aristocrat and his servants — for instance, Don Quixote and Sancho Panza, the musketeers and their servants. Aristocrats fight for abstract, chivalrous ideals, which are real for them inasmuch as they are "transcendent." The servants complain about this "irrationality" and try to rationalize the structure of events in a war: to provide provisions, to collect more trophies, to devise ways of preserving their lives and harming their enemies in secret and from afar (herein lies the origin of technical inventions for distant wars). The *narod* is formed by the aristocracy, the nobility. The nation is formed by servants, armor-bearers, orderlies, attendants. The traditional state is an affair of the hands of Don Quixote, d'Artagnan, Athos, Porthos, and Aramis. The nation is created by Sancho Panza, Planchet, Mousqueton, Bazin and Grimaud.

For an aristocracy, there is no big difference between one's enemies and one's own masses. They are merely varieties of the "other": internal and external. That is why it was so important for the representatives of the higher estates to marry partners from their own caste, even if they belonged to a different *narod*. Moreover, such marriages were regarded as preferable, especially for princes and kings, since they reinforced the distance between the elite and the masses. For traditional society, there was no need to lie to the populace toward the end of its "national mobilization." In its hatred against the "other," the elite acted entirely sincerely and the masses, who had to participate in military campaigns, did not have much of a choice: they had either to be in solidarity with the belief of their masters or they were simply compelled by brute force. In war, one can survive and earn fame; the punishment for disobedience can be quick and humiliating. No instrumentalism is required here. Those who believe in their mission act in accordance with their belief and the rest have to submit.

From an ethnosociological perspective, it is incorrect to apply the concept of "nationalism" to phenomena that do not belong to modernity and are not connected with the "modern society" and the social arrangements of the third estate.

Patriotism

Let us consider a few varieties of nationalism, which can be divided into a few categories.

The first form of nationalism is *patriotism*.

Patriotism is the mobilization of all citizens (of the nation) for the defense of the state from external aggression or for attacking an external enemy. Patriotism is built up from the emotional, affective representation of a society (nation), a "we-group," opposed to a contrasting model of an "adversary" ("they-group"). The term "patriotism" is formed from the Latin word *patria*, i.e. "fatherland." It is directed toward the cultural and historical identification of the nation. More often than not, "patriotism" is based on a partial and ideologically censored account of history, called on to produce conviction about the famous past of a given nation and the evil and inhuman (foul) deeds of its enemies. Victories are emphasized (and sometimes made up), defeats are softened (and sometimes altogether forgotten). At the same time, the algorithm of patriotism can in some cases be entirely "invented," which does not change its efficacy.

In the structure of patriotism we are dealing with the symbolic instrumentalization of the root energies of the ethnocentrum and the historic self-consciousness of the *narod*. But both (the ethnocentrum and the *narod*) are present in patriotism "symbolically," i.e. in a completely different, "national" context and for the realization of concrete political aims.

The distinctive feature of patriotism consists in the fact that this form of nationalism is most often directed against external enemies, real or imagined.

In national states, patriotism is most often regarded as a virtue and a fully legitimate quality. Moreover, upbringing in the feeling of patriotism is almost always included in the curriculum and tasks of state education as an instrument of state control. Patriotism helps the ruling (bourgeois) class to consolidate the *demos* for possible confrontation with a competing state, most often in a struggle for material resources, colonies, etc. Although appealing to organic and historic roots, in modernity patriotism fulfills purely political and pragmatic functions.

Xenophobia, Chauvinism, Racism

Xenophobia is an extreme form of patriotism. The term comes from the Greek words "ξὲνος," a "foreigner," and "φοβὲω," literally "I fear," "I detest," "fright." Xenophobia is a sociocultural affect that forces a person or social group to relate with hatred and fear to foreign nations and their symbolic attributes (external look, typical articles, etc.). Like patriotism, xenophobia can be analyzed on three levels: it can reflect a traumatic — spontaneous or provoked — rise of ethnointentional thought (of the ethnocentrum); it can be a vestige of the "transcendental" passionarity of the *narod*, constituting the figure of the "other" beyond its borders; or it can be an extreme form of political manipulation by the authorities in the service of some political aim.

It is important to note that in all cases the qualities and character-istics of the "foreigner," or the one towards whom hatred and fear are directed, have nothing in common with the model of him formed in the mass consciousness of a given "nation." This model is nothing more than a sociological construction, raised (artificially or spontaneously) to an "anti-type."

If patriotism is accompanied by the conceit, boasting and limited and narrow cultural horizon characteristic of the members of the "third es-tate," it is called "chauvinism." This pejorative name is based on the name of a character from the comic play by the Cogniard brothers, *Cocarde Tricolore*, the recruit Chauvin, who exclaimed: "France and nothing but France!" This character is based on a real historic person from Napoleon's army, the soldier Chauvin.

Racism in its narrow sense (as opposed to multidimensional racism: cultural, technological, evolutionistic, methodological and so on) is a form of xenophobia and chauvinism raised to the status of a worldview, which asserts that the members of other nations, cultures, races and *ethnoses* (other than those to which the subject himself belongs) are "lower," "infe-rior," "retrograde" or "evil," "foul" and "needing extermination or destruc-tion." If xenophobia and chauvinism are an emotional state, an affect, then racism is the attempt to build an independent "theory" on these emotions, which "avows" and "secures" them in the form of a system and ideology. And in this case, as in the case of xenophobia, the "hetero-stereotype" with which the racists operate most often has nothing in common not only with the real picture of the other society towards which hatred is directed but also with the auto-stereotype, built on arbitrary suppositions, erected into a dogma.

The ethnosociologist Muhlmann introduced the concepts "a-race" and "b-race" to describe this phenomenon.[21] An "a-race" is a scientific

---

21 Wilhelm E. Mühlmann, *Rassen, Ethnien, Kulturen* (Neuwied, Berlin: Luchterhand, 1964).

reconstruction on the basis of the anthropometric, genetic and serological methods of determining a human's belonging to one or another racial community. This reconstruction itself is to the greatest extent a problematic and hypothetical procedure, since there is no single method for determining the "a-race" among scientists, nor agreement concerning the racial classification and taxonomy. These studies require special preparation and science-intensive apparatuses. But even if the "a-race" could be established, it is entirely unclear how it should be classified, since different schools of anthropologists, biologists and geneticists dispute this question fiercely. Any element of the phenotype or of serological or genetic facts can be interpreted in different ways. All of this impacts the value of the determination of the "a-race"; even after establishing it, it is extremely different to interpret the given information correctly, due to the multitude of competing hypotheses. All of this concerns only biology and paleoanthropology. If we try to correlate the (extremely hypothetical and problematic) scientific data about the "a-race" with sociological peculiarities of typical behavior, linguistic characteristics or cultural patterns, we will simply fall into an abyss, since there are no reliable data about the interaction between the biological "a-race" and the sociological characteristics of a society. Thus difficult and expensive studies of the "a-race," which are entirely inaccessible to those without professional scientific preparation, even if they were carried out correctly, have not the slightest worth for the sociologist. In other words, the "a-race" is irrelevant for sociology and cultural studies.

Muhlmann also has the concept of a "b-race," this time as a sociological phenomenon, i.e. a "symbolic" object. The "b-race" is not biological but imagined. Man can identify himself as part of some "race" and for him this fact has definite sociological significance (to be valuable, to raise his status in his eyes, etc.). The same is true in the case of a b-race to which "others" belong. That is as arbitrary and "symbolic" but also actual. Essentially, this procedure is nothing other than the distribution of "auto-" and "hetero-stereotypes." The difference of the "b-race" from the "we-group" and "they-group," and also from the "antitype" and other forms of nationalism and chauvinism, consists only in the fact that those who operate with the b-race are inclined to regard belongingness to it as a fundamental and inalienable inborn status, with decisive significance, like gender, for instance. Racism is built on manipulations with the b-race, though it often tries to pass the b-race off as an a-race with the aim of inculcating this view.

In Nazi Germany, racism was politically instrumentalized as a means for the greatest possible consolidation of the higher and lower classes of a national-bourgeois society in a situation of extraordinary political mobilization. Racism also played an important role in the dogmatic justification of slave-holding practices in relation to Africans in the colonial era (sixteenth to eighteenth centuries). The idea that the autochthonous inhabitants of America (natives) are a "lower race" was at the basis of the practice of their systematic destruction in North America and their harsh enslavement and repression in the South.

Like all other forms of nationalism, racism is a modern phenomenon and appears together with bourgeois reforms in European states. Racism is a purely modern phenomenon and developed in parallel with modernization. From a class perspective, the phenomenon is unambiguously bourgeois.

In the legal codes of a majority of modern bourgeois democratic states, racism, chauvinism and xenophobia are outlawed and their appearance carries legal sanctions by the state.

Big Nationalism: Conservatism and Radicalism

Let us now consider manifestations of nationalism within the nation state.[22] They divide into two elements: *the nationalism of the ethnic majority* (the *narod* or the *ethnos*, on the basis of whose language and culture the artificial national identity was built) and *the nationalism of ethnic minorities* (who strive to create their nations, separate from the composition

---

22 Anthony Smith, *Nations and Nationalism in a Global Era* (Cambridge: Polity Press, 1995).

of the existing modern state). We can call the nationalism of the ethnic majority *"big nationalism."*

The purpose of big nationalism is to strengthen the unity of the nation by political methods, to stabilize and consolidate it. As a rule, big nationalism insists on absolutizing the sovereignty of the state and maintaining and strengthening its territorial integrity. This is often (though not always) combined with tendencies toward strengthening the vertical of power and political centralization, though in some modern federal states (the US, for instance) big nationalism can accomplish its aims by other means, without additional centralization and weakening the administrative autonomy of the regions.

Big nationalism, in turn, is divided into the following types: *conservative and radical.* Both conservative and radical big nationalism theoretically aim to solve the same tasks but they do so with fundamentally different methods.

Conservative big nationalism insists on preserving the impulse on which the nation-state was built in the form of a "social myth," vital enough to fasten together the autonomous individual citizens of an industrial society but "conditional" enough not to provoke "excess" enthusiasm in them, thanks to which "nationalism" could acquire radical features (xenophobia, chauvinism, racism) or affect the ethnic and *narodni* layers of society. Conservative nationalism strives to keep full control over the integrating methodologies of society in the hands of the political leadership and, accordingly, the ruling class (the bourgeoisie), increasing the level of nationalism in a nuanced way each time society is threatened by disintegration and collapse, entropy and decreasing it as soon as the threat ceases to be acute.

Conservative nationalism is euphemistically called simply "conservatism" and in many modern states has legitimate representatives in party members, ruling coalitions or big political actors. Conservative nationalism often (if not always) is combined with liberal ideology, the market and bourgeois democracy, and is a sociopolitical byproduct of modernity.

Radical nationalism also stems from the political style of modernity and is a modern and rather artificial phenomenon.[23] The purpose of radical forms of big nationalism is to intensify integrating processes in national society, to extirpate the remains of local ethnic cultures, languages, customs and traditions, and to move the feeling of national identity to an exalted phase. The aims of radical nationalism are the same as those of conservative nationalism: to rally the citizens of a nation state and to increase the extent of homogeneity in the society.[24] But conservative nationalism reaches this through methods of the unification of the legal area, economic space and administrative control, while radical nationalism does so through the suppression of local and regional uniqueness, cultural and linguistic aggression, demands for the introduction of discriminatory practices against ethnic minorities and migrants, and the mobilization of educational, cultural and informational strategies. As a rule, radical nationalists insist on depriving ethnic and cultural minorities of full rights and on the partial deprivation of rights of those citizens who, in the opinion of the nationalists, do not show enough enthusiasm for integration into the national society or who oppose such integration knowingly.

If conservative nationalists prefer to act by legal methods through democratic procedures, radical nationalists often turn to extreme practices and methods, including direct violence and sometimes terror. Radical nationalism most often takes the form of xenophobia, chauvinism, and even racism, merging with these phenomena. They should be distinguished only according to one marker: xenophobia and chauvinism are emotional-affective forms, racism is the attempt to theorize the affects and radical nationalism is the conscious and rational political strategy at the basis of which is neither emotion nor ideology but concrete calculation. Radical nationalists calculate that with the help of their actions they

---

23 Anthony Smith, *Nationalism and Modernism: A Critical Survey of Recent Theories of Nations and Nationalism* (London: Routledge, 1998).

24 Louis Dumont, *Essais sur l'individualisme. Une perspective anthropologique sur l'idéologie modern* (Paris: Le Seuil, 1983).

will reach an entirely concrete political result (precisely like the conservative nationalists): an increase in the level of the sociocultural and political homogeneity of society on the basis of the national factor.[25]

Different societies regard radical nationalism differently. Sometimes, it is used to solve concrete political tasks but most often it occupied a marginal position and its representatives balance on the edge of the law. Because of the specific character of their professional activity, those who come from military ministries and departments are close to radical nationalism, for, on one hand, they partially share the style of the "nationalists" and, on the other, partially use them on a limited scale in "delicate" operations as their conscious and willing (or unknowing) agents. In some cases, radical nationalists unite in political parties — far right, as a rule.

In South Africa until the end of the apartheid regime, radical nationalism, with a number of openly racist features, was the official political ideology. It is easy to discover analogous features in the modern politics of the democratic and overall modern state of Israel. In the US, rudiments of the radical nationalism of the white colonizers are present to today in the form of ethnic reserves, where members of the native population, aborigines, live. The fascist regime in Mussolini's Italy and Hitler's National Socialist regime represent the apogee of radical nationalism in the twentieth century (National Socialism was also based on unconcealed ideological racism).

Conservative nationalism in one form or another is characteristic of all modern states and bourgeois-democratic regimes. In the US, the members of the Republican Party are considered its traditional bearers. As a rule, in European politics, parties of the "center right" fulfill its functions.

Small Nationalism: Autonomism, Separatism

Let us now consider little nationalism. This is a phenomenon characteristic of small ethnic and cultural groups that are within a nation state with a

---

25   Louis Dumont, *Homo Æqualis II: l'Idéologie allemande* (Paris: Gallimard/BSH, 1978).

unitary national policy and that have preserved the will and ability to have some form of resistance against big nationalism (in all its forms).

Gellner describes this situation with the help of conventional conceptual ethnosociological objects, which he calls Megalomania and Ruritania. In the transition from the traditional state, the *narod* (= Empire), to the modern state, the following situation arises. The third estate of the former empire, having received political power in the capitals and main cities, based a nation-state, Megalomania, on the basis of the Empire (tolerating its polyethnic and polycultural character, including the polyglossia of rural regions). Its builders devise a style, history, and origin for it, and with the help of the state apparatus, the economy and a print monopoly, they unfold the project of big nationalism. So in the place of society-*narod* there appears the society-nation. The purpose of the nation is the project the norm of the city *demos* onto the entire territory of the state. Megalomania strives to be total in the national borders.

The rural regions (comprising the majority of the territory of the state) form the space of Ruritania (in Gellner's conceptual terms).[26] This is not a uniform but a multiform social field, in which there are areas that easily adopt the big nationalism of Megalomania and areas that reject it. Parts of Ruritania that reject big nationalism and, finding themselves in new sociopolitical conditions, advance their own project of nationalism, copied from Megalomania but directed against it and having as their goal exit from out of it. That is *small nationalism*.

Small nationalism is always a response to big nationalism. There is no such phenomenon in a traditional state. Separate ethnocultural regions begin to create their own nationalistic constructs only in response to Megalomania's offensive; before this moment they have no need, since traditional society relates to the ethnic uniqueness of the mass rather indifferently and hence tolerantly. Aristocracy has no need to mobilize the population through special ideologies; force, will and conviction in the need to fight the "other" are enough for it. Megalomania, by contrast, reaches to the depths of the regions and begins systematically and

---

26 Ernst Gellner, *Nations and Nationalism* (Oxford: Blackwell, 2006).

methodically to extirpate their individuality, which undermines the general cohesion of the structure of the nation. Ruritania can respond to this with a counterattack and elaborate its own national project.

Small nationalism is as artificial, mechanical and pragmatic as any other nationalism. Its social customers are the Ruritanian bourgeoisie and its executors are the intelligentsia, which has been educated either in the Empire or in Megalomania. This intelligentsia, having become familiar with big nationalism, builds its analog in a small form. It is as much a political, instrumental, and pragmatic project as is big nationalism and it has the same bases for its realization. Everything depends only on whether small nationalism has enough force to oppose big nationalism. Often, the historical context decides everything: favorable conditions for the success of small nationalism are produced either by a state crisis or by external circumstances. Then a new nation is formed (with a new ethnic minority that necessarily suffers from this) and part of Ruritania in turn becomes Megalomania. In the new nation state there is always a population that belongs to another ethnocultural or religious group and the process repeats again but only in the framework now of a modern nation state. At the same time, the principle of Empire continues to lie at the basis of the new phases, predetermining the polyethnic and polycultural character of Ruritania overall, i.e. of all rural territories in general that were within the traditional state (Empire).

Small nationalism is a political phenomenon that always sets as its task building an independent and sovereign nation state. This task can be realized in two stages: receiving relative administrative-political autonomy (autonomization) and final exit from the composition of the given nation and the formation of a new nation with full independent statehood (separatism).

The same scenario, the same logic, the same algorithm underlies both stages of small nationalism. A class of regional bourgeoisie appears, interested in establishing direct economic control over the regional masses. The civilized intelligentsia works out a national project, i.e. a project of the "imagined community,"[27] consisting of real data, mixed with prag-

---

27   Benedict Anderson, *Imagined Communities: Reflections on the Origin and Spread of Nationalism* (London, New York: Verso, 1991).

matic "myths," called on to "justify" the right to independent statehood, ties with some or other *ethnoses*, *narods*, states, civilizations, religions of antiquity, etc. On this basis, some spatial area begins to make claims to autonomy — at first administrative, cultural, linguistic and economic. Later, the political moment is added: a demand for the creation of a federal unit, a "national" republic, etc.

The second phase of small nationalism is the demand for separatism and secession (setting aside existing statehood and forming a new nation). In this phase, things can reach armed struggle, separatist guerrillas, illegal armed units and terrorism.

In the case of separatism, there arises a legal clash that is typical of the national order. The nation is nothing but the product of an agreement, a social contract entered into by a group of citizens. The representatives of small nationalism are a group of minority shareholders who wish to reconsider the agreement (in which they most likely had no part or of whose conditions they were insufficiently familiar, conditions that in other cases were simply changed by the majority shareholders, i.e. the representatives of big nationalism). Can they do so? Theoretically, yes; this is secured in the structure of "international law" and "the right of nations to self-determination." But in practice the realization of this right inflicts damage (political and commercial) on the big nation (Megalomania, according to Gellner). The resolution of domestic problems is recognized as the sovereign right of the nation, so no one can interfere from without in the process of clarifying the relationship with the minority shareholders.

An ambiguous situation is created, which is resolved differently in each concrete case. In Western Europe, we know of typical examples: the separatism of the Basques in Spain, who led an underground armed struggle for national independence, the conflict in Northern Ireland between Irish Catholics and English Protestants, and guerrilla separatists in Corsica. In Eastern Europe, the collapse of Yugoslavia recently demonstrated all the hues and nuances of the politico-legal aspects of this conflict. The fall of the Yugoslavian nation-state (built on a federal basis) happened in accordance with the domino principle, creating newer and newer nations with newer and newer minorities, clamoring for separatism.

In all cases, the presence of small nationalism — in harsh and soft forms — is a direct threat to the territorial integrity of the nation state. If we define some part of the nation state as a "nation" or "national republic," we automatically understand by this the possibility and likelihood of its sovereignization, separation and transformation into an independent state. The moment when this happens depends on many factors: the concrete balance of forces between big and small nationalism, the might of the central authorities, the stability of the socio-economic situation, external conflict, etc.

Irredentism

Irredentism is another type of nationalism. This phenomenon signifies that one state has pretensions to control the territories of another state on the basis of a presumptive "ethnic" homogeneity of the populations of those territories with the "ethnic majority" of the state, or on the basis of real or imagined historical precedents of these territories joining the composition of the given state. As in the case of all forms of nationalism, the issue concerns not authentic "ethnic" homogeneity but artificial reconstructions, used instrumentally by the national bourgeoisie in their practical interests. When a nation is created, the actual ethnic factor is ignored and the "community" is imagined on a purely pragmatic, constructivist foundation. "All similarities to real historical figures are an accidental coincidence." In the same way, nationalism produces the concept of "kindred" enclaves on other territories of nation states or brings historical evidence of its right to those territories (creating another "myth," that the modern state is a successor to a traditional state, an "Empire," from which Megalomania arose).[28]

Irredentism bears as pragmatic a character as do the nation and nationalism as such. In certain cases it can become a pretext for the formation of separatist tendencies and small nationalism, differing from it only in that in this case there is a neighboring state that can give the irredentist

---

28 Gellner, *Nations and Nationalism.*

tendencies political, dogmatic, moral and economic support. In some cases, irredentism becomes an occasion for the military aggression of one state against another.

Irredentism often arises when a newly formed nation (Megalomania) includes in itself a population culturally similar to that which comprises the core of a different, neighboring nation (another Megalomania). This often occurs after the collapse of an Empire (a traditional state), when members of the core *ethnos*, spread throughout all territories and mobilized by historic deeds, prove to be the minority in the context of new nation states.

Colonialism and Anti-Colonialism

Many other phenomena connected with nationalism, especially its practical side, require clarification.

Colonialism is a phenomenon characteristic to modernity and the creation of nation states. Sometimes among superficially educated people there is the impression that colonialism belongs to deep antiquity and that modernity began with the process of decolonization and granting independence to colonies that have roots in the "dark" period of the Middle Ages. In fact, the situation is precisely the contrary. Colonization is a modern phenomenon, relating to modernity and emerging in the period of the rise of nation states in Europe with the domination of the bourgeoisie as a class. The capture of colonies is a historical deed of the Western European bourgeoisie, which began the process of capturing the territories of the planet, valued as sources for additional resources and gain. At the basis of colonialism lies the principle of the optimization of the economy, the broadening of the zones of trade and competition. Liberal-democratic racism, formed in a cultural-educational spirit, became the ideology of colonization. European colonists represented high culture, humanism and Enlightenment around the world, while "savages" and "barbarians," populating the other corners of the planet, had to pay for the civilizing mission of the white man with slave labor, submission and the "voluntary" handing over to the colonizer of whatever he considered "valuable."

Europeans regarded colonization as the modernization and humanization of the world, since all non-European cultures were thought of as less human and developed. The purpose of colonialism consisted in uniting to the nation state additional "no-man's" lands, populated by "subhuman" beings of a lower sort, who did not have to be taken into account. So colonies were immediately organized along the principle of nations. Colonial capitals were at the center, where the administration was focused; the periphery was thought of as a "desert, populated by savages." It was much more comfortable to build the nation as an artificial instrument in the "empty" territories of the colonies than in the territories of Europe itself, where each meter of space was connected with history and culture and where a similar homogeneity of "laboratory" conditions was not as easy to attain. With this is connected one of the theories of nationalism (Anderson, Chatterjee), which asserts that nationalism as a project was originally realized precisely in European *colonies*, in the first place in the USA, and only then returned to Europe.[29]

Colonialism can be regarded as an inseparable feature of the nationalism characteristic of the first phase of the formation of nations. We can interpret colonialism as big nationalism, in the area of activity of which are included, admittedly, "no one's" territories, located at a certain distance from the main location of the nation (Megalomania).

Anti-colonialism, the struggle for national liberation, is in this case a manifestation of small nationalism and a total repetition of the scenario we considered with respect to Ruritania. It is important to emphasize anti-colonialism certainly carries in itself a purely nationalistic program, with all its necessary elements: the creation of a simulacrum in the form of a "national idea," the appearance of a local bourgeoisie, the elaboration of rational, secular, economic strategies aimed at acquiring concrete gains, etc.

---

29 Anderson, *Imagined Communities*; Partha Chatterjee, *Nationalist Thought and the Colonial World* (London: Zed Books, 1986).

Ethnic Cleansing, Ethnocide, Genocide

"Ethnic cleansing" is also connected with nationalism. We should understand by "ethnic cleansing" the deportation, displacement, expulsion, artificial placement into ghettos, or relocation beyond areas of political control of sociocultural groups that hinder the realization of nationalistic projects.

In the process of the creation or defense of an already created nation, its political leadership can encounter the opposition of separate ethnocultural groups that reject the process of national formation. As a rule, this is expressed in claims for the creation of their own nation, insistence on the preservation of a given area in the structure of the previous state model, or insistence on uniting an enclave with a neighboring state (irredentism). Such groups show an absence of loyalty toward the nationalists building or securing the nation and they refuse to play by their rules. "Ethnic cleansing" is used among diverse means aimed at overcoming and breaking the opposition.

Their purposes consist in freeing territories from the compactly living groups in them that are not loyal to the dominant nationalism of the group. Since the nation is based on total control over territories and borders comprise its essence, in extreme cases control over territorial space and the creation of a homogeneous *demos* over the entire national territory is realized by freeing problematic areas from an intractable, rebellious population.

We can consider as an example of ethnic cleansing the creation of the system of reservations, concentration camps of a milder kind for local residents (Indians) who refused to integrate into the American nation established by the colonizers.

The extreme form of ethnic cleansing is *ethnocide* or *genocide*, the physical annihilation of people because of the fact of their sociocultural, religious and ethnic belonging. The goal of ethnocide (genocide) is the same as the goal of ethnic cleansing: the establishment of full control over national territories and strengthening the degree of homogeneity of the nation at the expense of the annihilation of foreign sociocultural elements.

Ethnocide and genocide are modern phenomena and have meaning only in the context of the nation and those rational-pragmatic problems that it solves. The genocide of the Jews in Hitler's National Socialist Germany, in which nationalism and racism were raised to the rank of a political ideology, was the largest-scale case of genocide in the twentieth century.

The Example of Turkey as an Illustration of the Ethnosociology of the Nation

We can illustrate a number of ethnosociology's theoretical principles and the phenomena it considers through the example of the political history of Turkey.[30]

At the basis of the modern Republic of Turkey we see the Ottoman Empire, a traditional state, in which the descendants of the Turk-Ottomans (mixed with members of the most variegated but willful and passionary *ethnoses*) comprised the ruling estate, the elite. The core of the Ottoman Empire was the polyethnic Turkey *narod*, comprised of many sociocultural, linguistic, and religious groups. Ethnically, this *narod* was built around the Turkish-speaking ruling elite of the Ottomans, with the participation of a number of other Turkic groups. Iranian and Arabic culture also exerted a great influence on the Turkish elite, which impacted in particular the Ottoman language, full of Arabisms and Iranianisms.

After conquering the Byzantine Empire, the Turks preserved its external form, replacing the Orthodox religion with Islam and the ruling elite of the Greco-Romans with the Ottoman nobility.

The Ottoman Empire, the Sublime Porte, preserved the paradigm of traditional society right to the start of the twentieth century. But already at the end of the eighteenth century, the secular nation states of Europe (England and France), and also imperial Orthodox Russia, began to support the separatism of Christian *ethnoses* (Greeks, Bulgars, Serbs, Macedonians, Armenians, Romanians, Moldavians, etc.) to weaken

---

30   Tancrède Josseran, *La nouvelle puissance turque* (Paris: Ellipses, 2010), 314.

their geopolitical and economic competitor. England actively provoked anti-Turkish tendencies in the Arab world, giving attention thereby to the creation of Arab nationalism (recall the epopee of the British agent of influence Lawrence of Arabia, one of the key figures in the construction of Arab nationalist movements). Ethnocultural and religious minorities periodically raised rebellions against the weak Ottoman rulers and these actions often ended in harsh ethnic cleansing, right up to ethnocide (Serbs and Armenians especially suffered from this) and all possible repressions.

When the Ottoman Empire weakened at last, the "Young Turks" group arose in it, which included the young Mustafa Kemal (the future Atatürk), who set himself the goal of forming a bourgeois nation. The Young Turks produced the model for Turkish nationalism and, when the Empire started to collapse, they acted as creators of the nation.

Under the leadership of Mustafa Kemal, the inhabitants of Anatolia (Turkified, followers of Islam but ethnically with diverse origins, from descendants of the ancient Anatolian *ethnoses*, from Levites and Hittites to the Greeks and Slavs who had spread there at a later date), mobilized in the face of the fall of the state, fought the Greeks, Armenians (representatives of small nationalism) and the English (who helped finish off the competitor) and won control over a number of territories that had earlier been the core of the Ottoman Empire. An entirely new phenomenon was built on Atatürk's victories and the geography of these victories: the Turkish nation.

Although in the period of the Ottoman Empire the small nationalism of the Christian *narods* and Arabs was punished brutally, the new nationalism of the Young Turks with distinguished by an even more radical brutality. In Atatürk's republic, nationalism became the basis of the political machinery and all cultural-linguistic, confessional and ethnocultural minorities (Kurds, Armenians, Slavs, Greeks, etc.) were harshly suppressed. The Ottoman Empire was on the whole indifferent to how the ethnocultural areas of the empire were arranged, which language the population spoke and what belief it professed. The repressions only began when the minority took up the project of small nationalism and separatism. In the new nation state of the Republic of Turkey, everything changed: there begins the broad and massive Turkification of the population, the harsh inculcation of a uniform cultural, social, political type. Religion became a private question, since secularism is a generally compulsory norm. An official version of the history of modern Turks (inhabitants of Turkey) was constructed, stemming in an unbroken line from the ancient nomadic European steppe through the Ottomans to modernity.

In such a situation, the compactly living ethnic groups of the Kurds, preserving their ethnic, linguistic and cultural identity, found themselves in the worst circumstances. The Kurds, the largest minority in modern Turkey, began to fight and to create the project of a Kurdish small nationalism (goal: autonomy and separatism).

On the territory of the former Ottoman Empire, other nations were formed around the Republic of Turkey, realizing other national projects. Modern Greece, the Federal Republic of Yugoslavia, Bulgaria, the Arab states (Egypt, Syria, Iraq, Saudi Arabia, etc.) were created. In these nation states, Turks are now subject to repressions and ethnic cleansing, and in the majority of cases are banished from these countries. Only in Bulgaria is there a qualitatively significant Turkish minority and positive relations with Turkey are developed only in Bosnia.

At the same time on the island of Cyprus, a confused situation takes shape in which both Greeks and Turks live on the island: both have their nation states nearby. The tension of the two nationalisms spills over into the Cypriot events of 1967–1968, when in a compact area of Greek inhabitation there is a pogrom of the Turks and in the area of Turkish inhabitation, a pogrom of the Greeks. As a result, the army of the Republic of Turkey invaded the island and created two states: the Republic of Cyprus (recognized) and the Turkish Republic of North Cyprus (not recognized). Here we see all the classic stages of the formation of a nation and all forms of nationalism.

Everything begins with the fall of the Empire. It attacks from within the various projects of small nationalism, to which we must in the first place ascribe the small nationalism of the Young Turks, which strove to build a modern Turkish nation state in place of the empire. Then the other nationalisms demand the establishment of independent states. They find external support. Relations with Russia and the support of its military plans in the region become one of the causes of the Armenian tragedy, the victims of which were hundreds of thousands of Armenians, subject to repressions first from the side of the dying Ottoman Empire and then by the Young Turks.

The collapse of the empire allows for the realization of a few Megalomanias at once: the Republic of Turkey, Greece, Yugoslavia, Bulgaria and other countries become independent nations. In the course of the clarification of national borders, a bloody war is fought, combining radical nationalism and ethnic cleansing. This is complicated by England's interference for exclusively colonial considerations of trying to limit the independence of the Turks and not allowing them to return their empire or even build an independent power (a potential competitor of England in the Middle East).

The Turks of Bulgaria and other countries become minorities and small nationalism and irredentism takes shape among them. Small nationalism also forms among Turkish Kurds. We can observe in the example of the Cyprus crisis how the ethnic overlap of the imperial structure of the Miletians finally breaks down in the last splinter of the ethnosociological area where the Turks and Greeks lived side by side and where norms of the coexistence of the *narod*, not the nation are preserved. Here we see how through ethnic cleansing and ethnocide the division of territories into two unequal areas (Turks on the island in the minority, Greeks in the majority) occurs and how the irredentism of the Turkish Cypriots provokes the invasion of Turkey.

This picture shows us practically all the aspects of nationalism and all the main moments of the formation of the nation from an ethnosociological perspective.

CHAPTER SIX

Civil Society and Global Society (*Socium*)

SECTION ONE
The Sociology of Civil Society

Civil Society as the Main Subject Matter of Sociology

We come now to the next derivative from the *ethnos*, civil society. Here, we move to sociology proper as such, without the addition of "ethno." Precisely sociology studies society as a whole, understanding by this a complicated and complex society but examined (theoretically, at first) separately from the state and, hence, the nation. This pure form of "society" (*Gesellschaft*, according to Tönnies) is civil society, consisting of citizens as the smallest social units, capable of uniting into small and large groups and realizing various forms of interaction.

Sociology, which arose under conditions of developed modernity in Western bourgeois societies with a developed industrial structure, rational science, well formed political-economic classes (the bourgeoisie and proletariat), a secularized culture, etc., examined the society in which it appeared as the basic given liable to study and unwittingly gave it a normative status. This is obvious in August Comte: he proclaims the irreversibility of progress, leading society from religion through metaphysics to the triumph of positive science.[1] Consequently, social history has a telos, a goal, realized in stages, from the worst and less modern forms of society (traditional) to its best modern forms. At the same time, as a socialist and student of Saint-Simon, Comte sees the essence of history not so much in the appearance of modern states and nations as in civil society, which can and must be thought of outside the state as something independent and (conceptually and teleologically) primary. Only later, applying methods and principles based on the study of modern society as civil society, did sociologists begin to study the state (the sociology of politics), religion (the sociology of religion), archaic cultures (social anthropology and ethnosociology) and their historic transformations (the sociology of history). The basis of classical sociology was and remains precisely modern societies and the processes occurring within them.

Thus, classical sociology studied civil society thoroughly, deeply and from many perspectives. It was created for this purpose and for more than a hundred years it managed its task well. In this respect, we know much more about civil society than about any other society, thanks to the great bulk of sociological authors and schools, identified with sociology as such.

But this wealth also has a negative side. The huge body of sociological theories, schools, teachings, authors, conceptions and methodologies can create the impression that the society studied by sociology, i.e. modern civil society, is *society as such*, was always like that or tried to become like that. So in other societies, distinct from modern Western European and highly differentiated society, we will knowingly encounter something imperfect, unfinished, rudimentary, primitive and of only relative interest. Everything "non-modern" in this case will be thought of as something fundamentally discarded, rudimentary and atavistic, as a source of dysfunctions, aberrations and anomalies. From here the *progressive* model stems, characteristic of some schools of modern sociology, which asserts that society should be not only studied but also developed, modernized, improved. This is clearest in Marx, who advanced the method of "active sociology," in which the study of social relations and social regularities

---

1   Auguste Comte, *A General View of Positivism* (London: Routledge, 1908).

should be identical to the ideological and political struggle for the creation of a "better world." In this case, non-modern societies are studied in accordance with the principle of residue and in the context of an overall "negative" program. The pragmatic purpose of the study of the archaic consists primarily in tracing and overcoming its influence on the modern.

In other words, modern sociology looks at society as such with the eyes of modern society and adopts the norms of the modern as truth, not subject to doubt and demanding only enhancement, development and modernization. Thereby, civil society and modernity in some sense lose their historic content and can become an "abstraction" or ideologized and politicized discourse.

The Significance of Anthropology and Ethnosociology

Taking into account the specific character of classical sociology, which studies modern civil society taken as a norm, we can better understand the significance of social, cultural and structural anthropology, as well as ethnosociology itself (earlier, we showed that these are essentially identical, so later we will speak only of ethnosociology in the broad sense). The distinctive feature of ethnosociology consists in the fact that, in contrast to classical sociology, it rejects the basic assumption of the normativity of modern society and builds its theories on the basis of the equal right, equal significance and equal worth of all types of society, ancient and modern, simple and complex, highly developed and "primitive." This approach is based on a broad, "inclusive" ("all-inclusive") humanism, which recognizes that we are dealing with "human society" (Thurnwald's "*menschliche Gesellschaft*"), beginning not only with the era of humanism and modernity but even earlier, in all types of society and all stages of history. If something in some society seems to us, modern people, "inhumane" or "not humane enough," this means only that we, in the spirit of cultural racism and uncritical "ethnocentrism," project the notion of man characteristic of our society onto other societies and insist on the universality and exclusivity of precisely our interpretation.

Ethnosociology rejects precisely such an approach, considering it unscientific, non-objective and immoral.

Ethnosociology outlines (as a first approximation) a specific scientific topic, in which sociology itself is examined as a phenomenon of social history and a manifestation of only one type of society alongside others. After all, it sees the projection of the methods of classical sociology onto non-modern societies as an uncritical and unreflective expression of sociological myths about progress, the universality of Western European culture and the technological, sociological and economic superiority of complex systems over simple ones.[2]

Thus, ethnosociology sets as an agenda the theme of *the sociology of sociology itself* — what is more, distinct from the attempts made by sociologists themselves.[3] The ethnosociologist's task consists in the description and correlation among themselves of different types of society as finished, juxtaposed structural phenomena, without attempts at hierarchizing them and constructing a historical teleology.

Simple societies exist in time not only *before* complex societies but also *together with* and *after* them. Social history is reversible and if we are in one or another phase of a cycle, we should not hastily accept it as something constant and unidirectional, as something "monotonic" (in the mathematical sense of the constant growth or reduction of quantity). The eminent Russo-American sociologist Sorokin demonstrated precisely this reversibility of society in his writings (especially his later writings).[4]

If classical sociology studies non-modern societies from the position of modern ones (i.e. in general, from the position of civil society), ethnosociology, by contrast, begins with the study of archaic and traditional societies through the unprejudiced search for the criteria that determine these societies, without relating them to modern societies

---

2   Dugin, *Sociology of the Imagination,* 261–311.

3   Anthony King, "The Sociology of sociology," *Philosophy of the Social Sciences* 37, no. 4 (2007): 501–524.

4   Pitirim A. Sorokin, *Social and Cultural Dynamics,* vols. 1–3 (New York: American Book Co., 1937).

and, accordingly, without any evaluation whatsoever. And only after this preliminary procedure does ethnosociology transition to the examination of modern societies, entering the area of classical sociology. Despite all similarities of methods and terms, this is nevertheless an entirely inno-vative approach: civil society (modern society) is thoroughly examined only with the instruments of civil society itself, i.e. by means of itself. It does not allow the "other" into the sociology of itself; i.e. modern classical sociology is *auto-referential, exclusive and "solipsistic."* Only structural-ism and some postmodern methods call this circumstance into question and propose other approaches. Ethnosociology goes even further and proposes to consider complex society (civil society) through the eyes of simple society; i.e. in the term "ethnosociology" the emphasis is not on "sociology" (as in the science of high modernity) but on "*ethnos*" (as the primary type of simple society, the *koineme*). So when we speak of civil society in the context of ethnosociology, we not only bring to light the place of the *ethnos* in this complex and highly-differentiated society but also evaluate and analyze this society from the position of the *ethnos*. The simple tries to explain the complex.

This comprises the novelty and unexpectedness of ethnosociological analysis, which examines post-ethnic social forms as derivatives from the *ethnos*. Having reached the third derivative in the form of civil society, we maximally abandon the simplicity of ethnic society. But what is important is that the distance is measured from precisely this simplicity and not from the complexity of modern society. Thus, while making our instruments more complex, we obtain the possibility of preserving an uninterrupted link with the *koineme* and its primordial structure during the examination of civil society, just as in the case of the *narod* and the nation.

Civil Society as the Antithesis of the *Ethnos*

From the perspective of ethnosociology, civil society is an actually exist-ing type of society that is as distant as possible from the *ethnos*. In other words, civil society is ethnic to a lesser extent than all other societies. If the *narod* is a complex polyethnic society and the nation is "pseudo-ethnic" (the nation as a simulacrum of the *ethnos*) society, civil society is thought of as lacking an ethnic dimension. We underscore that we are talking about an "actually" existing society, since theoretically we can imagine a sociological model even further removed from the *ethnos*, which we call "post-society" or "postmodern society." We will consider it in the next chapter as a possibility and tendency but at present "post-society" has the status of a project, which might or might not be realized in the future.

Post-society is conceived of as even less ethnic than civil society, but in contrast to post-society, civil society exists actually and is subject to empirical analysis, while post-society is represented in actuality only in some separate details. So in actuality we have three derivatives from the *ethnos*: the *narod*, the nation and civil society. A fourth derivative is possible and is studied theoretically but is realized socially only in laboratory conditions in narrow, limited segments of civil society.

Taking this correction into account, we can speak of the opposition and contrast of the model of the *ethnos* and the model of civil society. But this opposition will be interpreted entirely incorrectly if we ignore (as often happens) two intermediate phases: the *narod* and the nation. It is entirely incorrect to compare civil society and ethnic society. In practice they can and do come into contact with one another in certain circumstances. But to reproduce the structure of their correlation reliably, it is necessary to consider those transformations that occur with the *ethnos* in the stages of the *narod* and nation. Moreover, it is necessary each time to thoroughly specify what precisely we are holding up against civil society: the *ethnos* proper (as the simplest society, the *koineme*) or one of its derivatives, the first or the second? Without this, any analysis will turn into misunderstanding.

With these comments in mind, civil society can be juxtaposed to the *ethnos*, the *narod* and the nation. But first we should contrast it with precisely the nation, since civil society is the first derivative in relation to the nation and its structure is constructed in connection with precisely the nation, as its continuation, overcoming, removal and rejection.

Civil Society and the Nation

The concept of civil society arises almost together with European nations and inside European nations. At its basis lies the same basic model of the individual identity of the typical city-dweller of the third estate as in bourgeois nationalism. The "citizen" is the "city-dweller," the inhabitant of a city as a specific sociological phenomenon. It is not the *ethnos* (rural social groups) or the higher estates (clergy and aristocracy). Etymologically and in its meaning, "citizen" means strictly the same thing as "bourgeois." So civil society is conceived of as bourgeois society, as the society of the city-dwellers of the third estate. We saw that national society, the nation state, is built on the basis of precisely this social and political identification. Thus, civil society and the nation have strictly common roots and belong to a shared historical "moment." They arise in modernity in Europe and are consolidated alongside the clarification and broadening of the paradigm of modernity. The nation consists of citizens, so the nation state is the sociological instrument that creates the preconditions for civil society, makes it possible and brings its establishment nearer. The existence of a full-fledged bourgeois nation and, accordingly, bourgeois nationalism, which as we saw in Gellner[5] is not a *consequence* of the nation but *the instrument of its establishment*, is a necessary condition for the appearance of civil society.

The similarity of civil society and the nation consists in the fact that both are based on the individual principle of citizenship. Both the nation and civil society are an aggregate of citizens who have voluntarily united. Both are a Western phenomenon and belong to the modern era and the paradigm of modernity.[6] Both communities are based on the principle of voluntariness, rationality, benefit, equality of opportunity and the normative (innate) status of all members (natural right). Both the nation and

---

5   Gellner, *Nations and Nationalism.*

6   Louis Dumont, *Homo Æqualis I: genèse et épanouissement de l'idéologie économique* (Paris: Gallimard/BSH, 1977).

civil society are artificial constructs, worked out by the intellectual elite of modernity (philosophers, politicians, economists).

But at the same time, civil society differs from the nation in that it rejects the substantiality of collective identity (national in the modern state), denies its normativity, obligation and inevitability. This is directly connected with civil society's attitude toward the state. If the nation has meaning only and exclusively in the context of the state, civil society calls into question the inevitability and historical justification of the existence of the latter.

Civil society represents a kind of organization of society that is possible outside the state, outside any sort of artificial (and even more so, natural) forms of collective identity. Moreover, in theories of civil society, this possibility is regarded as positive, desirable and, in a certain sense, predetermined. History is the path of social development, directed toward civil society. Civil society is thought of as the crown of social progress.

The Figure of the Citizen (Kojève)

The Hegelian philosopher Kojève, who devoted a number of works to civil society, applied Hegel's Master/Slave dialectic (as the general form of the model of social stratification) to civil society.[7] In traditional society, this pair comes across clearly and directly: the master is strong and courageous; the slave is weak and cowardly. The master looks death in the face. The slave turns his back to it. The master pays for his rule with death; the slave receives life as compensation for his slavery. In the nation state, this pair — elite and masses — softens its opposition and transfers it into the sphere of economics. But as Marx, with whom Kojève is in full agreement, showed, the contradictions are not thereby removed but only intensified. The master becomes richer and richer, an exploiter, a capitalist, a bourgeois. The slave becomes poorer and poorer, exploited, a proletariat. There is a transition from rule based on force and feudal estates to rule based on wealth. The specific character of bourgeois nations as a sociopolitical and

---

7   Alexandre Kojève, *Esquisse d'une phenomenologie du droit. Exposé preliminaire* (Paris: Gallimard, 1981).

economic formation consists in this new configuration of rule as a purely *economic* factor.

According to Kojève, civil society should overcome this opposition dialectically; not through a proletarian revolution, as Marx proposed, but through the replacement of the figures of master and slave by a third figure, which Kojève calls the "citizen." The citizen is a synthesis of master and slave. The citizen does not encounter death face to face but he also does not run from it. He refuses the extrapolation of violence. Death becomes his own individual problem. The citizen creates a society that has abandoned inequality. Inequality is located within the person.

It is significant that Kojève takes as the synthetic figure precisely the "citizen," i.e. the "bourgeois," while Marx proposed to create a classless society ("socialism") on the basis of the figure of the "proletariat." Kojève conceives of civil society as a liberal society, in which the figure of the representative of the third estate continues to dominate but only the differential between the rich and the poor and the extrapolation of fear and death onto neighboring competitor nation states is softened and gradually rendered "null." The master (the rich) shares his "rule" with the slave (the poor) and artificially pulls him up to his level. This is possible because of the fact that bourgeois society by its nature is rational and calculating. And at a certain moment it can rationally weigh the costs that it must incur for international conflict (the world wars of the twentieth century and the preceding history of modern Europe) and class struggle within nations divided into antagonistic social strata. To divide surpluses with the needy, to refuse the exteriorization of terror and international conflicts, to leave "national myths" to the side and to move to peaceful coexistence, to diffuse power from the point of its concentration (in the hands of the economic elite) to all citizens is much more *rational*, advantageous, profitable and economical than to continue to exist in the context of international conflicts and class warfare. It would have been untimely and absurd to appeal with this idea to feudal lords moved by the "will to power." But the rational bourgeois on the basis of a critical and calculating consideration of the costs of the politico-economic history of modernity can full well take this step voluntarily and establish the figure of the citizen as an alternative to master and slave, as their synthesis.

The replacement of the pair Master/Slave (bourgeois/proletariat) by the synthesizing figure of the citizen is the most distinct modern generalizing project of building civil society. In it we see two fundamental moments distinguishing it from the nation and permitting us to say that we are dealing with precisely a derivative of the nation. This is the rejection of collective identity in the form of the nation (hence the abolition of states as the subjects of rights and history) and the abolishment of social stratification (which remains in the modern state from the traditional state, though in a derivative form).

Egocentrum

The form of pure individual self-identification, in which a person identifies himself only with his own individuality and nothing else, can be defined as a specific form, the *egocentrum*. By analogy with the *ethnocentrum*, the picture of the world unfolds here around a certain axis. But if in the ethnocentrum this axis is the *ethnos* itself as an organic, universal, whole, integral principle that precedes all individuality, in the *egocentrum* the individual is the axis. The egocentrum is as "subjective" as the ethnocentrum and builds a world around itself as "naively" as does the intentional process. It operates with noesis and noemata that are not universally ethnic but deeply individual. The life-world in the egocentrum is individual and uncritical. It is subject to a certain logic that is built not on the collective norm but on the elaboration of arbitrary associations. This phenomenon of the egocentrum is thoroughly examined in the phenomenological sociology of Schütz[8] and in Garfinkel's "ethnomethodology."[9] The egocentrum

---

8   Alfred Schütz, *Izbrannoe: Mir, svetyashchiysya smyslom* (Moskva: Rossiiskaya politicheskaya entsiclopediya ROSSPEN, 2004).

9   As we have already said, the term "ethnomethodology" in Garfinkel's sociology does not refer to an *ethnos* in the literal sense but to the totality of individual, randomly taken units within the framework of civic ethics, the influence of the normative and social structure on which are extremely weak and fragmentary.

constructs its temporal and spatial horizons, operates with its subjective truths and validities. Moderating, it lets pass through itself the torrent of "public opinion," as a rule, without any concern for its validity.

In contrast to societies of nation states and all the more so the *narod* (with its clearly expressed hierarchies and estate paradigms), the egocentrum is considered as free from the pressure of non-individual norms. It configures the world as it likes and is "handy" without any non-individual imperatives. If in the nation the state is the basic bearer of rationality — it supports and finances science and education, makes laws and ensures they are followed, forms strategies and configures identity, develops and modifies the national idea — in civil society rationality is transferred to the individual and becomes an internal matter of the egocentrum.

"The egocentrum is rational and acts rationally," says the law of civil society. The representatives of Weber's "understanding sociology" and the majority of the sociologists of the American Chicago School take this position. But this rationality of the egocentrum is fixed for certain while we are dealing with a strong society (national or socialistic), which somehow or other cares for the formation of precisely a rational citizen. In the more liberal model, the rationality of the egocentrum, being a given, not subject to question, is considered a personal matter, which opens paths of the autonomization of this rationality, its individual and subjective interpretation. What seems rational to one individual in the context of his egocentrum might seem irrational to another, etc. In civil society this problem is resolved on the side of the ever-increasing borders of rationality, i.e. in favor of admitting as "rational" what the individual himself considers rational.

This is clearly manifest in questions of the diagnosis of psychic illnesses. In a strong society, the psychic norm is rather strictly described and deviations from it are classified as "illnesses." This norm has a social character and fully depends on the social criteria of sickness in a given society. In civil society, the criteria of "psychic illness" are significantly enlarged and a person is recognized as actually "psychically ill" only in the case of complete, permanent, inadequate behavior (such as catatonia, imbecility or sever psychic disorders) or when he himself takes his condition to be an "illness." All other cases full under the category of the "individual with 'peculiar conduct,'" an "eccentric," "extravagant type," etc. In other words, the sovereignty of the egocentrum in civil society tends to its maximization. Finally, the rational, logical and justified is regarded as whatever the individual accepts as such.

Another example of the egocentrum is gender voluntarism, i.e. the possibility of the choice of gender in civil society. If we extend the line of trust in the egocentrum, at some moment we will be forced to admit that a person has the sex to which that person relates himself. Civil society is based on the presumption of non-interference in the internal affairs of the egocentrum, in respect for its sovereign individuality. The general criteria socially fixed in all other types of society are here subject to doubt. Thus, that which in other forms of society is regarded as a perversion and pathology is perceived in civil society as fully acceptable, so long as it does not directly affect other individuals, does not invade the territory of other egocentrums. Remaining within his own individuality, anyone can think as he pleases, regard himself and others as he pleases and do as he pleases.

Civil Society and Pacifism

The most important principle rejected by civil society is the principle of nationalism as an integral attribute of the nation, the nation state.

Nationalism is an exteriorization of the concept of the "other" as an enemy and as such always presupposes potential or actual military conflict. War is the natural form of existence of nation states; it is their integral function. To a significant extent, states are formed for defense from aggression and for carrying out (in certain cases) this aggression. In the majority of historical situations, the line between defense and attack is extremely unstable. So the nation presupposes the possibility of war and the main attribute of the state's sovereignty is the ability to repulse external aggression.

So long as bourgeois society is built on the principle of nations, war remains an intrinsic part of its fate and nationalism (in its soft or radical forms) is a necessary aspect of political ideology.

Against this, civil society advances the opposite principle of *pacifism*. It is the crucial point of civil society. Pacifism has a few dimensions. It asserts that:

- The conduct of wars between nations is expensive, disadvantageous and irrational, while peaceful agreements can always solve problems more profitably, so it is necessary in international politics to move entirely to the economy and to abandon power methods of solving disputable situations;

- No material gains should be put above human life, since there are no values more weighty than the life of the individual, the citizen, and he should not sacrifice it for any aims (this stems from strict individual identity and the absence of faith in forms of life other than individual, earthly existence);

- Modern bourgeois states, based on a shared socio-political and economic logic, have more in common than they have differences and, according to the extent of their modernization and rationalization, should realize that for them integration and cooperation are an expression of a socio-historic fate.

Thus, pacifism cancels the main aspects of the nation, namely:

- Nationalism and the extrapolation of the image of the enemy onto another nation ("anti-type");

- The weight and significance of (artificial) collective identity (the nation as such) for the individual;

- The self-identification of the nation as an independent, sovereign formation, capable of defending the national model of society in its borders.

Civil Society and Liberalism

If pacifism is the basic form of civil society in the domain of international relations, liberalism is the ideology that lays claim in general to the fundamental principles of civil society in a normative key.

Liberalism stems from the principle of the strict individual identity of the citizen. The very word *"libertas,"* meaning "freedom" in Latin, implies "freedom from"[10] all forms of non-individual identity: ethnic, religious, state, estate or national. "The individual is only an individual," liberalism insists. And all forms of "social contract" entered into by individuals can be dissolved and entered into anew. The optimal society would be one that is built on the principle of the absolute freedom of the individual and the absolute voluntariness of the social, political and economic constructions made by him.

As a priority, liberalism examines precisely the economic activity of the individual. Man is a *"homo economicus,"* "economic man." Everything in man is a deeply individual matter; he can be whoever he wants to be and however he wants to be but he encounters others precisely in ensuring his material needs and as a result he intrudes into their private sphere. So here there is the demand to establish rules that will guarantee all participants in the economic process the observance of their freedoms and guard them from encroachments on the part of other individuals. These rules are called "the free market." The market is the domain of individuals' interactions that excludes the use of force. Competition, contests, antagonisms — all of this remains in the sphere of entrepreneurial economic activity and should never transition into the domain of physical violence. Abolition of the principle of violence in favor of the principle of economic freedom is the goal of liberalism.

There are various versions of liberalism and some of them combine full well with the nation and the strong state. Thus, for instance, Thomas Hobbes, basing himself on the liberal-individualistic understanding of man, considered human nature "sinful" and "evil" (whence the principle

10   John Mill, *On Liberty* (Indianapolis: Hackett Pub. Co., 1978).

"man is a wolf to man"), and he was certain that only a voluntarily formed but strong state, with the right to legal violence, could ensure freedom for all and the security of one from another.[11] Stemming from a pessimistic view of the nature of the individual, liberalism demands the creation of a strong nation. But if we regard human nature as something virtuous or at least neutral (as Locke does, for instance),[12] we get another version of liberalism, which allows that a man raised and educated in a normal social environment will most likely not require the violent subdual of his "evil impulses" and will begin to act toward others as he would like others to act toward him.

Precisely this "optimistic" version of liberalism (developed by Locke and, especially, the late Kant) lies at the basis of civil society. Individuals are regarded as good or neutral in themselves. They can coordinate their interests and build a free society along the market principle and without a state. Moreover, at some point the state begins to hinder them. Thus, liberals of this kind think that society should immediately be built on universal principles of economic freedom and individual identity and move gradually to the abolition of states and nations, like other forms of previously abolished collective identity.[13]

Civil Society and Socialism

Socialistic theories were a specific orientation of civil society. In the first stage (in the first half of the nineteenth century) they did not come into direct conflict with liberalism and represented [with liberalism] two sides of a shared "progressive" orientation in bourgeois thought. Socialists were the most consistent supporters of civil society; they stood for equal civic rights, pacifism and the smoothening out of social contradictions in society. If what was fundamental for liberals was initial equality of

---

11   Thomas Hobbes, *Leviathan* (Oxford: Oxford University Press, 1998).

12   John Locke, *Two Treatises on Government* (Cambridge: Cambridge University Press, 1988).

13   Louis Dumont, *Homo Æqualis I: genèse et épanouissement de l'idéologie économique* (Paris: Gallimard/BSH, 1977).

opportunity, which could lead and always does lead to the inequality of the concrete and actual position of separate members of society (class differentiation), socialists strove to equalize not only opportunities but also to smooth out real differentiation, i.e. to artificially redistribute material wealth in favor of the poor, indigent, economically weak.

As a rule, precisely socialists were the most consistent opponents of the nation state and supporters of the unification of nations into a single supranational society. At the same time, they stood not only for the evening out of external (international, interstate) contradictions but also for the reconciliation of classes and the softening of interclass tensions. Socialists think that liberalism produces too much social differentiation between the rich and poor, which makes society overly conflictual and unstable. At the same time, class contradictions can grow into war and involve the state and its punitive political system in repression. Thus, socialists stood for the kind of state that would be pacifistic externally and would equalize rich and poor internally. Individual freedom should, in their opinion, be balanced by social justice; only then is it possible to build a "welfare society," i.e. civil society.

Civil Society and Communism

Communism is an extreme form of socialism, the basic principles of which were formulated by Karl Marx and Friedrich Engels.[14] The basic principles of communism consist in the sharpened conflictological approach to the examination of the socio-political history of societies, which finds its expression in the theory of class struggle, the most important theory for communist ideology.

Capitalism and the creation of bourgeois nations in modern Europe is for communists the highest form of social differentiation, transferred from mediated class contradictions to the immediate conflict of labor and capital. In pre-capitalist societies, class contradictions were veiled by other, non-material, non-economic forms: religion, estates, traditions,

---

14   Karl Marx, *Capital: A Critique of Political Economy,* vol. 1 (Chicago: Charles H. Kerr and Co, 1906).

etc. Under capitalism, the essence of the contradictions is revealed. The bourgeoisie and the proletariat embody in themselves the antagonistic moving forces of history in their pure form. The nation state is the highest historical form of capital. It is based on nationalism in relation to other nation states and on class opposition between the rich (the ruling class, holding the state in their hands) and the poor (in the first place, the city proletariat). For Marx, "good" are labor and the proletariat, the poor and oppressed, objects of exploitation, oppression and lies by the bourgeoisie, who are "evil." For Marx, the battle of "good" and "evil" must occur in the following way:

- The conscious industrial proletariat of developed capitalist countries creates a party;

- The basis of the party is an ideology at once anti-capitalistic and international;

- The communist parties of developed countries unite with one another to engage in a struggle against world capitalism wherever there is the possibility for doing so;

- Capitalism periodically enters the zone of crises and wars, which must be used by the parties of the proletariat for seizing power through revolutionary struggle;

- After seizing power in a number of developed capitalist countries, it is necessary to spread the revolutionary struggle to other countries (world revolution);

- As a result, world communism will be built, in which international frictions (states themselves disappear) and class contradictions (capitalists will be destroyed) will be abolished;

- A worldwide classless communist society will emerge, based on total equality.

As a result, a post-national, post-class society must arise, which differs from civil society in the following details: it will be based not on the normative figure of the "citizen" as "bourgeois" but on the normative figure of the "proletariat," the "worker," and will arise by revolutionary means through the destruction of the bourgeoisie. At the same time, the theory of "world communism" has many features in common with the concept of "civil society": both propose the removal of international and class contradictions (the abolishment of states and destruction of classes). The means, rate and forms of reaching this aim differ substantially in each case.

Civil Society and Global Society

Civil society is conceived of as the stage following nation states. At this stage, nation states slacken, are relativized and are then abolished altogether. Then civil society, being realized in practice, automatically brings with it the end of sovereignty, the abolition of states and the disappearance of nations.[15]

The form of collective identity prevailing in the nation is completely discarded in civil society. The nation and civil society are incompatible. The nation is that which hinders civil society from establishing itself fully.

Thus, civil society is conceived of as necessarily international and supranational. In other words, realized, established civil society cannot but be global. The global character of civil society stems directly from the relation of the concept "civil society" to "state" and "nation."

Civil society sees in the state and nation only a barrier, a hindrance, an obstacle. And although in relation to estate society (the *narod*, the traditional state) the nation played a "progressive" role (from the perspective of the supporters of civil society), from the perspective of further "development" and "progress" it is an obstacle. The nation breaks society up into individuals, i.e. it produces citizens. It facilitates the seizure of power by representatives of the third estate (the bourgeoisie). It moves social contradictions (elite/mass) onto the plane of purely class and economic contradictions (bourgeoisie/proletariat). It rallies the atomized mass (the

---

15   Thomas L. Friedman, *The World Is Flat: A Brief History of the Twenty-First Century* (New York: Farrar, Straus and Giroux, 2005), 328.

demos) and liquidates traces of the *ethnos* (urbanization) and the *narod* (the abolition of the estate privileges of the hereditary elite). It constitutes a democracy and transforms earlier heterogeneous local groups into a homogeneous *demos*. It promotes a secular culture and rational science.

That is, the nation creates the preconditions for civil society. But at the same time, the nation at some point becomes a limitation for the final development of these tendencies.

Artificial and technical national identity and nationalism begin to hold back the further liberation of the individual. It diverts the bourgeoisie to international competition away from the realization of a global rational project and the optimization of the resources of the Earth. It creates the preconditions for class struggle, which shakes the capitalist world from within. It limits democracy by concrete administrative and political borders, deflating its universal significance. So in order that civil society actually be established, the nation must disappear, die off. And a new society must replace the nation, which can only be called global.[16]

So civil society and global society are in a certain sense synonyms. When civil society will finally be built, it will become global. And even today, when it is only being built, it is already thought of as a global phenomenon. Thus, civil society and global society are the same and we consider them as the third derivative from the *ethnos*, although we distinguish two types.

We shall clarify this in some more detail.

Civil Society as a Transition Phase to Global Society

From the perspective of the theoretical concept, civil society and global society are essentially the same. But we are forced to distinguish them for the reason that civil society already exists (even if only partially), while global society so far only exists as a potential, a goal, a horizon. There are serious grounds for thinking that it can be realized in the near future but, since for now it still remains an intention (although fully realistic), we

---

16   Rafael Domingo Osle, *The New Global Law* (Cambridge: Cambridge University Press, 2010).

cannot consider it an empirical fact. The difference between civil society and global society consists only in the fact that the first exists and the second does not. Theoretically, when (and if) global society is realized, it will be nothing other than civil society on a global scale. But that is only in theory. In fact, we cannot be certain whether that will happen. History has many versions and the future is open. Hence arises the necessity of strictly distinguishing civil society from global society, despite their theoretical equivalence.

Civil society had already begun to ripen on the eve of modernity.[17] It accompanied the birth of nation states: during the Renaissance and Reformation in Europe, there existed projects of uniting all European states into a single confederation. These projects often became the bases for various mystical organizations, like the Italian neo-Platonists, German and English Rosicrucians,[18] and Masonic lodges at the start of the eighteenth century.[19] Moreover, on the eve of modernity the idea of civil society was more widespread than in the era of the flowering of nation states, so the project of civil society did not develop progressively but cyclically.

In any case, nation-states created the preconditions for the establishment of civil society, which gradually accumulated according to the extent of urbanization, industrialization, the inculcation of a national "idiom," the politicization of the broad masses and the diffusion of books and sciences. The elements of civil society especially developed in cultural, philanthropic organizations, social movements, Masonic lodges, progressive parties, centers of arts and culture, in universities and academies, in scientific circles, in professional associations and the free associations of citizens around any serious or playful pursuits and interests. Civil society gradually formed in those sectors of the modern state where national identity and statewide politicization were weakened and private persons or groups of people received freedom of conduct and action, separate

---

17   Louis Dumont, *Homo Æqualis II: l'Idéologie allemande* (Paris: Gallimard/BSH, 1978).

18   Frances A. Yates, *The Rosicrucian Enlightenment* (New York: Routledge, 2002).

19   Paul Bachelard, *Franc-maçonnerie et Europe: La Trahison?* (Paris: Vega, 2006).

from any normative-collective obligation. Traditionally, private clubs were one of the main forms of such association.

Thus, civil society gradually acquired mature social forms. Conceived of historically together with nation states, it went toward its embodiment through numerous dialectical transformations, spreading its influence ever more broadly over groups of nation states. At the same time, civil society acted overall as an opposition to nation states and as a form of social organization opposed to all kinds of nationalism. In precisely this environment of civil society there developed as a priority all anti-nationalistic and anti-national projects, and theories were formed that harshly criticized all forms of nation states. In particular, one of the most consistent projects of this kind was Karl Popper's theory of the "open society."[20] The "open society" is civil society in its global expression.

Civil society in its actuality can be considered a transition phase to global society, which has not yet occurred fully, since the nation state today still plays a decisive role in world politics and in the inner organization of nations. At the same time, the horizon of global society is becoming closer and more concrete and certain aspects of globalization have become facts.

The Ideology of Human Rights

The principle of the egocentrum is expressed politically and ideologically in the concept of "human rights." Despite all the apparent evidence of this concept, we are dealing with an artificial construct. The concept of "human rights" is a concrete module of transition from the principle of citizenship in its linkage to the nation (citizenship as a fixed legal, juridical quality) to citizenship in the sense of membership in global civil society, in which each person by the fact of his belonging to the human race possesses intrinsic civil rights. The theme of "human rights" knowingly bears a supranational (and in some respects anti-national) sense, since it aims to place the significance of the norm of civil society above the norm of national society. The citizen of the nation state is (theoretically) protected

---

20 Karl Popper, *The Open Society and its Enemies* (Princeton: Princeton University Press, 1971).

by a civic code, a constitution, guaranteed rights. He does not need an additional, secondary confirmation of his civic status. Only when a state does not observe its national legislation might he need the interference of rights organizations, called on to monitor observance of human rights. In this case of a power supporting human rights despite the nation state not observing them, an aggregate of nation states act, for whom the institutes of civil society and the ideology of human rights have a greater influence on policies and are thought of as the predominant normative socio-political type. In this case, a concrete national government is pressured by global civil society that is not yet precisely fixed but in the stage of its embodiment. The conception of "human rights" is the most important attribute of this society. Where there are human rights advocates, the processes of globalization and the desovereignization of nation states unfold. This happens because of the very content of the ideology of human rights, which strives to consolidate global and supranational norms in the sense of citizenship despite citizenship understood nationally.

The supranational character of human rights is even more vivid in the case of individuals who have problems with citizenship. This affects people who do not have documents, displaced people, deported people, vagabonds, refugees, illegal immigrants, etc. Their status from the perspective of national law equates them to non-citizens; i.e. they are disenfranchised in civil rights. The nation always distinguishes citizens from non-citizens; that is its principal political-legal arrangement. But from the perspective of civil society, any person is a citizen, if he is a person, and he has the right to belong to civil society. For the nation, he has no rights; he is a non-citizen. But for civil society, he has them; he is a citizen. Here it is obvious that we are dealing with two normative political-legal and ideological categories: national and global, all-human. The meaning of the ideology of human rights consists in putting the norms of civil society above national norms, subordinating the national understanding of citizenship to the global; forcing the nation to recognize civil society as a higher priority and, on this basis, spreading their notion of citizenship to those who from a state-legal and administrative perspective cannot have it. If the nation goes for this, it globalizes and desovereignizes. If it resists and puts the national understanding of citizenship higher than the global one, it is subject to pressure from those countries that have moved even further along the path of acknowledging the ideology of human rights.

In civil society, man is a legal status; he has rights. Man is a citizen. To the extent that the nation will admit this state of affairs, it will gradually globalize, desovereignize and transfer its authority to non-state, non-national authorities.

The European Union as a Stage of Global Society

The integration of European states into a single political and economic whole, the European Union, is an excellent example of how it is possible to transition from the theory of civil society to concrete political and economic practice. The creation of the European Union over the past 50 years has been an example of the realization of this project. In a relative way, the creation of the European Union at the limits of Europe itself can be considered a fact of the realization of globalization. In Europe in the twentieth century and especially in the period after the Second World War, developed institutions of civil society were created within the framework of nation-states and on the basis of a shared sociocultural type. These processes occurred even more successfully in the integration of separate fields of the European economy. Gradually, all of this led to European states making a political decision to transfer power, sovereign authority, to a supranational authority, the European Union. Henceforth, Europe is a state with a common President and parliament and shared political-administrative and financial structures. This is not only an example of the unification of a number of states into a single whole but also the first historical case of the creation of a new type of society on a supranational basis. European society is intentionally realized as civil, supranational and non-national. In a limited context, we can consider it an example of successful globalization. Of course, it is not entirely global society, since above the European nation states another state form is established, the European Union. But taking into account the serious contradictions between the nation states that tore up Europe in previous centuries, the very fact of going beyond these borders is extremely important. It shows that civil society can be strong enough to predetermine the political configuration of a post-national arrangement and that globalization — even if on a limited scale — is entirely possible; consequently, global society is acquiring mature features before our eyes.

The United States of America as an Example of a Successful Civil Society

The US can serve as another example of civil society. From the beginning, the structure of this state was built along artificial templates, as a laboratory experiment in embodying in life extreme Protestant utopias.[21] For many European sectarians, America was considered "the promised land," on which they contrived to establish a new type of society based on rationality, enlightenment, science and effectiveness, which were hindered in Europe by medieval traditions and cultural limitations. The US was created mainly by representatives of the third estate and the bourgeois model of social organization lies at the very basis of North American statehood. There was never an estate aristocracy in the US, i.e. the state was formed as a nation from the start, without the prehistory of a *narod* or traditional state. The US was created in an "empty place" (previously cleansed of the autochthonous *ethnoses*, the natives who had settled it before the arrival of the colonialists). The political system of the "states," which have a significant degree of legal and administrative autonomy, the whole system of American federalism and many other peculiarities of the American political and administrative system can be regarded as a model of decentralization, one of the main characteristics of civil society.

As confirmation of the idea of some ethnosociologists (Anderson, Chatterjee) that the first prototypes of European nations were precisely colonies and the US first of all, we see institutions of civil society developed in the US before anywhere else: sects, clubs, philanthropic organizations,

---

21 Alexis de Tocqueville, *Democracy in America* (Chicago: Chicago University Press, 2000).

Masonic lodges, professional associations, humanistic circles, sporting unions, etc. American identity was from the start connected with the egocentrum, with the recognition of the full freedom for any member of society to be anyone, to consider oneself anyone and to become anyone; American morality is based on this idea.

In today's America, these tendencies are as strong as in previous stages of that country's history and many analysts think American society is a model of civil society. This version differs substantially from the European Union; the histories of their emergence are entirely different. But in a certain context the US can be considered one of the most completed models, in which many sides of civil society were realized in practice.[22] Precisely this is usually called "the American way of life."

Globalization and the Regionalization of the Planet: The White North and the Non-White South

Globalization gradually delineates a new geographic and sociological regionalization of the territories of the Earth. According to the extent of the concentration of power in the hands of supranational authorities and the desovereignization of nation states, realities are exposed that geopoliticians call "the rich North" and the "poor South," or the "core" and the "periphery."[23] In the "rich North" are those countries where civil society is developed to the greatest extent and where the centers of economic life are. We can confidently refer to the US and the European Union, i.e. the countries of the Atlantic Alliance, as the "rich North." This is the "core," where the major financial, political and military-strategic resources of humanity are concentrated. From a sociological perspective, we can take the "rich North" as a synonym and matrix of "civil society," since we see

---

22   Michael Hardt and Antonio Negri, *Empire* (Cambridge: Harvard University Press, 2001).

23   Immanuel Wallerstein, *World-Systems Analysis: An Introduction* (Durham: Duke University Press, 2004).

in precisely the US and Europe successful examples of the embodiment of civil society in life. The "core" is the "core" of a global world.[24]

The "poor South" represents the states and cultures of the Third World. In this area, modernization is not complete, economic institutions are not developed and the socio-political system is in a transitional phase. Sociologically, the "poor South" represents the totality of countries in the earlier stages of forming nations, where ethnic societies and partially traditional societies are strong. But colonialism left a deep trace in them in the form of hurriedly formed nations and often the elite of these countries is "Westernized" and "modernized" (with rare exceptions). But what are definitely absent there are adequate structures of civil society. So the "poor South" represents a serious problem for the creation of global society, since in this area not only has the creation of bourgeois nations not been completed but often the structures of archaic *ethnoses* and traditional society (the *narod*) are also much stronger and more stable than formal democracies and market institutions. That is why the term "periphery" is fully fitting for this zone, not only in an economic but in a sociological sense. This is the periphery of global society, since here the necessary sociological structures and paradigms are absent.

From an ethnic perspective, we can note that the societies of the states of the "rich North," the "core," were in the majority of cases formed on the basis of Indo-European *narods* and speak some Indo-European language. Phenotypically, these societies, being poly-ethnic, are represented, as a rule, by "whites." The societies of the "poor South," the "periphery," are populated for the most part by members of non-Indo-European *ethnoses* and *narods* and have other phenotypic characteristics.

Although a significant and constantly growing percentage of the "non-white" population successfully integrates into the societies of the "rich North" and often occupies high positions in its elite (the phenomenon of Barack Obama is highly significant in this regard), on the whole the proportion remains like this: civil society is predominantly white and

---

24 Thomas P. M. Barnett, *The Pentagon's New Map: War and Peace in the Twenty-First Century* (New York: Putnam Publishing Group, 2004).

Indo-European, while peripheral, transitional types of society with weakly developed or altogether lacking institutions of civil society are predominantly "colored" and speak languages from outside the Indo-European group. In certain cases, this regularity can lie at the basis of new "globalistic" forms of racism: globalization is associated with "whites," while opposition to globalism or simply the inability to develop "civil society" is associated with all other *narods* and *ethnoses*.

The Semi-Periphery

The global regionalization of the planet reveals another specific area, which some sociologists (Wallerstein, for instance),[25] call the "semi-periphery." It refers to the BRIC countries (Brazil, Russia, India, China). From a sociological perspective, these countries represent rather specific societies in which modernization penetrated more deeply than in countries of the "periphery," giving them the possibility to develop high and effective industrial, scientific and military technologies, allowing them to compete with the "core," the "rich North." At the same time, these societies themselves reproduce characteristics of traditional societies; nations formed in them only partially and they preserved a number of archaic features.

This is a peculiar phenomenon that allows us to presume a possible alternative to a future global world. Here, we are dealing with a probable reversibility in the future. If the countries of the "semi-periphery" (BRIC) prove politically, economically and socially capable of competing with countries in which civil society was established and consolidated, the picture of the future world might look different. In the countries of the "semi-periphery," "traditional society," i.e. the *narod*, is preserved in one way or another. The process of forming a nation is in an earlier stage and capitalistic forms are not dominant, although they are widely present. At the same time, the potential of the BRIC countries from the perspective of economics, energy resources, territorial scale, demography, the cultural

---

25   Immanuel Wallerstein, *After Liberalism* (New York: New Press, 1995).

consolidation of the population and political autonomy is great enough to represent a serious and realistic alternative to the Western model of globalization.

In the countries of the "semi-periphery," civil society is very weakly developed or not developed at all, besides separate artificial inclusions, initiated by the "rich North." Instead, structures of traditional society were preserved, together with a significant number of archaic, purely ethnic local groups, untouched by modernization. So if these societies prove to be sound from an economic, military and political perspective, they can be models for a new phase of reversibility. Precisely this area can be very attractive to the "poor South," sociologically nearer to the "semi-periphery," which reorients the vector of its modernization in another direction.

Frictions and, perhaps, conflicts with the "rich North" are in this case inevitable. If the "periphery" comes out victorious, the process of the establishment of a global civil society will be set aside for an indeterminate period or removed altogether from the agenda. Instead of a unipolar West-centric world with the "rich North" at the center, a multipolar world will be built with a few centers equally great in influence but organized differently. There will be neither a "World Government" nor a "United States of the World," nor "human rights." The world will be divided into distinct "large spaces" on the basis of civilizational markers.

"Civilization," as we saw, relates in ethnosociology to the *narod/laos*. The political scientist and sociologist Samuel Huntington, who advanced the thesis of a "clash of civilizations,"[26] considers precisely such a scenario in his books. We note that the use of the concept "civilization" in the context of globalization already presupposes the reversibility of social history, since the factor of civilization is regarded as entirely overcome, removed and abandoned in the transition from the *narod* to the nation.

In this case, the "rich North" will lose its global significance and move to the format of one local civilization alongside others. This will mean the reversibility of Western society within its own borders. We see signs of

---

26 Samuel P. Huntington, *The Clash of Civilizations and the Remaking of World Order* (New York: Touchstone, 1997).

this possibility in the phenomenon of American neo-conservatism, the representatives of which openly reason in pre-modern terms, speaking of "hegemony," "Empire," the "elite," appealing to religious values, traditional morality, etc.

The future is open: there might prevail in it the tendencies toward global society and then the logic of the social history of the West will be spread to all other countries, or tendencies might prevail toward the return to previous forms, to the preservation of nation states or even earlier types of society, such as empire and civilization, including religious societies. It is not impossible that the processes of local archaization, i.e. a return to ethnic forms, will proceed in parallel. This phenomenon is noted in Roland Robertson's notion of "glocalization,"[27] meaning the fixation of processes accompanying globalization and occurring on a local level in the completely opposite direction: not to the further individualization, modernization, complication and autonomization of the egocentrum but to the revival of ethnic and regional communities or the appearance of new ones.

Demographic Processes in the Global World

In the modern world, many processes acquire a global character. In particular, this affects migration and demography.

Globalization launched the process of the active movement from vil-lage regions (the area of the *ethnos*) to the city on a planetary scale. The increasing flow of migration from the "periphery" to the "core," from the "poor South" to the "rich North," is related to this process. Urbanization and migration toward the "core" are from a sociological perspective one and the same process of modernization and movement toward civil society, since citizenship presupposes the "city" as the main social, technological and cultural environment. And the entire territory of the "core" can be regarded in turn as a "global city."

---

27 Roland Robertson, *Glocalization: Time-Space and Homogeneity-Heterogeneity* in Mike Featherstone, Scott Lash, Roland Robertson (eds.), *Global Modernities* (London: Sage, 1995), 25–44.

There has been an important shift in the present, statistically: more than half of humanity (51%) now lives in cities and 49% in rural areas. This means the majority of humanity is "civic" and the minority ethnic. This argument can be serious confirmation of the fact that the processes of globalization are fundamental and weighty. On the other hand, migratory processes and the growing concentration of the population in cities is balanced by the preservation in countries of the "periphery" and "semi-periphery" of the social structures of traditional society (there were cities, including large, densely-populated ones, in antiquity but in the nation, and all the more so in civil society, these systems were not outgrown) and the vividly expressed proletarianization of the city population (migrants and citizens in countries of the "poor South"). For now, there is enough potential for integration of the proletariat masses in "rich North" countries into the class of the petty bourgeoisie (this is done through inculcating clichés of "bourgeois consciousness" and the ideology of "comfortism," even in those milieus that endure a pitiful economic existence, and also through the system of the constant growth of consumer credit, which was a cause of the latest economic crisis). But there is clearly not enough potential for the growing wave of immigrants from the Third World. The low-qualified masses remain bearers of traditional or archaic consciousness and integrate into the civil society of the West with great difficulty, preferring to establish a ghetto or enclave within and taking advantage of certain social privileges but also ignoring the paradigms of the egocentrum, the ideology of "human rights" and other attributes of civil society. Thus, migrants become a counterpart to the national proletariat, an alienated class, an internal "other." Refusing to be integrated into civil society, migrants undermine the successful realization of the global project.

On the other hand, globalization directly influences demographic processes. The modernization of systems of healthcare leads to an increase in births and a decrease in infant mortality even in countries of the "periphery." At the same time, rural conditions of life and traditional religious injunctions prohibit "birth control." Hence the rapid demographic growth in population of the "poor South."

An opposite tendency opposes this one in the "rich North." There, the population is steadily decreasing and aging.

Together, these two parallel processes change the proportions of the social system on a planetary scale. The issue is not that there is a growth of the "colored" population and a decrease of the "white" population. In itself, this is not a sociological factor. But the issue is that demographic processes in the "periphery" increase the percentage of bearers of archaic or traditional society and decrease the number of adepts of civil society. As the core of globalization, the West becomes a minority sociological authority, a shrinking global elite. This elite recruits new members in the countries of the "semi-periphery" and even the "periphery" but here the sociocultural specificity of the new members makes itself known more and more. Huntington called this "modernization without Westernization."[28] This phenomenon is the typical case when the representatives of the higher class of traditional society receive a Western education but then return to their societies, preserve traditional values and use their acquired skills for the consolidation of their own cultures in competition with the West. From "modernization" they take only the technical side, they reject the ideological bases of civil society, human rights, the egocentrum, liberalism, tolerance, etc.

Overall, migratory processes and the demographic contrast present a challenge to global society, not through direct resistance to its establishment but through broadening the area of active globalization to those territories of the Earth with a social culture differing sharply from the social culture of Western countries. The intensity of globalization undermines it from within, creating new risks.

Global Society and Its Borders

Let us turn again, not to the practice of globalization, where, as we saw, there are a number of contradictory sides and uncertain tendencies but to its theory, to global society as a theoretical concept.

---

28   Samuel P. Huntington, *The Clash of Civilizations* (New York: Simon & Schuster, 1997).

"Global society" has a number of different synonyms: "one world," "humanity," "planetarism," "mondialism," etc. We can imagine it as a repetition of the experience of the European Union on a planetary scale or as the transfer of the American model of society to the entire world (the "United States of the World").

In this case, all humanity can be regarded as the populace (*demos*) of a single World State, governed by a single "World Government" and having other global political institutions repeating in their basic features the Western, American-European model.

This global state is thought of as minimally a state, and that only in the face of a figure that could be put outside of the limits of humanity, since the nation state has a purpose only in the face of another nation state. For now, there are claimants to this role only in fantasy novels and films about "aliens" who play the role of the "other" for a humanity that has become global. In some fantastic scenarios, the role of the "other" is played by an internal enemy; for instance, "robots," "machines," or "computers" that have escaped control and even cyborgs and mutants. Functionally, they replace the protesting classes of industrial political systems.

But these borders, capable of establishing the general parameters of collective identification — terrestrials/aliens, people/machines, etc. — are extravagant not at all by accident. On one hand, they are illustrated by a fantastic hypothetical character, an unlikelihood, an "imagined" character, and "irreality"; on the other, they fulfill the sociological functions of concrete limits, necessary for the constitution of any collective identity, even the most approximate. The "fantastic" and "exotic" figure of the "other" (external and internal) is called on to indirectly affirm that global society will not be a new version of the nation state on a planetary scale but rather precisely a non-political society, society as such, in which non-political forms will predominate. First, the world will become a "global market," i.e. an area of free exchange, without any economic barriers or borders. Second, this will be a network reality, uniting people not according to their location but according to their will: global communications facilitate instantaneous ties with any point on the planet, while real localization is secondary in relation to virtual localization. Finally, most important will be the egocentrum as an open possibility of the free, arbitrary constitution of one's own microcosm. The ideology of human rights will here reach its apogee and any inhabitant of the planet will automatically be considered a "citizen of the world."

If we cast a glance at the borders of the global world (inner and outer), we counter a new sociological construction, which we define as "post-society."

SECTION TWO
The Ethnosociological Analysis of Civil and Global Society

Post-Ethnic Analysis of the Derivatives of the *Ethnos*

It remains for us to examine civil society from the position of ethnosociology. At first, we will consider why it lacks the ethnic factor and what conceptual distance separates it from the simple society, the *koineme*, the *ethnos*.

Civil society is a maximally differentiated society. Moreover, differentiation, complexity, affects all its spheres and fragments it both vertically and horizontally. If the *ethnos* is something simple and whole, civil society is something extremely complex and fragmentary, split up, fractional.

The two intermediary derivatives from the *ethnos*, the *narod* and the nation, lie between the poles of integrity and fragmentation. During the transition from the *ethnos* to the *narod*, primordial wholeness is ruined and duality is produced in its place. A fundamental split occurs and the poles of this split extend to the furthest horizons. The reach of differentiation in traditional society (as compared to all other types of society: *ethnos*, nation, and civil society) is as great as possible. Precisely here arises Logos, transcendence, the highest exertion and the highest traumatism.

The wholeness of the *ethnos* splits, like the atom, and a massive flow of energy is released (passionarity). In its scope, the peak of qualitative non-simplicity is attained in the *narod*. Duality radically differentiates heaven and earth, elite and masses, "ours" and "theirs." This is embodied in the great empires, grand religions and glorious superhuman cultures of antiquity. All this is colored by extreme forms of heroism, the greatest exertion and encounters with the dizzying abysses that opened up in place of the all-inclusive, steadfast, eternal, harmonious ethnic being.

In the *narod* we transition from the greatest possible qualitative wholeness in the *ethnos* to the extreme duality of the split, which has no parallel to its exertion and traumatism in any other type of society.

During the transition from the *narod* to the nation, the structure of society on one hand becomes technically and mechanically complex, since the structures of power, economics, and technology become more complex, but on the other hand heroic exertion declines. The highest qualitative differential of heroic dualism, the exclusivity of Logos, is diffused onto a multitude of citizens, individuals, egocentrums. So the transition from the *narod* to the nation can be regarded as a complication of the system from a technological perspective but simultaneously as a lessening of exertion, the removal of dramatic tension and, hence, as a simplification. However, it is not a return to the *ethnos* (which also happens but not in the transition phase from the *narod* to the nation), which would be a real simplification, but the transfer of the heroic energy of traditional society into the spirit of capitalism, entrepreneurial activity, bourgeois nationalism, geographic discovery, colonization and the development of science and art.

Transcendentalism, the heroic encounter with death, logos, rationality: all of this is distributed among the third estate and through it the entire populace, the *demos*. This is the specific characteristic of democracy: it is simultaneously more complex than estate societies and simpler than them. Power moves from the elite, as far as possible from the ethnic masses, to the bourgeoisie, which becomes a half-elite (in the class sense) but remains a half-lackey estate recruited from below. The nation is the subtle path of the city bourgeois, the citizen, away from the dramatic split and the uttermost qualitative differential of the medieval elite but not to return to the ethnic simplicity of the village and *Gemeinschaft*. That is why the nation is an "imagined community": the bourgeoisie "imagined" it in place of the estate model and rural ethnic societies.

In civil society this impulse, vividly expressed in the birth of nation states, continues to develop in the same spirit. Civil society is even more technically complex than national society but "simpler" than it qualitatively, from the perspective of heroic, transcendental potential. Here logos, rationality, transcendentalism, the pair *subject/object* and also confrontation with death and the "other" are fully and finally delegated to the individual, without collective expression (as in the case of the nation). Henceforth, the individual becomes the "world," split like the *narod* and its poles but closed like the *ethnos* and its structures. In the individual of civil society, all the responsibility is placed exclusively on the individual but real potency is curtailed in direct proportion to the growth of responsibility. The individual can do anything; he is entirely free. But the realization of his will is blocked by the will of another, exactly similar omnipotent individual. Thus, virtual space as a new area of maximum complexity becomes the optimal sphere for the realization of freedom. In it, the individual is indeed free and cannot do harm to an "other," since each is for the other located on the other side of the screen where all the events occur. At the same time, the dramatic tension working on the individual and the technologism of the surrounding environment grow but they are also scattered, dispersed entropically into a soulless confluence with high-precision apparatuses: computers, mobile phones and multifunctional devices.

The egocentrum of civil society is a complex fragment, but one with weak energy and its face turned toward entropic virtuality.

Civil Society in the Chain of Ethnosociological Derivatives

The entire chain from the *ethnos* to civil society is set out as an irreversible process only and exclusively in European history. In other cases, we quite often see a transition from the *ethnos* to the *narod* but in the case of a crisis of the *narod*, there is a return again to the *ethnos*. The *narod* breaks up into *ethnoses*. Gumilev gives many examples of this cycle in his works (if we factor in that he calls "ethnogenesis" what we call "*narod*" or "laogenesis"). At the same time, in traditional states developed cities populated by a *demos* are often created and a significant third estate forms. But this class practically always shares the fate of the *narod* and does not step out independently into the historic arena in the form of a nation.

The transition phase from the *narod* to the nation and not to the *ethnos*, as happens in the majority of cases, was realized only in Europe and only in modernity. And although separate nations and modern states also break up into *narods* and *ethnoses* in certain moments, on the whole the European system of bourgeois nation states proves relatively stable and the second derivative from the *ethnos*, the nation, is consolidated in it.

The stability of the nation permits the development of tendencies directed toward the appearance of civil society. It is obvious that civil society can be built only in the context of European bourgeois nations or their post-colonial zone. Today, we live in the era of the next transition phase to the third derivative, which should historically confirm or disconfirm the very possibility of its realization and stability. Elements of civil society without doubt exist. But global society in the full sense has not yet been built and there is no certainty that it will ever be established. For now, at issue are tendencies, theories, ideologies (human rights) and the formation of separate supranational institutions. We cannot be sure whether or not a full rejection of nation states will occur and when this might happen.

The Transformation of Language:
Koine-Idiom-Artificial Language

We can observe the transformation of language in the chain of derivatives from the *ethnos*. The *ethnos* speaks a language. During the appearance of the *narod*, the phenomena of the *koine* and polyglossia appear. The nation carries with it an "idiom." But the "idiom," a relatively artificial construction, is formed on the basis of some concrete dialect, taken as a norm.

Civil society should work out an even more abstract model, which can be called an "artificial language." We are talking about the elaboration of such a system of signs as would correspond to various articles of the objective world, acting as a kind of instrument for the semantic nomenclature of things. Language in the *ethnos* is an auto-referential system: sense and significance, intentionality and extensionality, were contained in it. Language was the world and man simultaneously.

In the *narod*, the wholeness of language is broken up. There appears in the sign as an element of language an internal sense and external significance. Language changes its nature.

The "idiom" in the nation strives to fasten precisely the significance of the sign to the detriment of its internal sense but, since at the basis of the "idiom" there lies after all a living language, this can only be done in part, in separate linguistic zones (science, jurisprudence, politics, education, etc.). Where the state is strong, a concrete significance or group of significations corresponds to the word, while inner-linguistic and psychological associations are placed at the disposal of artists, poets, writers, etc.

The shift to the egocentrum presumes a fragmentation of the "idiom" into separate individuals. The state removes from itself the responsibility for providing words with meanings. So the subjectivity of the derived language in civil society increases sharply; theoretically, each gets the right to speak his own individual language.

But to preserve inter-individual interactions in civil society, alongside the individual pseudo-language with its arbitrary meanings and associations and voluntary, changeable structure of intentionality, another language is required, a language of things, a coded system that allows various individuals to operate with the same things. For this, the thing must be named. But the question arises: how? If civil society strives to leave the national context, an "idiom" does not help. Hence the idea of the creation of an "artificial language." The concept of an "artificial language" is based on the idea that it must consist of signs with significances (extentionalities) assigned to them. There should be no senses in this language (neither intentional nor textual and contextual ties with other signs). Some artificial languages used by science (sometimes called metalanguages) are an example of such a construction.

Esperanto, Ido and Interlingua are other example of this language and in the nineteenth century Volapük acted as an "artificial language." All these languages were created on the basis of Indo-European languages and can sound like something faintly recalling Italian or Spanish to those who do not know them. Just as an "idiom" is created on the basis of some *narodni* language (most often the *koine*), so "artificial languages" are based on societies where civil society is historically more developed, i.e. Western European languages. But an "artificial language" is not simply a firmly fixed dialect with a legal and compulsory political status, like an "idiom." It is a kind of "anti-language," since it is built as a construction, called on to facilitate egocentrums' contact with each other concerning relatively non-linguistic objects. This is a language of tallies, price-lists or individual numbers assigned to things and classes of things. This language has no generalizing structure, no semantic field, no context. It is impossible to write a text in an artificial language; it is only possible to designate a number of articles of the external world and to propose their composition. This is not a language of people, of society, but a language of things, articles, goods. It is fitting for technical instruction for an apparatus purchased from a store; i.e. it has a strictly utilitarian significance.

Modern English as an "Artificial Language"

In our days, "artificial languages" have so far not received their due diffusion. Perhaps we should expect even broader versions of "artificial languages," which would include the signs, sounds and morphemes of not only Indo-European but also non-Indo-European languages. So far, English acts as the "artificial language."

In its roots, English is the ethnic language of the Germanic group. But during England's history it was exposed to the serious influence of the Celts (whose languages were preserved in Welsh and Irish), autochthonous to Britain, and, to an even greater extent, Latin, through the language of the Norman conquerors (Old French), the Catholic mass and medieval erudition. English was for a long time the *koine* of Great Britain, which preserved polyglossia (Celtic languages) — the typical case of a traditional state. In the next period, around 1500 CE, i.e. during the transformation of English society into a nation, modern English formed as an "idiom" on the basis of the Middle English dialect. In the period of the British Empire, this "idiom" became a norm for the populations of all colonies. This is still the case in India, for instance, where the upper classes communicate in English and a significant part of the national press is in English. English became the "idiom" in the US and the dominant "idiom" in bilingual Canada (alongside French). The aftermath of British colonialism and the global strategy of the US, as well as the active diffusion of technologies, goods and methodologies produced in English-speaking countries led to the fact that English is today the most widespread language and can be considered the preferred language of global society. Since members of the most diverse national, *narodni* and ethnic groups, most often with their own languages or derivatives (*koines* and "idioms"), communicate in English, the semantics of this once natural ethnic language are substantially changed and to a significant extent simply lost. Many citizens of the Earth who use English well enough in the technical sphere and can speak it freely clearly have difficulties understanding the classical English of nineteenth century literature: Dickens, Chaucer or Thackeray. Planetary English, as a purely "artificial language," is a language of things, instructions, technical recommendations. It is not a language but a meta-language. In it, senses are reduced to a minimum; associations and inner connections are banished. No one knows the contexts for the correct use of terms or the rules of grammar. In the US, English has already been exposed to de-semanticization and acquired many artificial and purely pragmatic characteristics. When it became the language of global society, it took another step in this direction.

However, as a language of natural origin, despite all of its transformations English cannot be considered an "artificial language." It is more correct to say that at present it fulfills the function of an "artificial language," without being one fully. So as the pace of globalization increases, the introduction of an "artificial language" will become a more and more acute and urgent problem.

As long as English remains a substitute for a "global language," the line between Western cultural imperialism and properly global civil society will remain indefinite and uncrossed. On the whole, precisely this state of linguistic affairs reflects the specific character of the historical period in which the modern world lives. The transition to global civil society continues but has not yet been completed.

Ethnos–Laos–Demos–Idiotes

We will now trace the transformation of the anthropological type through the entire chain of societies we have considered.

In the *ethnos*, the norm is the figure of the shaman; in the *narod*, the hero; in the nation, the bourgeois. To this there corresponds the sequence: *ethnos-laos-demos*. In civil society, all collective forms are fractured into individual units. The citizen of the world represents no collective except himself. He is not a member of an *ethnos*, not a part of a *narod*, not a link in a nation. He is only himself.

In Greek there was a specific term for the description of the similar social status of an individual: *"idiotes"* ("ἰδιώτης"), formed from the root meaning "the same," "that same one." The *"idiotes"* represented only himself. The inhabitant of the city-state was considered part of the *demos* and belonging to the *demos* comprised the essence of his civic status. Only someone who had a historical relation to it, who shared a special history with it — connected, for that matter, with local cultic gods and who met certain property requirements, etc. — could be a citizen of the *polis*.

Citizens were only free, mature, independent males, historically rooted in the structure of the polis. In other words, citizenship was a qualitative category and an indicator of a rather high status.

Citizenship was defined in approximately the same way on the eve of the nation state. At that time, only males with a certain property qualification and belonging to the third estate — the bourgeois — were considered citizens.

Everyone else in the *polis* was divided into *"metics"* and *"idiotes."* *"Metics"* were non-citizens who, however, were allowed to settle in the *polis* and do certain kinds of work. In contrast to slaves and women, they had certain rights, though seriously truncated in comparison with citizens' rights. Everyone else was regarded as *"idiotes,"* as people who represented only themselves as individuals. *"Idiotes"* was not at first an offensive term. It described wanderers, newcomers, migrants or guests of the city, who did not represent a distinct collective community or society. They were neither bearers of sacred status (like pilgrims) nor representatives of another *polis* (amicable or inimical), nor were they members of some strictly defined profession or estate. They were individuals, "egocentrums," identical to themselves.

Precisely the *"idiotes"* comprise the fundamental, normative type for a member of civil society. The ideology of human rights calls us to concentrate on the figure of the *"idiotes,"* the individual as such, without any collective, social characteristics whatsoever. It is significant that the philosopher Martin Heidegger, describing the processes of globalization, employed for their definition the special term "planetary idiotism," having precisely this meaning in mind. Separated from all forms of collective identification, the citizen of the world can only be an *"idiotes."*[29]

Thus, we can add to the chain of the normative socio-anthropological types of different derivatives from the *ethnos: Shaman (ethnos) — Hero (laos) — Trader/Bourgeois/Citizen (demos, nation) — Idiotes (civil society, global world).*

---

29 Martin Heidegger, *Introduction to Metaphysics* (New Haven: Yale University Press, 2000).

Discovering the *Ethnos* in Civil Society

The theory of civil society does not have any ethnic component or dimension. It is created strictly after the nation and capitalism have completed their work of fracturing the natural collectives and estate structures that existed in other types of society. The nation is an agglomerate of individuals but at the same time it describes itself as a historical "collective" without being one. Civil society rejects this "simulacrum" and calls on bourgeois society to be recognized as what it essentially is: civil society.

The *ethnos* disappears long before the appearance of civil society. The socially differentiated structure of the *narod* already replaces the *ethnos* as the fundamental form of society, qualitatively complicating social structures many times over. But the ethnic beginning is still alive in the *narod*, especially in the *narodni* depths, in the masses, which continue to remain an *ethnos*. It is relatively easy to discover the *ethnos* in the *narod*. We have only to look at its lower strata. In the nation, things become more problematic. The nation is something entirely different from the *narod* and all the more so the *ethnos* but it claims that it is a continuation of the same thing or simply the same thing. According to Anthony Smith,[30] in the nation the ethnic beginning is present "symbolically," as an intellectual concept and in artificial symbols. On the other hand, not all of the norms of the nation are actually embodied in reality. It is one thing to normatively equate all citizens to the city industrial and trade bourgeoisie and another to deprive the inhabitants of rural regions of their sociological peculiarities. So we can find ethnicity even in the nation, especially in the rural regions or among separate ethnic groups resisting the universalization and fragmentation of the nation state. It is difficult to find ethnicity in bourgeois nations but it is nevertheless possible;[31] one has to pay attention to the "symbolic" myths of bourgeois nationalism and to separate processes of rural communities. Moreover, many signs of traditional society

---

30 Anthony D. Smith, *Myths and Memories of the Nation* (Oxford: Oxford University Press, 1999).

31 Anthony D. Smith, *The Ethnic Origins of Nations* (Oxford: Blackwell, 1987).

are preserved in culture: religion and civilization, and the relation towards the modern nation state among the lower strata can full well continue the relation of the masses toward the traditional state.

In civil society the ethnic layer is abolished. The furthest corners of sparsely populated territories are included in a single informational space through the development of transportation, communications and network technologies. This space actively completed the work of the bourgeoisie of fragmenting natural and historical collectives, fracturing identity to the level of the egocentrum, the "*idiotes*."[32] And this time the entire population is dragged into the process (not just the urban but also the rural). But the more aggressive the striving to finally uproot the *ethnos* is, the livelier the protests from the ethnic depths of society become. In this situation the *ethnos* no longer acts for itself but as a general vector of opposition to the global strategies of civil society.

The *Ethnos* and the Global Proletariat

In this sense, the proletariat can be considered a dialectical expression of the ethnic principle [beginning], opposing on a new stage the atomization of organic wholeness. Sociologically, a proletarian is someone who arrives in a city later than the bourgeois. Consequently, there is a great peasant principle in the psychology of the working class, since the proletarian almost always comes to the city from precisely the country. But the *ethnos* is not the same as the nation, so the proletariat can have an ambiguous attitude toward the nation. On one hand, the national bourgeoisie can play on the ethnicity of the proletariat, proposing a class pact in the name of the interests of the nation (the German National Socialists and Italian Fascists used this strategy). On the other hand, the proletariat can become aware of their class kinship with the proletariat of other countries, since the bourgeoisie and bourgeois nationalism are an "other" for the proletariat. Hence proletarian internationalism, representing the consolidation of the "ethnic" principle against the national principle, i.e. the

---

32   Louis Dumont, *Essais sur l'individualisme. Une perspective anthropologique sur l'id ologie modern* (Paris: Le Seuil, 1983).

bourgeois, civil principle. In conditions of globalization, this connection between the ethnic factor and the global proletariat becomes even more manifest. The "poor South," as we saw, is represented primarily by colored *ethnoses*; the "rich North" by "whites." European *narods* embodied their sociological construction in civil society, which has become a synonym for global capitalism and global capitalists (white = capitalist, bourgeois). Non-European *narods* form the major mass of the global proletariat.

All major communist and labor movements and parties in the countries of the "poor South" combine anti-capitalist motifs of war against economic imperialism, globalization and the universalization of the "Western way of life" with ethnic, religious, cultural and civilizational themes.

The *Ethnos* on the Periphery of Global Society

Similarly to the way we discover the *ethnos* in the lower layers of modern civil society, including in the figure of the proletariat, we encounter them in the geographic outskirts, in the area of those societies that belong to the global "periphery." The issue is that even now there are enclaves on the Earth (in Asia, Africa, Latin America, the Arctic zone and the Pacific region) where *ethnoses* live in primeval conditions. Just as such *ethnoses* paid no attention to their integration into the differentiated structure of the *narod*, so they ignore globalization and the expansion of civil society. Maintaining the integrity of the ethnocentrum, they mark all articles that have come from without as known and familiar and include them in their integral structure, without thinking about their purpose and meaning in other societies. They still do not know an "other."

So the *ethnos* can be found not only at the depths of civil societies but also at their side, in the "global reservation," the population of which still composes a significant percentage of the Earth's population. In precisely the same way, there remains a significant purely archaic area in more differentiated, religious and socially stratified societies. And even in the territory of the most modern societies, the US for instance, there are islands of purely ethnic culture (for instance, areas of compact settlements of native Indians).

This synchronism of archaic societies is very important for ethnosociology, since it clearly shows that it is not possible to prove a strict succes-
sion in social development. If in one part of the Earth a change of social
structures occurs, that change might well not occur in another part. It is
not possible to apply the logic of one social group, which has transitioned
from the *ethnos* to civil society, to all other social groups in the world.

If we now consider the phenomenon of globalization precisely as
propagation of the historical experience of Western European society
onto the rest of humanity, we can easily understand the nature of such a
phenomenon as Robertson's "glocalization," which we mentioned earlier.[33]
The increase of ethnic identity on a local level accompanies globalization
as a universal Western social code, as the spread of civil society as an all-
obligatory norm, precisely because the pressure of a cultural form foreign
to the majority of the population of the planet (civil society) provokes
a natural reaction. Having maintained themselves full well, ethnic and
narodni traditional societies strive, not passively but actively and insis-
tently, to change the course of globalization in the direction of localization. And the more it insists on its globality, the more strongly the archaic
enclaves, for their part, accentuate locality and turn it into a program, a
project, a conscious policy. *Glocalizations* appear in result.

If globalization were a natural phase for all or the majority of societies,
it would experience resistance only from nation states. But in this case the
issue is not only the nation, since globalization is resisted both by those
social forms immediately preceding globalization and by all other ethnosociological layers, whose weight in societies of the "periphery" and even
the "semi-periphery" remains decisive even in the present. Regarding only
its own Western time as universal, civil society forgets that in other societies time flows differently and often even in a different direction. Striving
to consolidate its standards, it comes up against the fact that localities
begin not simply to resist but erode the globalized code, to undermine the

---

33   Roland Robertson, *Globalization: Social Theory and Global Culture* (London: Sage,
     1992), 346.

very essence of the processes of globalization, to saturate it with entirely foreign elements.

As an expression of the imbalance of the world system, territorial space comes into play. Glocalization can well be considered a counter-blow by *ethnoses* and their first derivatives. This same energy feeds nations too, persevering in not finally disappearing before the face of global civil society and the ideology of "human rights."

So for global civil society, the following formula will be just: the *ethnos* is not only at the bottom of the socio-economic system (in the form of the global proletariat) but also alongside this system, next to it, beside it, parallel to it.

The Ethnic Lifeworld and the Lifeworld of the Egocentrum

Finally, we can discover the ethnic dimension at the very center of global society; neither beneath nor alongside but *within* it. In this case, we are talking about the structure of the egocentrum.

The figure of the "*idiotes*" as the norm of civil society represents the view of an integral and self-conscious social system toward those lacking any of the characteristics that correspond to its criteria. But the "*idiotes*" himself, having come to the city (*polis*), into the sphere of the "*demos*," came from somewhere. That is, he necessarily must have belonged to some concrete ethnic community or to some *narod*. As an "*idiotes*" he does not display these signs or they are simply not noticed, not identified by the city-dwellers, the *demos*. In other words, the "*idiotes*" is always a "thing-for-others." In himself, as a "thing-in-itself," he is not an "*idiotes*" but possesses certain qualities of a trans-individual kind. In other words, a person cannot but be the member of an *ethnos*, *narod* or nation. He can fail to accentuate it and pay it little or no attention, giving it no heed, but he cannot fail to have this dimension. The *ethnos*, *narod* or nation, and sometimes all of them together, form the entire content of the egocentrum. The specific character of the consciousness of the individual is one way or another predetermined by the *ethnos* (in this case, he is a bearer of ethnonationality, language, faith and customs), the *narod* (in this case, he speaks and thinks either in the *koine* or in one of the ethnic glossia, shares the cultural and differential, has a place in the stratification and a status), or the nation (in this case he is a product of his education, political upbringing, indoctrination, a bearer of the "idiom" and a subject of rights). All these levels of socialization predetermine, in the final analysis, the content of the egocentrum. The individual can perceive these formative influences in a weakened form, grasping only separate fragments and letting the rest split through his consciousness but he remains in any case coded by social algorithms, since socialization begins from the moment of birth.

OTHER BOOKS PUBLISHED BY ARKTOS

OTHER BOOKS PUBLISHED BY ARKTOS

OTHER BOOKS PUBLISHED BY ARKTOS

CPSIA information can b[...]ned
at www.ICGtesting.com
Printed in the USA
LVHW091216070322
712811LV00003B/260

9 781912 079216